MW01595043

Iris Novak

AN INDEPENDENT WOMAN IN YUGOSLAVIA

A Memoir

Published by:
Leila d.o.o.
Mencingerjeva 7
1000 Ljubljana
Slovenia
https://www.leila.si

Ljubljana, 2021
100 copies

Readers can send their questions, opinions and remarks to:
info@leila.si

An Independent Woman in Yugoslavia: A Memoir
Iris Novak — 1st edition

Some persons and/or names were changed.

CIP — Katalozni zapis o publikaciji
Narodna in univerzitetna knjiznica, Ljubljana

821.111(73)-94

Novak, Iris, 1953-
An independent woman in Yugoslavia : a memoir /Iris Novak. — 1st ed.
— Ljubljana:Leila, 2021

ISBN 979-877-32180-3-6
COBISS.SI-ID 90691075

1
My Family

I was born in Yugoslavia almost ten years after the end of the Second World War when our country broke its close liaison with the Soviet Union and started to introduce a milder form of communism than the one practiced behind the Iron Curtain.

In the fifties, Yugoslavia had a very low standard of living, but I don't remember the lack of money ever causing us major problems. On the contrary, many people spoke and wrote enthusiastically of how we citizens were going to live better. My mother, for example, always liked to describe the beauty of Ljubljana, the capital of Slovenia. She was proud that she worked in one of the biggest Yugoslav enterprises and she was convinced that people should be pleased with the life in Yugoslavia. Our teachers indoctrinated us with the idea that Comrade Tito, the lifelong president of Yugoslavia, did his best to help us develop our economy, as well as our comradery. Some twenty years later, when I started to work in the National and University Library, whose archives held the publications of Slovenian emigrants, I still had no idea that thousands of Slovenians were killed after the war. I spent all my youth fully convinced that Yugoslavia was a wonderful and safe country. All of its people were employed. There were no beggars in the streets and no common criminals.

Before the Second World War, my father's parents had a big farm in the northern part of Slovenia which was one of the six republics in Yugoslavia. My father's mother was considered an educated woman because she was a nurse who specialized as a midwife. At the beginning of 1941, her husband was killed by German soldiers while she and her children were sent to the concentration camp on the island of Rab. The soldiers tried to pull my father onto the truck, but he managed to run away and hid in his uncle's house. When my grandmother returned from the camp, she entrusted her children to her relatives and joined the Partisan movement. They offered her work as a nurse, but she refused. She quickly learned how to use a gun and blow up bridges, and then instructed the Partisans to deploy her for the most difficult tasks.

Many years after the end of the war, my mother used to tell me: "Look, this bridge was blown up by your Styrian grandmother."

The war must have changed her very heart, because the woman who was supposed to help people became a person who had no mercy, neither towards herself nor to her children. At the end of the war, the Partisan Army promoted her to a high rank, gave her a veteran pension, a villa in the country and quite a large estate.

She was a busy and strong woman who had to bring up three children, manage the estate and provide for the housekeeping. Besides this, she was often called to help women in labour. Her children hated her teaching because it was too militaristic. She was always ready to slap someone's face or at least provide a long lecture on how things should be done. My father was the first to get sick of the old general woman and he left for Ljubljana where he quickly found employment. His sisters married young and left my grandmother's house as soon as they could. When my grandmother was left alone, her children having fled, she adopted an orphan who left for Germany as soon as she was able. So, my grandmother remained quite alone. For some time, she complained about how everybody left her, but then she accidentally met her first boyfriend of many years past, a man she believed to be dead. After some months, they married and thus caused a great scandal among near and distant relatives, friends and neighbors. My mother and I were among the few who visited and congratulated her in her new home. I quite frankly didn't want to go because the old bat teased me whenever she could, often calling me a "wretch". However, my mum convinced me to forget my hard feelings.

My mother's family lived in much poorer circumstances. My maternal grandparents had only about two hectares of land with a house and a cowshed. The buildings and most of the land were ten kilometers from Ljubljana, quite near the street that ran from Ljubljana all the way to Trieste in Italy. The house was built in the Slovenian rustic style with the roof covered with brown tiles and a white façade with pretty little windows. The old carved door, decorated with wrought iron, led to a hall with entrances to all the rooms in the house. Right behind the main door, you could enter a broad room with a tiled stove, old cabinet and a big table with chairs. The tiled stove was not heated during the winter months because my grandmother found it too expensive. The only exceptions were for Christmas and Easter, when my grandmother made cakes with carob powder and raisins. The main place where the family gathered was the kitchen, which was equipped with a cupboard, a kitchen-range and a table with chairs. The most beautiful part of the kitchen was a small copper kettle from which somebody could wash or quickly make a cup of coffee or tea. On the windows and the cupboard, there were embroidered curtains made by my grandmother. Beside the kitchen was another small room that was filled with beautiful old furniture. This became my grandfather's room when he had to leave the bedroom he shared with my grandmother. The other half of the house contained two big rooms. My mother and my aunt slept in one of them and another was used for storage.

Right in front of the house were two plum trees. My mum made jam every year—so much that we sometimes had to throw it away. On the west side of the house there was a small orchard with old high apple trees that gave us enough apples to last us until the next autumn. The southern part of the house was covered with vines. Across the street there was a moor in which my grandparents produced the rest of their food: potatoes, carrots, parsley, turnips, cabbages, lettuce and corn. Though a small choice of products, even their use was limited because my grandmother had rather precise definitions of what could be eaten by people and what was meant for animals. It was quite clear that people should eat orange carrots while animals got the yellow ones. Corn was eaten only by pigs and hens and was not meant for people. Turnips could be eaten only if they were sour, and so on.

On the northern side of the house there was a stable overgrown with vines. The ground floor was used for one or two cows, two pigs and hens and the higher floor for hay. Behind the stable there was a forest that started with birch trees and continued with huge, dark pine trees.

I am still not sure which side of our house I liked more: the moor with its fog that covered the fields in the early spring and summer mornings or the forest in which I knew every tree.

My grandfather worked on his small farm and for the local railway. My grandmother sold milk and eggs and tried to earn some money through knitting, so that the family could have lived quite well. But my grandparents had neither the time nor the will to improve their standard of living. My grandfather used a lot of his time and money for drinking in the local pub and my grandmother was more eager to change her husband into a reliable and sensible one, than think of how to get some more money for her family. I still don't understand how it came to such a situation. My grandmother was a hardworking, smart girl from a big farmhouse who knew how to cook, work in the field and take care of the animals. And I was always convinced that my grandfather was a good soul, one of the best I have ever met. He tried to do what my grandmother required, worked in the field, helped his children and his neighbors. His only fault was drinking. From time to time, he sat in the pub and drank whole days away and my grandmother raged like a dragon when he arrived home. Sometimes he remorsefully sat behind the table and then went to the field, but occasionally he just returned to the pub. In our house there was not much talk about love, but my grandfather often said that he loved us, especially if he'd had a glass of wine before.

My grandparents had two daughters: the first born was my aunt and, after two years, my mum. God was rather unjust when he divided His talents between both girls. In those times, when men liked big fat girls, my aunt was small, thin and wore glasses. When she was a baby, she was very ill, and thus started to walk later than other children and did not do well in school. The majority of their neighbors found her rather simple. However, if she learned that somebody spoke ill of her, she got revenge in full measure. She usually waited until she met the person in front of the church and then naively said that she heard one or another unpleasant thing on their account. When telling such a story, she produced a silly giggle and looked as if butter would not melt in her mouth. People suspiciously watched her and were never sure if she was simple or very smart. My grandmother took every effort to teach her how to please other people and how to work in the house and in the field. But when she had to weed the lettuce in the garden, she plucked out the lettuce along with the weeds. If she was told to hoe up potatoes, she hoed up turnip. She never learned how to milk a cow and she never wanted to touch hens, because she found them disgusting. She could not sew or knit because her sight was poor. She never learned how to cook. And she also never wanted to marry, although she had a good opportunity, as my mum told me. She was proposed to by a decent farmer who lived in a remote village. My aunt mostly enjoyed just sitting on a chair and chatting. Since my grandmother was sure that such a waste of time was a big sin and because my aunt's speaking got on everybody's nerves (not just because she never said anything important, but also because she had a harsh, unpleasant voice), my grandmother usually shortly ordered her to shut up.

My mum was her direct opposite. She had dark hair, blue eyes, a beautiful oval face, a pretty round figure. She was entertaining, lively, smart and flirtatious but also kind, hardworking and compassionate. As soon as she was about fifteen, she became one of the most popular girls in the parish. My grandmother wanted her to become a dressmaker, which was a profitable and respectable occupation, but she had to break up her schooling because of the Second World War. After the war, there was no money to continue school. My mum was never sorry about it, because the teachers required much more patience and precision than she possessed. But she bought a sewing machine and continued sewing to the best of her ability.

My mum was a great help to my grandmother. My grandmother had tuberculosis and could no longer work in the field. She was the first in the house to get up, she fed the cow and the pigs, prepared breakfast, made lunch and dinner, washed the dishes and knitted. But the most difficult work had to be done by my mum and my grandfather. If my grandfather did not drink, he was working his fingers to the bone, but those were rare weeks. My aunt was no special help and my mum preferred to work without her. Although my mum had a lot of work, she managed to do everything and did not miss any entertainment. My grandmother did not like parties, but my mum was always invited to help with cooking and serving during garden parties, weddings or a priest's first Mass.

All the boys from the near and far-off villages were in love with her, partly because she was so beautiful and liked to laugh and partly because she could just look at a man and already manage to twist him around her little finger. My grandmother never understood this art and also never appreciated it, but she could not convince my mum that girls should modestly look down and not into boys' eyes.

To prevent my mum from marrying too soon or choosing an unsuitable man, my grandmother asked her about all the boys who walked around the house and quickly discovered and described their faults.

Later in her life, my mum was sorry that she believed her mother and refused so many suitors. She sometimes showed me one or another wealthy man from the village and said: "Just take a look at what a big house and car he has. What a fool I was that I listened to my mother and stopped dating him, even though he was in love with me."

My mum's family was very lucky because they did not lose any family members during the war or in the post-war purges. During the war, the family had to give up half of their house as the headquarters of the Italian and later Partisan army, but they got the rooms back. Neither my grandparents nor my mum and my aunt ever said that the soldiers did them any harm. Quite the opposite, they often gave the girls something to eat and even sweets, if they had them.

When my mum suggested that she might like to find a job in Ljubljana, my grandmother sharply opposed. It would be a scandal if young girls in those corrupted communist times tried to find jobs outside their houses! My grandmother thought that decent women should stay at home, take care of their family, fields and animals in the stable and go to church. Young women should be modest and never expose themselves in any way. If my mum were employed in Ljubljana, she would certainly meet a number of "worthless fellows without estates," without money and without serious intentions to marry. But the Yugoslav government did not work in favor of confirmed church mice like my grandmother.

Representatives of the village government simply came to the house and told my grandmother that two young, healthy and strong girls should not sit at home without employment. The girls should be employed, or the government would include them in the work brigades. Although young people who joined the work brigades helped to rebuild the broken country, my grandmother was convinced that the brigades were organized just to bring young men and women together. Work brigades were, according to the opinions of many old village women, places of absolute immorality, because young people sang and danced every evening, and some girls were so indecent that they wore trousers, some of them even shorts! So, my grandmother was forced to let her daughters find jobs in Ljubljana.

My mum could not have been happier. Her greatest wish was to come to the city among new people, earn some money and have a good time. She enjoyed her daily travel to Ljubljana, because she met always new young men and women of the same age, with whom she could discuss things quite different from those she shared with her embittered mother. It was pure happiness to get acquainted with the new city environment, where everything was well-organized and where a young woman could go to a cinema, to a park, a pub, to shops or simply walk along the river or admire the beautiful old houses. When my mum got her first salary, she went to a sweetshop and bought so many chocolate cakes that she had to vomit.

My grandmother quickly took action. She required that her daughters come home immediately after their jobs were finished and work in the field. My grandmother also expected that both her daughters would give her all the salary that they earned. The girls could keep just a bit of the money so that they could buy one or two pairs of shoes and material for a couple of dresses.

My mum first worked for the Yugoslav railways but, after a year or two, she gave them her notice. She had liked the work, but often had to work during the night and fell asleep. Her boss kindly said that she should find a morning or afternoon job. She then found employment in Iskra, a large factory for electric products, and remained there for almost twenty years.

My father worked for the Yugoslav railways, too, and that's where he and my mum met. Quite a number of people said that they never understood why she fell in love with him. He was probably quite a handsome young man. But my mum said that he attracted her with his words. He didn't hide his emotions and often remarked on his difficult childhood.

When my grandmother heard of my father, it was too late to convince my mum that she should leave him. My mum confessed that she was pregnant. My grandmother furiously boxed her ears and scolded her, but she agreed that the young couple should marry. They did not have a place to live together, so my grandparents gave them half of their house—two big rooms in which my mum and my father organized their kitchen and bedroom.

Not just my grandmother, but also other villagers refused to welcome my father. Why did my mum marry somebody who was not from the parish, but wandered in from who-knows-where? Many village boys had been members of the Home Guard that had opposed the Partisans and collaborated with the German or Italian army. After the war, they were shot by Partisans or emigrated, which led to many of the villagers hating them. And my father was the son of a rather well-known Partisan! No one could believe that the most beautiful girl in the parish would marry a Styrian with that kind of background. And besides, it was such a scandal that my mother got pregnant before the wedding! The priest did not want to marry them until my father went to Confession and took Communion. My father could have done that because he was brought up as a Catholic and his bosses would not control his going to church. It was just a question of power. The priest had his principles and my father had his. At the end of the conversation, my father shouted that he would marry somewhere else.

The wedding took place in Ljubljana and was very simple. When my parents returned from the town, there was a lunch at home and only family members were invited. My father's relatives—his mother, both sisters and cousins—were quite different from those of my mother's. My grandmother talked about, for several years, how unusually they spoke, how they laughed and hugged the new relatives and how they brought tasteless, strange sausages and cakes.

If my father had thought that the marriage would have brought him independence and the opportunity to become his own master, he was mistaken. His mother-in-law was a strong and sharp woman who was very conservative about what was right and what was wrong. And my father committed many faults in her eyes. He married my mum when she was already pregnant and was almost without money. Perhaps my grandmother could have forgotten about it, because my father really loved my mum and spoke about it all the time. And he could still become heir to his mother's large estate in Styria, but he refused to go to church, so my grandmother considered him a sinner who would go to Hell when he died. My grandmother did not expect that men would go to church every Sunday, but her son-in-law categorically disapproved of all priests and did not want to visit the church, even for Christmas and Easter. The young man also did not want to work in the field. He was ready to help with the most difficult work, but it never entered his mind that he should quickly eat his lunch and then work in the field, like his wife and sister-in-law. My grandmother considered him very lazy and it made no impression on her when he maintained that he worked hard in the morning. She also did not appreciate when he started with smaller joiner's work in the afternoon.

The Yugoslav government was against private businesses and everyone who established a firm was under strict control. But they did not care if people performed a trade if it was not registered. My father often claimed that he was able to do any joiner's work and people started to ask him if he could make a table, a cabinet and the like. My grandfather gave him a place beside the stable and my father created a small joiner's workshop. At first, he wanted to make modern kitchen furniture for my mum. He produced a big cupboard and painted it in white and blue—two colors that my mum hated—and she started to cry when she saw it. Similar things happened also with the neighbors. My father made wooden products according to his own knowledge and taste. If anybody argued that he had not ordered such a product, my father raised his voice, explained that he graduated from joinery school and that people should consider his professional opinion. Such discussions usually finished with a loud quarrel and the client left the product in the joinery, without paying. There were fewer and fewer orders. My father never admitted that this might have been his fault. No, the villagers were not worth of his efforts. As a result, he had quite a lot of time in the afternoon, so he decided to sign up to attend a school for professional drivers and then tried to get a driver's job with a higher salary. He quickly finished school and became a driver for a general manager. It was a considerable promotion and he was very proud of it. He paraded his achievement to everybody who would listen.

After some months, people were fed up with the reports on his professional success and my mum had to tell him to stop boasting. What a horrible mistake! He burst into a rage, because she did not "appreciate" him, hit her face and then started to weep.

My mum took to her mother, but received no solace, as she stated: "I told you what he was like. You did not listen and now you have got him. Get divorced from this savage so that we will live in peace."

But my mum still loved him and tried to save her marriage. When my father hit her the next time, she ran away and hid in one of the neighboring houses. I was small, but I still remember that I was quite desperate. My beautiful, adored mum, for whose smile I would wait from the morning until the afternoon, left me. My father said that she would never come back again, and I had no courage to ask questions or oppose or weep. But after some time, my father waited for her in front of her factory, promised that he would never hit her again and she returned home.

Although my father worked as a driver and often returned home in the evening (he had to drive his directors whenever, and for as long as, they wanted), there was no peace in our house. Quarrels broke out again and again. If my grandmother did not scold my grandfather or my aunt, there were more serious quarrels between my mum and my father. They did not just shout. My father very often hit my mum, threw dishes on the floor and almost every month broke the glass of the door. As a three-year old girl, I started to tremble with fear when my father raised his voice because I knew that he would not stop before he hit somebody or broke something. When he broke the glass door, he usually hurt his hand and it started to bleed. This made him feel sorry for himself. He would weep and, exhausted, slowly stop raging. But we were all so distant from him that nobody felt sorry for him. His relatives-in-law sneered, my mum said that it was his fault and I could not sympathize with him, either. Although I was only three years-old, I knew that it was him who always started the fights.

2
Small World and Big Fears

I still don't like to remember the first years of my life and sometimes I can't understand how I survived. My father always threatened to kill or beat one person or another, so I feared him all the time. I also felt sorry for my mum and my grandparents because I knew that they suffered. My grandmother seemed a strong woman who did not show her feelings, but she was unhappy when my parents quarreled. A couple of times, when we sat in her kitchen and listened to my father's shouting, she mumbled what a wild father I had, but when she noticed how unhappy I was, she stopped. She pressed her lips, continued with her knitting and sent me out, if it was possible. My grandfather remained silent and frowned. He once said to my father that he should stop raging and shouting, because I was nervous and trembled with fear whenever I heard him coming home. My father furiously called me in front of him and started shouting what a wretch I was.

The crisis broke out when I was about four years old. While my father was shouting and threatening my mum, I asked him not to beat her. I still remember how I begged him: "Daddy, please don't hit mum."

I repeated the sentence again and again, although I was afraid that I would get my share, too. And he really lost his temper, because I meddled with things that were no concern of mine and because I was not on his side. He took a bicycle pump and roared that I should be quiet or else he would break it on me. It was a big iron thing and I thoroughly believed that he was going to kill me. I fell on the floor as if I were dead. Both parents were frightened that he had really hit me.

My mum called the ambulance, while my father cried: "My God, what I have done? Iris, wake up, do not die, I did not mean to do it!"

Although the doctors found out that I had only fainted, my father never tried to beat me again. But he scolded me, because I did not show him real love and respect, as a decent child should.

I spent my first years mainly with my grandmother. She loved me very much, although she never showed it until I was twenty and I saw her crying when I left for Great Britain to learn English. I regularly walked with her from the kitchen to the stable, watched how she prepared lunch or dinner, put in order the rooms, knit, fed her cows and pigs. I helped her to put the hens in the stable and went with her to the field. In the morning, she placed coffee with milk and bread on the table and when I ate, she did my hair. My mum never wanted to cut my hair, so it grew down to my knees and I could not do it myself. My grandmother usually made two braids and fixed them on the top of my head. Then we went to the field and I tried to help her plant or weed. I must admit that I did not like it, because it was so boring. I worked just to help my grandmother. I showed even less talent and skill with the animals. Pigs smelled so horribly that I did not even want to look at them. My trials at milking the cow (it was not easy, because she kicked and flailed her tail) were quite unsuccessful. I was good enough with the hens and I knew how to collect their eggs. But even with hens, I had an accident. Our house was below a forest in which there were hawks. When a hen had chicks, hawks liked to quickly come down and steal them. My grandmother once told me to take care that the hen would not go to the orchard, but the hen was stubborn and led her chicks from the stable directly to the orchard. In a moment, a hawk descended and stole a chick. I started to cry and ran to my grandmother. She got very upset because of the stupid behaviour of the hen.

"I will teach this shameless animal to obey" my grandmother scolded and took the poor thing in her hands to fasten her to a tree. The hawks circled above the hen the whole afternoon, and though she was frightened, she was too big and they did not attack her. I don't know if my grandmother's teaching methods had any influence on the hen, but I certainly learned how dangerous the world was.

I sometimes asked my grandmother to teach me how to knit. She was the best knitter in the village and could produce all kinds of cardigans, sweaters, coats, gloves and caps. Villagers brought her wool of all colors and she made beautiful things. When she was knitting, she did not have to look at her hands, but could knit and chat, order, and listen to the radio. However, she didn't manage to teach me knitting. I never managed to produce even such a simple thing as a shawl. Perhaps I would have slowly learned to do so, if I had not considered knitting to be so desperately boring.

Around noon, my grandmother started to cook. She did not know many recipes, but she did her best every day: very often a vegetable soup with potatoes, cabbage, pie, dumplings, potatoes with carrots and kohlrabi and salad. In summer, we had a lot fresh green salad and in winter we ate cabbage and pickles. On Sundays, we always ate beef broth, fried potatoes, meat from the broth and salad. For Christmas and Easter, she made two big cakes with carob and raisins. Not a very large choice, but I liked everything.

Among the most important social events in which I participated before I went to school were visits to the village shop that was about 300 meters from our house. Before my grandmother and I went to the shop, I had to wash my face and hands and put on a better cardigan. Young women who sold just the most basic food products seemed so beautiful and important that I, too, wished to become a shop assistant. But my grandmother quickly taught me that I should not even think about it. We did not have so much money that my mum could send me to a vocational school. And I was also not very intelligent, she would say, so I should not have too rich an imagination. According to her, I would have to find a job in a factory, like my mum.

My grandmother sometimes took me to the church and taught me prayers. She put me on a small seat on her bicycle. On the way to the church, we met a lot of people and there were even more inside the big building. It was a great performance with wonderful music. In the middle, I usually fell asleep and, when I woke up, other children laughed at me. I was interested in everything and asked a lot of questions about God and the Church, but my grandmother was not a very good teacher. Whenever I asked a question, she said that I should not ask about God and that it was necessary to simply believe things, otherwise God would be angry, and His smallest punishment could be thunder and storms. Once there was a horrible storm with lightening and even my grandmother seemed scared, so I asked her if it might help to say the Lord's Prayer. She answered that one Lord's Prayer was not enough. I generously offered one thousand prayers, but she was even less pleased with me. She said that I could not even count to one thousand and besides, this would be making fun of God. There was nothing that I could have done.

I loved her, despite the fact that she was so pessimistic. Each year, when she had to go to the hospital because of her tuberculosis, I hid in the stable and cried because I was afraid that she would not come back. When she was away, my grandfather took care of my brother and me. He was much more optimistic, relaxed and of a much better mood than my grandmother. When he looked after us, he told us stories from the history books that he liked to read. He also cooked and his food was so good that we always ate a whole bowl of potatoes. He watched us, smiling and smoking. But he did not find it necessary to wash or comb us. When my grandmother was in the hospital, he sometimes managed to endure without a drink, but one time he went to the pub and left us alone in the house. We thought that my mum would be happy if we waited for her at the railway station. We went out in heavy rain and were almost run over by a car. When we got there, we were so dirty that my mother was ashamed when our neighbors saw us. Then she ordered that we should by no means go into the streets again but should wait for her in the kitchen. To illustrate her order, she told us the story about the wolf and the seven little goats and said that someone could come and take us if we were not in the house. I believed her every word, but my brother did not and ran around the village whenever he could. My brother was three years younger than I. From the moment he started to walk, one could find him everywhere except in the house. I was supposed to look after him and set an example for him, but I was not very successful. He did mainly what he wanted and did not listen to my suggestions.

Once a year, we visited my father's mother and his sisters in Styria. It was a long journey, almost to the end of the world, it seemed. The train chugged on for so many hours that my brother and I were dead tired when we arrived. I liked the big and beautiful house and the surroundings, meeting my cousins and tasting new foods. My favorite member of the family was my father's sister, Fani, who spoke with me as if I were an adult. Once she gave me a wonderful pink scarf with white flowers that was perfumed. Up until that time, I'd never seen something so beautiful. I wore it only when I went to the church. Fani was also the first person to give me a chocolate and a cake and I couldn't believe how delicious they were.

The only trouble in the house was my father's mother. She usually sat in the living room and ordered people about, telling them what to eat, what to think, how to behave and what they were not supposed to do. She had different approaches to the members of my family. She never ordered my father and spoke to him in a friendly manner. If she addressed him in too tender and attentive a way, my father sharply answered that he had needed her tenderness when he was young. Each time we visited her, my father reproached her, saying that she had left him alone, and this made her cry. She liked to offer him delicious food as they prepared enough dishes for a wedding when we came, but he often scornfully refused it. My grandmother was also very kind to my mum and it seemed that she loved her more than her own daughters. She praised my mum's beauty, her liveliness, her hard work, her sewing skills and so on. My father liked this, and I still remember how he raised his head and brandished a confident smile. My grandmother was rather tolerant towards my brother, although he was a naughty, little boy who always did something stupid.

But she only laughed and sometimes poked him in the rib: "You are a real boy, aren't you!"

But she did not like me. She found me an ordinary wretch and tried to change me into a stronger person. She was always prepared to say that I was fat (and she, the old bat, must have weighed about 120 kilos), that I did not know how to smile, that I did not behave well because I did not kiss her in the morning (we never kissed at home and I did not want to kiss her because she was so wicked and she stank). One day I ate too much, the next day not enough, I was a coward and so on. I do not know if my mum noticed how my grandmother teased me, but my father listened to all her remarks with his ears up. As soon as he realized that she teased me, he told her to stop and leave me alone. Then she teased me just when my father was not there. I am still sorry that she died before I was independent enough to make her respect me even more than my father.

Anyway, we can still meet in heaven and discuss things on equal ground. When she grew old, she changed into a pious lady who often made donations to church and perhaps God forgave her shooting so many people during the war.

My world enlarged and life became more pleasant and interesting when one of our neighbors asked my grandmother if I could come and play with her daughters. I used to go there every day and we played with dolls. We sewed their dresses, fed them, sang, taught them how to walk and never tired of it.

My neighbors must have been fed up with my staying with them the whole day and even bringing my brother, but they almost never said that we should go home. Just the opposite, actually, my neighbor claimed that she liked children playing around her. Therefore, her house was usually full of children who made a lot of noise while she quietly prepared lunch, baked bread and fed the cows. Her husband sometimes looked at us and, with a slight smile, mentioned that our parents missed us. Only then did we leave. My neighbor's husband did not speak much and did not show his love to his wife and children, but he and his wife never quarreled the way my parents did. I still remember the day when he made me cry. When his eldest daughter had a birthday, he made her wooden equipment for her doll: a small bed, a cabinet, a cradle, and a kitchen-range. When I saw those marvellous things, I burst into tears. Her mother was alarmed and asked me what was wrong. I answered that I would also like to get something like that from my father. My neighbor's father said that I should ask my father— after all he was a joiner and knew how to make such things much better than him. They taught me how to politely ask my father and I repeated the words in front of him. But my father only murmured that he had no time. After two years, he remembered my wish, made a bed for my doll and was very proud of his gift. I did not care, because by then I did not play with dolls any more.

I always adored my mum, but we started engaging in longer conversations only when I was five years old. Once my neighbor tethered his dog at another place than was usual and, although they warned me not to come in its vicinity, I forgot the warning and the dog snapped at me. It caused quite a big wound that bled and my neighbor brought me home, most unhappy and apologizing. My mum took me to the doctor and he ordered that I should lie down for some days. My mum bought me caramels and stayed at home so that she could change the bandages and take care that I would not jump around. She moved her sewing machine to the room with my bed, sewed and spoke with me. Finally, my brother and I had her just for ourselves. How good it was that the dog bit me!

She also tried to teach me to write, but without success. "Well, I think you will not do very well at school. Never mind, you will find work in a factory, as I did," she lectured. Some weeks later she spoke with her friends, and with much regret said that I would probably not be good in school. These words made me sad, but I was not worried. I felt that I would be a good pupil. But I got angry when her friends said that I was too big, too fat, and that I could not produce a kind smile like other little girls. If I now take a look at a photo of my first year in school, I can see quite a normal girl, a bit taller than her classmates, but not so much that it was worth mentioning. However, they often spoke about it and I was so stupid that I started to believe them.

3
The School

Our village was very small and located between two bigger ones, each of which had its own school. We had the choice to go to either the school that was nearer to Ljubljana or to the other one that was farther from the town. The village near Ljubljana was quite large, its school, too, and it was about three kilometers from our house. It had been built after the war, the building low and long with a grey roof. It had large halls, big classrooms, a very extensive gym that served also as celebration hall, a room for the teachers, a kitchen and a dining room. The school had a good reputation because it had severe teachers and a strict headmaster. The other school was a pleasant yellow villa that was one or two kilometers from our house. The kitchen and the dining room were in the cellar, the ground floor had two big classrooms and a room for teachers and, the first floor had apartments for two teachers. This school taught only the first four grades. When the children finished the fourth, they had to go to some other school. People said that the quality of this school was rather low.

I dreamt that I could go to the school near Ljubljana, together with Rozi and Zala, two pretty and polite girls who lived about a kilometer from our house. I rarely had the opportunity to play with them. We actually met just when their mothers brought to my mum materials for dresses or jackets. Both girls had such beautiful faces, were so well-dressed and behaved so politely that I always remained without words when I met them. I had no idea how and when to say please, thank you, excuse me, goodbye and so on. Zala repeated these words in every sentence and always offered a kind smile. Rozi was not so polite, but she was even more beautiful than Zala and everybody admired her.

When it was time for me to be enrolled in the first class, a teacher from the smaller school paid a visit to each family with a seven-year-old child and tried to convince them that they should send the child to her class. She explained that children would feel better in a smaller school, where the headmaster and the teachers were kind and not so severe. My mum presented me to the teacher, and I liked her because she was kind, had beautiful blue eyes and a pleasant smile. However, I still wanted to go to the larger school with Rozi and Zala. I also did not want to attend an easy school but thought that I would like the challenge of a really difficult one.

My mum knew my wishes, but she told me that I was to go to the smaller school, the one with no reputation. I resisted with all my power, but she clearly explained her view: "The smaller school will be closed if it does not have enough children. We have to do something to keep it for the next generations of children. The smaller school is nearer to our house and the teacher in a small class will be able devote more time to you and teach you at least something. Mind that you are not very clever and that you will probably have difficulties. If you go to the larger school, Rozi and Zala will tyrannize you. Don't think that they are waiting to be your friends. I heard them say that they would not go around with a dull and clumsy girl like you. You will find better friends in the small school. This week, I will acquaint you with a girl who would like to be your friend. She will come with her mother, because they want me to make some dresses for her. You will see that Tereza is much better company for you than Rozi and Zala."

All my dreams crumbled into ruins. I would have to go to a school of low quality and Rozi and Zala did not like me. I would never achieve anything and nobody would like me because I was so ugly and stupid. Such were the lessons of my childhood.

My mum tried to cheer me up and started to sew two skirts and aprons for me. The skirts were made from my mum's old dresses, while the cotton for the aprons seemed new. Whenever my mum cut materials for skirts, blouses or dresses for her friends and neighbors, I stood beside her and sometimes sighed that I would like at least one dress made from new material, bought just for me. But my mum always said that the materials cost a fortune and that I could not even think about a new dress until I went to Confirmation. So, the new clothing for school did not cheer me up.

Only when I received a brand-new bag with a book, two notebooks, a pencil and ten colored pencils did I get over my unhappiness. The bag was made of red plastic and I found it very beautiful. However, the book interested me much more. It contained short stories, poems and drawings and I was dying to learn what they were about. I started to trouble everyone to explain the letters and numbers or read to me.

My mum did not want to teach me, because the teacher said that she should leave this to her. My grandparents sometimes showed mercy and told me one or two things. So, I learned at least a couple of letters. But nobody knew how to teach reading. All I could do was copy letters and the binding of the notebooks. I placed the bag beside my bed every evening, so that it was the first thing that I could see in the morning.

My grandmother accompanied me on the first day of school and we were soon joined by Tereza and her mum. Some girls from the second grade went to school alone and did not want to join us. I was so afraid that I hardly breathed. The next day was even worse, because I had to go to school alone. One of the older girls looked down upon me and said that my grandmother should still come with me if I was such a baby. But my parents and grandparents thought that it was time for me to stand on my own two feet.

In about a week, my fears died away because school was so interesting. I expected that the teacher would show us how to read on the very first day and was a bit disappointed because we made just a couple of drawings. But the teacher praised me, saying that my drawings were marvellous. She asked me if my parents taught me how to draw and did not believe that I had never had a colored pencil in my hands until I came to school. I wanted to draw, but my grandmother said that I should save my colored pencils for school and not use them for my entertainment. Still, when the teacher asked us to draw an animal or a plant, I could do it in a moment. It was quite obvious what an apple or a pear or a cat was like, wasn't it? All you had to do was to imitate what you saw, didn't you? I found it most strange that the majority of my classmates waited until the teacher told them how to begin, how to make a circle for a cat's head or even made drawings on their behalf.

I enjoyed when the teacher taught us how to write letters. Each time she brought a drawing that she had made herself, told us an interesting story and then we started writing. I wanted to write at least ten pages with letters and drawings, but the teacher said that two or three pages were enough, especially because she was pleased with my writing. I was disappointed when she told me that I should do just as much as she told me and not more. She taught us mathematics and singing, read stories and I enjoyed everything. The only problem was that the teaching process was so slow. The school did not demand from me even half of what I was prepared to do. That's bad, I thought. When I met Rozi and Zala, they told me that their school was very difficult and that they had to learn all day long. In their opinion, it was not likely that I could ever start going to their school, because I would simply not possess enough knowledge to achieve their level.

I did well at school, and I brought home excellent marks, but my life became difficult. I had two classmates who always tried to pull my hair and Tereza's, and even beat us. I do not know why they chose us as victims. Tereza suggested that we should quickly put things in our bags when class was over and run to escape them. The boys soon noticed that we tried to escape and chased us with even more pleasure. I told my parents what happened, but my mum abruptly said that we should beat them back. Neither Tereza nor I knew how to do so, because we had no experience in fighting. The boys followed us for several months and it was so unbearable that I wanted to die. Then Tereza told her aunt that the classmates followed and beat us every day. On the next day, Tereza's aunt took her bicycle and saw us running and and both boys chasing us. She stopped, threw her bicycle in the grass, caught both boys and gave them a good beating. She threatened that she would drink up their blood next time if they even tried to look at us. The villagers never spoke well of Tereza's aunt, but I will hold her in kind remembrance until the end of my life. She was the only one who understood our distress and saved us. God bless her.

My life became pleasant again. I was in seventh heaven when I found out how to connect sounds represented by letters and how this brought about a word that meant something. It occurred to me, without the teacher's assistance, that I could make this procedure with all the words until the period, and thus understand a thought. When I realized that this might be the secret of reading, I sat at the table, took a children's newspaper and tried to read a short story. My grandfather sat in the vicinity and helped me, if I got stuck. After I finished, I ran to my mum and to my grandmother and cried that I could read.

They both doubted me, but my grandfather said: "Iris, do not take their opinions seriously. I have heard you and I swear that you know how to read. Continue reading and you will soon be able to read large books, like me."

When I proved to my family that I could read, they did not consider it the miracle that I did: "That's why you go to school."

My teacher did not believe me at first, but then she praised me, opened a cabinet and gave me a book of fairy tales. She also promised that I would be able to get a new one when I finished with this first one.

From that day on, I did not want to play with my neighbors any more. I had no time for playing and I also hardly found time to help in the field. As soon as I came home, I quickly completed my homework and then read the whole afternoon away. My teacher again did not believe that I read all the books that I borrowed. After I retold some stories and after my mum told her that I read all day long, I was allowed to borrow all the books from the teacher's cabinet.

At the end of my first class, I brought home a certificate with top marks and my family was quite surprised. They thought that I was a poor stupid creature but look at me now! My father got tears in his eyes and bought me a bicycle (and, of course, he boasted all around that I had top marks). He still claimed that I was not as clever as my younger brother, but I was certainly hard-working.

My father tried to contribute to my intellectual capacities by teaching me chess. He criticized each of my mistakes and very rarely uttered a word of praise. One time when he mocked me, I knocked over the figures and told him that I did not want to continue with chess. He made a loud lecture and required that we started playing again. But I intentionally placed my figures so that it came to checkmate in five minutes. When he saw that I sabotaged his self-sacrificing teaching efforts, he got even more furious, but finally my chess lessons finished. I never wanted to play chess again.

Children in the first grade started also with religious education and had to go to Mass every Sunday. My religious lessons took place in a small cold church on a hill behind the school. It was very far from my home. Walking about two kilometers, with one part through the forest at six in the morning, was a difficult task for a seven-year-old girl. The priest told us, during the very first hour, that it was absolutely necessary to go to religious lessons and to the Mass, otherwise we would commit a mortal sin and end up in Hell. I did not want to be a sinner, so I went to the lessons every week, although I was afraid that there was a robber behind every tree en route. My grandmother did not let me go a couple of times, because it had snowed heavily, and assured me that this was definitely not a sin. But I did not believe her and when I first went to Confession, I admitted it as a sin.

The lessons were interesting, because the priest usually explained the stories from the Bible. I also enjoyed when he wanted us to say prayers by heart, because I knew them all. But he made me sad and angry, because he often asked pupils if and which family members went to Mass, and if we prayed before and after lunch or dinner. I could say that my grandmother, my aunt and I went to Mass, but I had to shamefully admit that my parents did not. Each time I asked them to go with me, my mum answered that she was too tired, and my father remarked that I should tell the priest to mind his own business. So, I could not insist on encouraging my parents to go to church, although it seemed they would go to Hell. I once asked the priest if I could pray so much that somebody who did not go to church would come to Heaven, but he said that everybody should decide and pray for himself. Just as I had been told years ago, that my fervent prayers would not calm a thunder storm, I could not pray my parents into Heaven.

There was some solace in the fact that I could always answer all the priest's questions, that I always completed my homework and that I knew all the prayers by heart. The majority, especially the boys, did not do their homework and could not recite prayers. The priest usually asked them why they did not do their work and told them to learn from me. I did not like it, because the boys were then angry with me and pulled my hair when we went home.

Very soon I had to come in front of the whole class and admit a much bigger sin than what was ever committed by the most mischievous boy. One day, Tereza and I went to Mass together and stood in front of the altar while my grandmother and my aunt sat in the back row. Tereza suggested that we should go to Communion together with other people.

"Do you think that we are allowed to go?"

"Why not, can't you see that other children go?"

That was true, so I gathered my courage and followed her. When we ate the Host, the priest stopped and looked at us, because he remembered that we had not been to the First Communion yet. He watched us disapprovingly for a long time and then continued with Mass.

Tereza did not go to religious lessons as regularly as I and she missed the next lesson. So, the priest called just me to come in front of all my classmates, pulled my ear and told everybody what a horrible sin I had committed. I came home in tears and told my grandmother what had happened. She gave me a lesson, too: how could I be so stupid that I went to Communion before I was allowed to? I was very sorry and thought that it was my fault, although I really did not know that one should wait for First Communion. I didn't even know what First

Communion was. But we faced even more shame next Sunday, when the priest sermonized that some parents did not tell their children even when to start with Communion. When my grandmother, my aunt and I left the church, we did not know where to look, because we were so ashamed. A group of village women stood in front of the main door and watched us disapprovingly. One of them asked my grandmother why she allowed me to commit such a horrible sin.

In that moment, my neighbor came out of the church and answered in a loud voice: "Why didn't the priest teach her anything? It is easy to stay high in the pulpit and present oneself as a saint. But I would say that the priest should teach children and not just play judge. And besides, such a good little girl has no sins and deserves to go to Communion much more than many other people!"

The priest was in the vicinity, but made no comment because he knew that my neighbor was an energetic and loud lady who was ready to discuss religious things for hours. When my grandmother heard her, she said that my neighbor was a wise woman and stopped scolding me.

At the end of the first schoolyear, I received First Communion and went through Confirmation. In those times, children who finished their first school year went to First Communion, and in the next one or two years they were Confirmed. But the priest made an exception for me, because I knew all the catechism and all the prayers by heart. He even said that I was more religious than many older children. My father was not interested in it and considered it an unimportant event. My mum liked it because she had to buy just one dress and one pair of shoes for both events.

Some villagers disdainfully said that this was too soon because a girl of seven could not know what First Communion and Confirmation meant and that at least my Confirmation should have taken place later. But I am still convinced that I understood all the religious lessons in the right way. My faith was, of course, a bit childish, because I thought that angels had wings and that there was fire in Hell and so on. But I knew everything about the Bible. I was aware of what the church demanded of people, I prayed every morning and evening and tried to do everything to remain without sin.

There was a tradition that children received gifts for Confirmation. My mum told me in advance that I was not to expect anything, and I was aware of it also myself. I was quite pleased that I could go to such an important sacrament, although I was only seven years old. Besides, I was very happy because my mother's most beautiful and kindest cousin agreed to become my godmother. My godmother brought me a whole box of biscuits, a small wristwatch and a necklace (they were not made of gold, but I liked them as if they were). And I got wonderful material for a new skirt. I did not know how I deserved it. I remembered that my mum made doughnuts and a cake and invited some relatives to the house. One of them was not respectful enough towards my father, so he loudly explained how insulted he felt. The guests quickly left, and my mum tried to convince my father to suppress his anger at least on such an important day. My brother and I went to our grandmother and then everything finished as usual: my father broke the glass of the door and then wept because of his hard and unhappy life. He could have bled to death and no one would have cared. No one even apologized to him or showed compassion.

"To Hell with such religious people!"

4
Self-Confidence and Arrogance

During my first four years of school, my small class was always joined with a higher or lower grade because there were only about ten of us. At first, I was in the class with older pupils and then with younger ones. When Rozi and Zala learned about it, they shook their heads, saying that they had never heard of such a school. If they had known that the teacher sometimes left us in the class alone for one or two hours (I suspected that she went up to her flat to prepare lunch), and that we had to repeat the multiplication table or declensions of words, my friends would have been even more indignant. But this never came out and didn't cause any harm. We repeated multiplication and declensions so many times that I still do mental arithmetic and I am accomplished with irregular declensions, which are common in Slovenian. I even still use the dual to indication the specific verb form for two people or things whereas many Slovenians today simply use the plural form.

In second grade, when I was eight, I had no more fears. To the contrary, I was aware that I was at the top of the class and I felt rather proud. All girls in the second grade pretended that we were not at all interested in boys, but that was not true. I liked a boy from the fourth grade who used so many bad words that the headmaster always called him to his office.

But I disliked Boris from the first grade, who followed me everywhere and sighed whenever he saw me. As a pupil of the second grade, I did not even notice him for a long time. On the day when children of the first grade were accepted among pioneers, a national socialist youth group a bit similar to Boy Scouts, he put me in such an embarrassing situation that I could not forgive him for years. The second grade pupils had to put caps on the heads of the new pioneers, bind red bandanas around their necks and congratulate them for becoming a part of the organization of the Yugoslav president, Tito. During rehearsals, I chose a pretty girl from my village whom I would equip with the basic uniform of the pioneers, but during the real celebration, my teacher pushed me in front of Boris and ordered me to put a cap on his head, bind his bandana and congratulate him.

It was hard enough that I had to touch him but when Boris saw me, he produced a happy smile and sighed: "Oh, Iris, you!"

Everybody laughed, especially his parents, whom he told how very much in love he was with me. And I, silly girl, got angry each time he came in my vicinity, instead of being proud of such a great love!

Tereza and I were no longer best friends after first grade. Once, I accidentally hit her cousin with my bag and Tereza became protective and boxed my ears. Some weeks had to pass before she was ready to hear that I did not do it intentionally. Then she suggested that we should be friends again and I accepted, but very coldly. I also started to distance myself from other classmates. I became as proud as a peacock. I had my reasons. In the class, I was far ahead of my classmates. I could solve any task and the teacher praised me all the time. If we learned a new song, I could repeat it in a matter of minutes, while others needed days. I had my world of reading, which occupied me all day and on all occasions. I retreated to reading if I heard unpleasant criticism, if I was bored or if my family quarreled. I frequently thought that I was wasting time in that small school and that I should have been in the larger one near Ljubljana. There I could really use my abilities and show my knowledge. I was sure that I would also find new and better friends. I felt that Rozi did not like me, but perhaps she would change her opinion if she saw how good I was in school.

In the fourth grade, we got a strange teacher and I started to hate the school. The teacher had a stupid habit of asking pretty little girls to sing something and he then put them on his knees as a reward. I was very happy that I was neither small nor pretty. I was looking forward to finishing the last year in that school and leaving both teachers and classmates.

It was not a simple matter to come to the larger school near Ljubljana. Our village did not belong to the municipality of Ljubljana, so I was supposed to continue school in another small town. But my parents now yielded to my requests and my father decided to convince the headmaster of the school near Ljubljana to accept me. The headmaster was known as a hard, iron man. My father borrowed an official car, of which he was a chauffeur, and we both put on our best clothes and left. My father behaved so politely and humbly that I was embarrassed. The headmaster had nothing against accepting a child with excellent marks who had been yearning to visit the best school in Slovenia since she was five. He even smiled and said that I would have to learn more if I wanted to have similar marks. I finally achieved what I wished for so many years and considered myself the luckiest person in the world.

I was looking forward to entering the new school and finding new friends with whom I would never quarrel. I knew that I would have to work hard, but I was ready to do it with my heart and soul. My parents bought me a new bicycle, because the way to school was quite long, at least three kilometers. I got a new bag, books, notebooks and slippers (all children wore slippers indoors, even in school). Of course, I wished to get at least one new dress, but my mum told me that we would start building a new house, therefore we had to save money and forgo everything that was not absolutely necessary.

5
Getting Sober

My start in the new school was not very successful. Zala and I were together in one class, while Rozi was placed in the parallel one. On the first day, I came in at the last moment because I waited for another girl who arrived late. I did not find the right place for my shoes (because we had to wear slippers) and during the break, I left my bag in the wrong place.

The headmaster noticed it and said: "Here we are used to discipline. If you forget your bag again, it will disappear."

On the next day, Zala and I had such an interesting discussion that we both forgot our bags in the hall. When we wanted to take them home, we could not find them. Other pupils had similar experiences and told us that the bags were probably taken by the headmaster. We had to go to his flat, apologize and promise that we would never be so careless again.

I had no idea how to behave or apologize, but Zala suggested that we should go together, and she would apologize on our behalf. Scared stiff, we went to the headmaster's flat in the school and stood in front of him in a piteous state. When I recognized that Zala was so scared that she could not even open her mouth, I stammered that we left the bags in the hall, that we regretted what we had done and that we humbly asked him to forgive us. Before I finished, I noticed that I repeated the words usually used during the Confession and was even more ashamed. I had a feeling that the headmaster was rather amused, but his face remained locked in a frown and he told us never to do it again.

I was not used to learning in a proper sense, so I had no real idea why my mum had to buy me so many books. I always did my homework, but I did not know why I should learn from books, as well. My teachers told the same things, some even read directly from the books. I also didn't know why I should repeat what I learned. In the afternoon, I preferred to go to the forest, pick up flowers and think about how I would meet my new friends again the next day, especially Zala and one of the boys whom I liked. I sobered up when I got an unsatisfactory mark for geography and just a satisfactory one for my Slovenian. It was a bit of a consolation that other classmates received similar poor marks, but I was aware that I should do something to improve my grades. However, I did not know what the best way forward was. My grandmother said that I should learn more and stop walking around as if I was dreaming. I looked at her with surprise:

"Well, I go to school every day and do my homework."

"You should repeat what you hear in school and what you put down in your notebook and you should read your books and remember their contents."

"But I remember everything the teachers say."

"No, you don't. Don't be such a fool and don't run around but sit at the table and read your books. Then close your eyes and repeat what you read. Do it again and again until you remember everything by heart."

Her standpoints were most old-fashioned, and I asked myself what my grandmother could know about learning, but I obeyed all the same. After all, I had no better solution. Over the next months, my grandmother asked me every day if I'd done my homework, if I'd really learned everything, if I'd prepared my bicycle and my bag for the following morning. I was indignant that she should control me like that, but there was no living soul who could convince my grandmother that some people did not need to be controlled.

"Shut up and learn" she said, sitting behind my back and knitting.

I soon became aware that I only sat at the table, looked at the book and thought of something else. To stop wasting time, I started to underline things that I found important. I repeated things in a loud voice and finally understood what learning was about. It took almost a year, before I recognized that I had to use this way of learning in every course.

It was English class that made me a star. I immediately remembered foreign words, pronounced them in the right way and used them in sentences. I understood everything (and quite frankly, I still do not know why many people cannot repeat words or express simple thoughts in foreign languages. You simply repeat what you hear, don't you?) Our English teacher was a daring, loud, young woman who was not afraid to tell anyone what she thought. If she did not like somebody, she used every opportunity to knock them down. But she liked me because I was living proof that she was a good teacher. Her classes were often visited by the headmaster and by the father of one of my classmates who had trouble with English. They came together to find out if the teacher explained things in the right way and if she was just towards the boy. If the boy could not answer and his father sighed that the question was too difficult, the teacher simply asked me, and I got the right answer. Then she shrugged her shoulders, saying that even a poor girl who came from a small school without a reputation knew more than his son.

Our math teacher was even harder. She explained math very well and often made us laugh. But she got mad if somebody chatted during her lesson or during exams. She'd start to shout and beat the miserable child. The worst pupils were beaten with a stick and they had to drop their trousers and show their naked backside to the whole class. I later learned that the parents of such pupils took their children out and sent them to another school. But the math teacher also liked me because I did not chatter too much and because I always got excellent marks. However, I soon faced trouble when I had to show my knowledge in front of the teacher and the whole class. After she had checked our homework, she usually gave us a frown, sharply said that we should close our notebooks, hold our tongues and then she called one or two pupils to the front and examined their knowledge. She asked her questions very quickly and expected immediate and quick answers. If pupils did not answer immediately, they got a low mark. After some months of such oral exams, I started to tremble when she called me, and my answers were rarely good.

The teacher of Slovenian could be sharp, as well. She understood if some pupils did not know all the grammar rules or if they wrote poor essays, but she could not stand if somebody yawned during her "interesting" lectures. I was very good in Slovenian because I knew grammar from my previous school (declensions and other rules stayed with me for ever) and I always wrote the best essays. Of course, I did, as I'd read so many books.

My worst nightmare was gym. Yugoslavia glorified athletics like half-mile races, exercises on different gymnastic equipment, ball games and the like. Sports were among the most important school activities, and it was much more appreciated than reading. Each school had to have a big gym, while it was enough if the school library contained one or two cabinets of books. During gym lessons, students had to compete in running, jumping over a vaulting horse, strange exercises on parallel bars, climbing a rope and so on. I was always last during races and that meant really the last one, the one who either never crossed the finish line or arrived minutes after, because I'd gotten quite out of breath. I hardly ever managed to jump over the vaulting horse. I usually fell from the parallel bars and I could not climb even one meter on a rope off the ground. During ball games, I was among the clumsiest girls and no competing team liked to have me among them. The sports teachers mocked me and, in the end, I usually got only a satisfactory mark, which was then corrected to "very good" by the teachers' council because all my other marks were excellent. All the same, I don't remember my classmates laughing at me. It seemed that the majority felt pity for me and they could not believe how somebody could suffer during a pleasant lesson like gymnastics.

6

Material and Social Development

I n the Sixties, the standard of living in Slovenia started to grow, but my family still lived in rather poor circumstances. We were in my grandparents' house, where we had only one bedroom and the kitchen. By then, my classmates' parents had built new houses or renovated the old ones so that they had indoor bathrooms and toilets. Some people had fridges, electric kitchen-ranges and black and white TVs. I once visited one of these luxurious houses and could not stop admiring how beautiful and ideal everything was. However, I could live without such expensive things.

But I was rather unhappy because I didn't have any trousers or a pullover and I was not dressed like other girls in my class. I had just one or two worn-out dresses that my mum had sewn from her old clothes. I convinced my mum, over the course of almost a year that we should go to Trieste, where many of my classmates got their clothing. In those times, how much money Yugoslav people could spend abroad without paying customs taxes was strictly defined, therefore the majority of people had a system in place. They did their shopping in Trieste wearing their worst clothes and shoes, bought new ones there, changed in the shop and threw their old garments into the rubbish bin. My mum and I followed this procedure. We bought polyester trousers, pullovers, ski boots and winter jackets for my brother and me. Our shopping was very tiring because we first went to all shops and, in the end, bought the cheapest things. I felt even more exhausted when we passed the border between Italy and Yugoslavia. I was scared to death that the customs officers might ask me if my clothes were bought in Italy and determine that my mum should pay tax. The customs officer gave us a rather severe look and then asked my mother what we had bought in Trieste. She innocently watched him with her blue eyes and answered with a pleasant smile that we bought almost nothing. He started to smile as well and when he was leaving the train, he was still watching her.

Although we came home very late, I immediately ironed the new trousers and pullover and put them on the next morning. My grandmother always suggested that I should wear the new clothes just for church. But when she saw that we had bought trousers, she did not insist because trousers were, in her opinion, not decent for church. When I came to school, my schoolmates watched me with a measure of new respect. The girls had to admit that I'd bought modern things and even some boys said that they liked them. One of my classmates, whose sister went to Trieste twice a month, asked me why I did not buy any jeans, chewing gum or at least some beautiful Italian notebooks. When I came home, I mentioned what important things we'd forgotten to buy, and my father promised that he would bring them the next time he went to Italy. He often took his director to the towns on the border, and while he was waiting for him, he could go to Trieste or to Gorizia. Just after a week or two, my brother and I got several boxes of chewing gum, beautiful notebooks and pencils. I noticed that the chewing gum raised my social status in the class. My teachers did not like to see me chewing, but my classmates sighed in admiration.

The girls in fifth grade were about ten years old and much more interested in boys than they had been some years earlier. Girls used to write to each other about the boys they liked. We wrote long letters and gave them just to those girls who were our best friends. My best friend, Zala, liked a different boy every week and she regularly reported to me how he had looked at her and what he had said. She wrote about great adventures, but at the end of her letter she usually added that she'd dreamt it or that she'd simply concocted the story. I did not write such things. The boy whom I liked did not care about girls (nor did he care about school and other things). I just saw him on Sundays during the Mass and during the break in the school. But it was quite enough. I was happy.

In the middle of the year, our teacher required that I sit with a boy who'd had to repeat a year, but who was very amusing and nice. It was *comme il faut* that I frowned when I had to change my seat, but I actually liked it. My new neighbor did not hide that he was very happy to have me as his neighbor. Among the strong reasons for his happiness was the fact that he could copy my homework. Whenever we expected an oral examination, I quickly told him how to answer and his marks improved. Because I obviously had a good influence on him, the teacher let us sit together until the end of the year. We were both sorry when his family moved away, and he went to another school.

My mum managed to convince my father and my grandparents that we should start to build a new house, just like our neighbors. My grandparents owned land and were prepared to give it to us, but we lacked money. My mother saved some, found a new job with a higher salary in the biggest hotel in Ljubljana and asked for a loan. My father decided to earn more money, so he got a driver's license for long vehicles and said that he would start driving to foreign countries. This meant that he would be at home even less, but he would receive a higher salary and additional money in foreign currency. My grandparents agreed that we could build our house on the place where my father once had his joiner's workshop.

At this time people did not care about building plans and building permits. My mum made the plans herself, bought the building materials, asked a neighbor who knew how to build houses to help her, and the first floor of our new home was raised in one week. My mum and my grandfather did the most difficult work, because they dug out the place for the foundation and made the concrete (with their own hands, of course). My brother, my aunt and I brought the building material and water, went to the shop and so on. As soon as the walls were made, one of the neighbors reported to the municipality that the house had no building permit and my mum received an official letter that required explanation. The Yugoslav government usually did not ruin buildings that were made without a permit, especially if they were extensions of the already-existing houses, like ours. The municipal clerk threatened my mum that she would have to pay a big penalty fee, but she persuaded him and he prepared the building permit for her. He did it quickly and my mum said that it was much cheaper than the regular way.

Then the money ran out and the building stopped. We took all our efforts to save more. We did not buy any new clothes and no food except bread; we did not go to Trieste or to the seaside anymore. My mother sewed more and more. The only luxurious things that we had were a TV (black and white) and a small fridge. My grandmother thought that both were unnecessary wastes of money, but my mother liked to cook new things and always tried to prepare something a day before, so that she could immediately serve lunch when my father came home.

When we first got the TV set, we watched almost everything, except the communist congresses which filled most of the program. The comrades in the Communist Party had very frequent meetings, they spoke for hours and the Slovenian TV broadcasted everything. I enjoyed watching the TV announcers, who were all beauties with big painted eyes, mouths and exquisite hairstyles. I still remember how modern it was that women quickly moved their eyelashes—like a butterfly. I found it funny and tried to learn, but it took a long time before I managed to imitate them. I noticed that make-up could completely change a woman's face and decided that I would also start to use cosmetics after I finished elementary school. I was so ugly that I desperately needed them: a fat girl with fair hair, green eyes and I often had a pimple on my face. I wished that I were thin, with black hair and brown eyes.

Although I enjoyed watching TV, I never forgot books. When I went to the school in the vicinity of Ljubljana and was acquainted with the place, I heard that the village had a library and I soon started to visit it. What wealth! They had one room with many shelves full of books, especially novels, and I borrowed at least five per week. As soon as I finished my homework and had learned everything for the next day I started to read and often could not wait until I learned how the story finished. Sometimes I had to hurry up because my family did not like that expensive electricity was used too long into the night. Therefore, I learned how to quickly read the last pages. I skipped lines and pages just to see what happened at the end.

My grandmother thought that such speed reading was not worth mentioning. She claimed that I could certainly not remember or understand what the book was about. My grandfather likewise doubted the benefits of such skimming through books. But I was sure that I remembered as much or even more than other readers. So, I once suggested to my grandmother that I quickly read a book which she had already read and then explain what it was about. She agreed with the experiment and was rather displeased when I retold the story and also answered all her questions. Then she stopped saying that it was necessary to read slowly.

Even the librarian at the village library did not believe that I read five books per week. When I once retold all the five books that I had read, she said: "You might have read them, but such reading is superficial. I am sure that you did not understand all the depth of the authors' thoughts."

I answered that deep thoughts were probably not included in each line but did not dare to say that the librarian probably did not remember each important thought, either. More than thirty years had to pass before the first courses on speed reading appeared in Slovenia and before at least some people believed in it.

When I was eleven years old, my mum and I sat in the kitchen and listened to the radio. The program was interrupted by news that there was a horrible traffic accident on the road to Novo Mesto.

My mum leapt to her feet quite pale and said: "My God, your father went to Novo Mesto today. What if something happened to him?"

She often expressed sudden fears and tried to predict things, so I quickly answered that she should not make up stories. Towards noon, two colleagues of my father appeared at the door. I knew them well, especially one of them who always joked. This time his face was serious, and he looked down.

My mum opened the door and cried: "Tell me if he is alive or dead?"

"He lives but is seriously hurt. He is in the hospital of Novo Mesto and waiting for an operation. We can take you there if you wish."

"Was the accident his fault?"

"No. There was thick fog and the other car drove on the wrong side of the road. It was a head-on collision. Just your husband survived. Both directors who were with him are dead. And so is the driver of the other car."

My mum collapsed on the chair and I, too, remained pale and without words. My father's colleagues tried to comfort us, but it was clear that it was a grave accident and a question if my father would survive. My mum took a couple of things and went to Novo Mesto. When she returned, she told us that he was unconscious. His legs, arms and ribs were broken, and doctors were afraid that they would have to amputate one of his legs. She was wringing her hands, because she knew that it was she who should sign the permission for the operation. She delayed it as long as she could, but then the doctors forced her to make a decision. My mum signed but required that the doctors amputate only his toes. The doctors thought that they would soon have to make another operation but did what my mum wanted. It was a good decision. My father did not lose his leg, and after some years, it was difficult to see that he'd had such a horrible accident. He remained in the hospital for many months and then spent another year in a rehabilitation center.

In my last years of elementary school, all our Sundays were the same: in the morning my mum, my brother and I would take a bus to Novo Mesto, drive two hours in one direction and two hours back and spend a couple of hours with my father. During that time, they did not quarrel so much because my mum was aware that my father was in pain.

When I learned that my father had an accident, I said a lot of prayers, asking that he would survive. But they were not just prayers. I often made an ultimatum: "Please, God, make my father recover, otherwise I will not go to church again. And during my father's funeral I will tell everybody that I do not believe in You anymore."

God heard my prayers. He did not only provide that my father completely recovered but he also kept his job. The accident happened on the last day of his work for the Slovenian Railway. On the next day, he should have started a new job in another firm as a lorry driver. But companies in communist times were kind-hearted, and nobody even thought that my father should leave the Railway. In spite of his accident, he was lucky enough: he survived, my mum had convinced the doctors not to amputate his leg, he kept his job and all his family members supported him. Even my grandmother and my grandfather started to visit him in the hospital.

I think that my father secretly enjoyed the consequences of the accident. He'd faced and survived a deadly car crash that was not his fault and everybody pitied him. The hospital personnel took care of him, he did not need to work and there was not less, but actually more money. And he had the right to sigh that he would be an invalid all his life and that he would limp. He liked to make people cry and he shed some tears, as well, on his own behalf.

7
Communism and Religion

When I was twelve, we began some new courses and got a new, beautiful and modern teacher. She taught biology and chemistry and her lectures were so good and interesting that even I enjoyed listening to her, though I could never understand why one should be interested in single-celled beings or how many electrons there were around a nucleus. Our teacher did not only teach us about science but tried to acquaint us with proper values. She often sent me to Ljubljana, where I borrowed short films that we would watch in class and then discuss what was right and what was wrong. Sometimes she mocked those who still believed in God, although evolution lessons proved that there was no God. Once she exaggerated and two girls felt so hurt that they started to cry and left school. Then she stopped mocking, but she continued with convincing explanations about Darwin's theory and about the many mistakes the Church had made in the past. However, I didn't feel hurt. I'd read that the Church did not oppose the science of evolution because it was actually not an important question. Even if development took place in the way Darwin had discovered, there was still the question about who created the first living being. I could not believe that the world developed by chance—I found too much reason in it.

During our lessons in religion, we often addressed that the Church excommunicated and burnt a lot of innocent people and the priest answered with regret that this was a bad mistake and that priests were sinners, just like other people. Since my teacher obviously didn't know these facts, I tried to explain them to her. When I started with this discussion, my schoolmates were silent and did not want to say anything. The majority went to church, but they were told not to oppose teachers. The teacher never punished me but just tried to insist on her opinion.

I still don't know if my objections were public expression of religion or spitefulness. I regularly went to religious lessons and to Mass, but

I often doubted if certain church lessons were right. I was not at all interested in dogmas or in differences among religions. Perhaps people who lived far from each other created their own images of God?

After many years, our priest went to another parish and we got a new, younger, very energetic and communicative one. Some people found him provocative and said that women liked him because he was tall and chatty. In about a month, he turned everything in the parish upside down and divided people into two sides. He attracted a number of new believers, who were amused by his sermons and because he told, very concretely, what people (including priests) were doing wrong. Of course, there was also opposition. He once mentioned that it was hypocritical if somebody sat in church but did not want to marry his pregnant fiancée and he would look straight at the person he was referring to. The whole family of the young man in question left the church and never came back. Some women did not accept his statement that slander was a sin. They enjoyed such a pastime and did not want to give it up. As we were twelve, we liked his provocative behavior. He knew how to answer our questions, made us think critically, encouraged us to go to Confession and so on. Our religious emotions grew exuberantly. At the time, I thought that I was deeply religious, but I don't think so any more. I am convinced that God did not like all those emotions and that He would have preferred more reason.

Up to that time, I was a moderate and rational believer. But then I started to read all the religious literature that I could find, I sang in the church choir, I helped arrange flowers in the church, I organized activities to clean and decorate graves, and I examined my conscience every evening. After some months of fanatic examinations of which sins I had committed, I started to feel guilty, even if I knew that I had not done anything wrong. Some school friends sneered that I was a stupid fanatic. But I could not immediately find the right path. I read and read and finally found out that repeated self-accusations could not bring anything good. When the priest left the parish after about a year, I started to think more rationally again. Before he went away, the priest said that he intentionally remained in each parish just one year. His goal was to introduce changes and when he achieved it, he went to another place and never came back again. He certainly changed the minds of many people, but not always for the better.

My teacher was sometimes disappointed that all her teachings about ethics and values did not bring any results. She once mentioned that she expected more from me. As the best pupil in the school, she thought that I would be a leader and would help my schoolmates advance in their knowledge, but I was obviously interested only in my own good marks. If she said that today, I would sharply answer that leading and developing knowledge was her task, not that of her students, but back then I took her words very seriously. I immediately accepted her proposal that I should become the class president and president of the youth organization. And I also made a secret personal plan to help schoolmates whose marks were poor. I started to carry out these tasks right away and with enthusiasm.

As president of the class, I didn't have much work. I had to organize class meetings, plan final excursions, offer suggestions to teachers if I thought that one or another of my schoolmates got too low a mark, and discuss things during meetings.

As for the youth organization, I didn't intend to enter, but I wanted to obey my teacher and do something good. Youth organizations should connect young enthusiastic and ambitious people who wanted to do something for society and could be later recruited into the Communist Party. However, it started and ended in a rather poor way.

I had to attend meetings in Ljubljana once a month. We were a group of about twenty students from the schools of Ljubljana and its environs and we discussed how we wanted to organize life in our villages or parts of the town, how we intended to arrange admission into the youth organization and the like. I think that we should have actually discussed the values of young people and then transferred them into our schools, but such questions were not on the agenda. The most philosophical question we ever spoke about was evaluation of our work. That was when I first spoke at greater length and said that we were not critical enough, that we should have done much more and that it was a waste of time to hold meetings if we could not speak about something other than the music that should be on during our admission into the youth organization. One of the boys did not like my remark and tried to sneer at me, but all the others refused to join him and agreed that we could have fewer meetings and that it would be better to learn more and speak less.

When I reported it to my teacher, she gasped but did not say anything. Then she obviously spoke to the regional leader of the youth organization, who was not at all satisfied that the number of meetings should be reduced. She warned me that I should not be so critical.

"What kind of Tito's youth are you, if you find it too difficult to even participate in some meetings? Is there any point in your entering the youth organization?"

I quickly found out that I didn't believe in such an organization, that it didn't mean anything to me, and that I didn't agree with some of its principles, so it was best not to enter it. When I explained my decision to the teacher, she looked at me as if I'd gone mad. Nobody had ever said that he was not ready to enter the youth organization. She started to argue that I should not be so stubborn, that the youth organization was nothing bad, that I would not be able to continue with secondary school if I did not enter the youth organization and so on. It took some time before I mercifully said that I would enter it, after all.

My personal plan to help schoolmates with low marks produced better results. A year earlier, I'd started to make short summaries of some of the courses, because I noticed that they helped me to memorize more effectively and to quickly refresh the most important facts before written or oral exams. One of my schoolmates, the smallest and a sometimes rather naïve girl, was often laughed at because she did not understand the teacher's question. I once noticed that she had been crying and asked her why she had such problems with learning. She sobbed that she was doing her best, but she simply did not know what was important and what to do to improve her marks. I gave her my summaries and she copied them. During the next weeks, she asked me to give her the summaries for all the courses and to tell her how to learn. I was happy that I could explain to somebody all the learning techniques which I'd discovered up to that time. She listened to me with an open mouth, but I wasn't sure that it would help her. After one month, her marks considerably improved, and the teacher asked her what had happened. She frankly admitted that she had started to learn with the help of my summaries. The teacher seemed surprised but did not say anything. After that almost all my schoolmates (even those with good marks) started to ask if they could get my summaries and if I could explain to them how to learn. I always complied with such requests and the average success of the class increased.

The headmaster, who taught us physics, once noticed how two schoolmates exchanged the papers with my summaries and wanted to see them. At first, they tried to hide them because they were not sure if they were allowed to use them. I knew that the headmaster could be very persistent and very sharp when he wanted information and I was also aware that the schoolmates would never betray my identity, so I said that they had my summaries for physics.

"You give your summaries to all your classmates?"

"Yes, also others find this method effective."

"Listen, don't be stupid and think that I'm going to bite off your heads if you show me the slips. And I also won't do anything to your beloved schoolmate who produced them. I would just like to see them. Can you please show them to me for a minute or two? Do you allow them to show them to me, Iris?" That was the first time that he'd called a student by name and it sounded most friendly, so the boys gave him the pieces of paper. He put them on his desk and read them.

"Yes, that's good, very good indeed. I like what you did. And I understand why the class is doing better. Go on in this way."

My position in the class thus became even better. Only two girls did not like me. They were not interested in either school or religion, just in boys. But even though they found me to be a dull swot, they still asked if they could get my summaries and copy my homework.

8
Better Standard and Happiness

When my father was in the hospital, my mum received his salary and saved it. She also applied for loans and thus gathered enough money to buy the building materials and finish the house. All the work was done by my mum, a neighbor who was a bricklayer, my grandfather, my aunt, my brother and me. The result was a small house with a balcony. A close look at it could show that it was not made by professionals. On the ground floor, there was a garage and a big room to store potatoes, cabbages, apples and pickles for winter. On the first floor, there was a larger space which served as a kitchen and sitting room, three bedrooms and a bathroom. My mum always liked to cook, preserve fruits and pickle vegetables, so she filled the store room with pickled French beans, cucumbers, peppers, mushrooms and she even experimented, like preserving sausages and eggs in fat. She made lots of stewed apples, pears, peaches, plums, and blackberries. There were all kinds of jams and bottles of juice. The storeroom had the appropriate temperature to preserve potatoes, carrots, kohlrabi, parsley, cabbages and even lettuce, which was taken from the field when snow began to fall and was wrapped in newspaper.

I liked to help mum by picking blackberries. Each year, towards the end of June, several friends, my brother and I would go to the forest and pick them. We left in the morning, took a piece of bread as a snack, and returned in the afternoon. I usually picked about 6 kilos of blackberries and tried to handle them as gently as possible, so that they remained a bit greyish and were pleasant to look at. My best friend once said that she would sell her blackberries to one of her neighbors and I quickly calculated that she would earn a lot of money. As she said that one could sell blackberries on the market at a much better price, I suggested to my mum that I should try to sell blackberries, too. But both my mum and my grandmother showed annoyance and opposition. My grandmother demanded to know where I got such stupid ideas: a thirteen-year-old girl going alone to Ljubljana to sell blackberries! In the town, there were murderers, thieves and all sorts of villains! My mum looked at her with a bit of disdain but said that we would eat blackberries at home and that I would not go to Ljubljana alone.

My father returned home from the rehabilitation center and the quarrels began again. They were louder than ever. In the years that he spent in hospitals and in the rehabilitation center, he got used to being served food, his friends often brought him wine, and everybody showed him empathy. He expected something similar now at home. He could certainly cook and do some work himself, but as an "invalid" (he repeated this word at least twenty times a day) he expected that his family would support him and try to cheer him up. My mum came home in the afternoon and then she had a lot of work with sewing, cooking and organizing the house. She could not sit with him and comfort him. My brother and I did not like to listen to his moaning about how unhappy he was. It was most tiresome because he not only wanted us to listen to his morbid stories again and again, but very often he began to weep. My God, he only lost some toes which couldn't really be seen, so why did he need to cry? Feeling so sorry for himself certainly did not help him. Couldn't he think about the accident in a different way: he survived, he could still walk, he had a job, a family, a new house and now he was going to buy a car, what else did he want? I tried to convince him that the reality was not as dark as he thought, but he told my mum that I had no heart and that I mocked his accident. My mum seriously asked me what I had said.

"Mum, you know that I never mock anybody! But it makes no sense that he sits in the kitchen and feels sorry for himself. It would be better if he started working and being happy that things are like this."

"Yes, you are right, but mind that he is still not well and be very careful with your words. Better to be quiet than say something that might hurt him. You know how touchy he is."

But he did not like when I remained silent. He said that my silence showed contempt for his misery. I had no more ideas about what to do and finally I asked the priest during Confession.

"Show him respect, be kind…" the priest started explaining what he obviously repeated very often and knew it by heart.

"I am respectful, and it has never entered my mind that I should show contempt towards invalids. I know that they suffer. I never feel ashamed if my schoolmates see me with him and he limps. I am also rarely rude, and I am careful with my words."

"Oh, come on, your father just needs some more signs of kindness and love. When you come home, go and kiss him, tell him something nice, smile, be his little daughter and he will be happy."

Not bad advice, but how could a teenager who was brought up in a family that did not show their emotions (we were not even used to saying "good morning" to each other) change into a smiling little girl kissing her father? Perhaps I would have tried had my father behaved differently towards my mum, my brother and my grandparents. But he scolded them all the time, and wrongly. No, I could not take into account the priest's advice.

After my father had a loud argument with my grandmother again, he decided that we should move to our own house. When I was about fourteen, we had a relatively good standard of living—at least in comparison with our neighbors. My brother and I each had our own room with brand new furniture, my mum had a pleasant kitchen and a living room which she cleaned all the time. My father started to work again and was very proud because he finally had his own car (the smallest and the cheapest one that was on the market).

But all this did not bring us peace or happiness. While my father stayed in his office it was quite pleasant. My mum, my brother and I sat in the kitchen, my mum sewed and we told her what happened at school. As soon as we heard my father's car, we went to our rooms and said that we had a lot of homework. My mum prepared dinner and continued sewing. My father often started shouting immediately upon returning home. If he did not like his dinner, he threw the plate on the floor and said that even pigs would not eat it. My mum silently cleared the floor and put something else on the table.

My father always suspected that his mother-in-law hated him and that she encouraged us to be silent and cold to him. It never entered his mind that he had any faults, especially now that he was an invalid, and he required that we stop seeing her. I impulsively said that we could not do it, because we shared the yard, and somebody had to comb my hair in the morning.

"You are fourteen and should have learned how to comb years ago. If you cannot, go to the hairdresser and have your hair cut. I do not want you to even take a look at the old witch, otherwise you will get what you deserve."

That was too much. It was not that I loved my long hair as I often thought that combing took too much time and that some other hairdo would suit me better. But my long hair was a part of me—a sign of the seriousness with which I was brought up. And now my own father required that I should have my hair cut, just because he hated his mother-in-law. Over the following days, he asked me each day if I'd gone to my grandmother or if I'd combed my hair myself. I had enough and said that I would go to the hairdresser. I think that he was sorry for this decision, but he wanted to have his family completely under his control and that would only happen when there was no more influence from his mother-in-law. Perhaps he was aware that women found their hair important, or perhaps he remembered that cutting women's hair meant punishment in many countries. His attitude changed. He offered me money for the hairdresser and asked if he could drive me, but I coldly refused and went by bus. He did not start shouting but looked down.

One of my mother's cousins was a hairdresser and she cut my hair. When she took the scissors in her hand, she said: "Now hold tight and do not start to cry. Think about the photo of the film star that you have brought with you. The new hairstyle will suit you much better and you will look more modern. And think about a woman who had cancer and will be able to cover her bald head with a wig made of your hair."

Tears entered her eyes when she started cutting and other women in the beauty salon seemed miserable. She styled me very nicely and everybody praised me. Even the headmaster took a look at me when passing by.

Some days after cutting my hair, I got very ill. I had such a strong headache that I could only lie in a dark room. I was not able to move, and I vomited. I lost ten pounds in a week. I was not sorry for the pounds, but I felt dangerously ill. I could not even stand up, because I was so dizzy. After a week, my headache slowly stopped but I remained without will and unhappy for weeks. I did not go to a doctor, but I am sure that it was the psychological trauma caused by my father.

9

Preparing for Secondary School

Although it became a repeating refrain among my family and my neighbors that I was not very clever, I decided to study—to go first to secondary school and then to the university. My grandmother tried to convince me that I should enroll in a vocational school and become a shop assistant or a secretary and not dream about universities that accepted only rich people.

Even if my father prohibited me from seeing her, I still visited her every day and I remained with her for hours. If my father came home when I was in my grandmother's house, I jumped out the window on the other side of the house, ran to the street and then said that I'd gone for a walk. My father did not quite believe me, but he could not make a fuss because he saw me coming from the street and not from my grandmother's house.

"How can you be so vain and dare to say that you want to become a doctor or study foreign languages?"

My mother often asked me if I was sure that I would manage well in secondary school. I answered positively at least one hundred times, but she repeated, again and again: "How do you know it? Here in a village school it is easy to be the best student, but secondary schools are much more demanding, and they accept only the best students from throughout Slovenia."

When I insisted, she finally agreed:

"I will try to save enough money so you can go to secondary school. Let's hope that your dad will contribute. But don't forget that you should do your very best. If you don't pass the first year, you will have to find a job in a factory."

My father and my grandfather did not oppose at all. My grandfather was convinced that his granddaughter was the most intelligent girl in the world and my father liked the idea that his daughter would enroll in the same secondary school as his director's daughter.

We had to sit for entrance examinations in Slovenian, Math and English. I was not quite sure that all my answers on the Math exam were correct, but I was almost convinced that I passed, so I read, sang and happily anticipated the results.

My mum nervously watched me and said: "How can you sing, if you do not know if you passed the exams? Are you aware that it is now too late to enroll in any other school?"

Other schoolmates were unsure if they passed the entrance examinations, so three of us made a vow that we would make a pilgrimage on foot if we succeeded. We intended to go to Brezje, to the Church of Mary, Helper of Christians. We did not know that we could have joined the national youth pilgrimage which took place every year towards the end of June. We decided to walk the 40 kilometers by ourselves. We passed our exams and then wanted to do what we promised. We first undertook some training, walking about ten kilometers, and then prepared our bags. When I told my father that we were going on foot, he was furious. That was too dangerous, there were all kinds of bad people on the streets, we would get hurt and so on. He forbade me to even think about such an expedition. I had to tell my friends that my father forbade the pilgrimage and they decided not to go either. We agreed that we would postpone the pilgrimage for a year or two. I bitterly resented his decision and thought that his goal was to prevent me from fulfilling my religious duties. It took years before I understood that he was worried about me. My father offered that he would take me and my friends to Brezje by car if we thought that God had something to do with our entrance exams, but I coldly refused. I made a vow to make the pilgrimage on foot and not by car, what did he think? God helped us to pass our exams and we had to show gratitude with something really difficult and not just with a comfortable drive.

During the holidays I had no real work, so I read. I tried to improve some of my weak points like my personal appearance and behavior. I borrowed a book on slimming diets and one or two on polite behavior. The first one did not help at all. I starved for a day or two and then I started eating everything that my grandmother put on the table. The books on polite behavior had a stronger influence. I realized that I did not know anything about good manners, and I discovered numerous habits I should change. I learned that I did not know how to maintain a witty and smart conversation, I could not smile when I was expected to, I could not provide arguments for my ideas and so on. I found new mistakes every day and before entering the secondary school I was convinced that I was a wretch.

In spite of all my faults, however, those times brought me my first marriage proposal. My neighbors more or less liked me and almost everybody said I had beautiful hair and that it was pleasant to talk to me. When I came home, my grandmother and my mum giggled. After some moments my mum solemnly said that one of our neighbors asked her if she were prepared to marry me with his son. I knew that my mother did not like that neighbor and that everybody would find a marriage of a fifteen-year-old girl absolute nonsense but both my grandmother as well as my mother behaved as if they took the proposal seriously. My mother started to explain that the boy was tall, handsome, hardworking and clever and that I should seriously think about the proposal. I was insulted by even thinking that I should marry a usual farmer. It did not enter my mind that my education in those times was no higher than his and it also didn't occur to me that I should have considered it an honour. My mum told my neighbor to ask the same question after ten years. From time to time she still scolded me that I was too choosy because I refused a rich suitor.

10

First Days in the Secondary school

I enrolled in a secondary school in the center of Ljubljana that was thought to be one of the best in Slovenia and was the only one that offered three foreign languages: French, English and Latin. I adored French and tried to imitate its sounds and intonation. Latin seemed eminent because everybody said that it was the right foundation for a classical education. I would have loved to learn German, since it was spoken by our neighbors to the north. But Yugoslavia did not forget that Germany had attacked it, so the majority of secondary schools did not offer the language. I did not know that my secondary school had one additional reputation, namely that it accepted mainly young girls and boys from rich families, children of doctors, lawyers, teachers and directors, which meant that the atmosphere was rather snobbish.

If one assumed that, in a socialist country, almost everyone was socio-economically equal, he would be wrong. In the socialist Yugoslavia there were considerable socio-economic discrepancies although everybody spoke about equality. People who were in the Communist Party, those who worked as managers in large enterprises, and many intellectuals had higher salaries than usual workers. They also knew how to get loans, building permits or cheaper flats.

The school had a marvelus location in the center of the city. Some classes faced a beautiful park and others one of the oldest churches in Ljubljana. In the vicinity there were also big shops, several schools and a number of student bars. The building itself was dark and serious: its walls were decorated with ugly black drawings and the floor was damaged in many places. The classes were big because they accepted up to thirty-five students. The tables and chairs were almost black from age and they smelled of mildew. The teacher's desk was on a low platform. The classrooms had no special equipment: they had just blackboards, some pieces of chalk and a sponge. Only the classroom for chemistry contained a number of strange tools.

On the very first day, we introduced ourselves: we had to tell our names, where we were from and the occupation of our parents. When we described the occupation of our parents, we immediately presented our social status. Mari and Mila were at the top of the class. Mari was the daughter of one of the best-known Slovenian doctors and Mila's father was director of one of the largest companies in Ljubljana. Both girls were beautiful, slim, smart, energetic, self-confident and could answer any question the very second they heard it. They were well aware of their position and treated the rest of the class a bit haughtily.

The next on the social ladder were Barbara and Stela. Barbara was the daughter of a lawyer and Stela of the railway director, whom my father drove to different places in Slovenia. In comparison with Mari and Mila, Barbara and Stela wore much prettier and more expensive dresses that could not be bought in Yugoslavia, but in the most expensive shops in Italy or Austria. During the break, they said that they enrolled in the secondary school just because their parents required it, and that they had no intention to study hard because they were interested in other things (and they smiled and looked at the boys).

The class elite further consisted of Miriam and Eliza, whose fathers were university teachers. Miriam was a star because she was good at mountaineering. Eliza distinguished herself because she had plenty of activities in the afternoon: she learned to play the piano, took ballet lessons, studied German and Italian and who knows what else.

The most striking among the boys was Luka, who was not only a handsome, tall young man with dark hair and blue eyes, but could also speak like a professor. He could discuss the latest pop songs, the latest essays by Slovenian philosophers or even women's fashion.

Janez was another boy who immediately showed that he was something special. He was handsome, too—tall, fair with blue eyes. But nobody ever noticed his appearance, because all gasped when they heard how self-confident he was. I still remember how surprised he was each time he got an average or low mark, although he had thought he'd said enough in oral exams or written everything that was necessary on paper tests.

Other girls thought that the most handsome and witty was Vito, but I never shared that opinion. I rarely found him funny.

Nikola was also noticeable because it was clear that he read a lot and that he was able to discuss rather complex topics. He had all the characteristics that could have placed him among the most popular boys in the class, but the majority of our schoolmates did not like him very much because he was not self-confident and simply let others suppress him.

There were two or three of us who did not come from respected families, who did not live in Ljubljana and whose success was doubtful. Everybody knew that village schools were much less demanding than those in Ljubljana. I was afraid that my schoolmates considered me to be at the bottom of the class. Stela immediately and loudly said that I was the daughter of her father's driver. I did not speak much, but the main reason for my low position was my appearance. I was not slim, I only had two old dresses made by my mum and my shoes were worn out.

After the first week, I was desperate. How should I be successful among so many beautiful, communicative, exceptional classmates who came from well-situated families, wore fashionable clothes and were much more intelligent than I—or so I felt. It seemed that my schoolmates were of the same opinion, because some mocked me quite plainly and others in a more discreet way. Mari and Mila were high above the others and did not even speak with me. Barbara and Stela mocked everybody who was not well-dressed. Miriam and Eliza criticized me because I avoided gym class. Gym lessons took place in the late afternoon, so those who lived outside Ljubljana did not have to participate. The boys did not have so many remarks, but they were not interested in girls who were neither pretty nor communicative.

The teacher organized a trip outside Ljubljana very soon after classes started. We would first visit a factory and then have a picnic to get better acquainted with each other. I knew that this would be too demanding for me, because I would not be able to participate in the discussions of my schoolmates. When the picnic started, the class divided into several social groups. Young, aspiring intellectuals discussed the values of contemporary young people, class beauties spoke with the most handsome boys, Miriam, Eliza and Stane discussed their sporting and cultural achievements, Luka described a very good new song that was on Radio Luxembourg and Nikola ran from one group to the other and tried to bring the company together. Margareta noticed that I sat alone and invited me to her group of girls, who already had serious boyfriends, but I did not know how to contribute to their conversation either. After an hour, I asked the teacher if I could go home, because

I had a headache. She allowed this and my schoolmates did not even notice my departure.

If I had had any self-confidence, I would have lost it when I got the first marks. I received only good and low marks and my knowledge of math and physics were unsatisfactory. The teacher of these two subjects was a sharp old lady who had very poor teaching methods. But she effectively convinced the class that we were stupid and not talented in her subjects. She often said that math was essential for the development of logical thinking and that one could not succeed in life if one did not understand it. She was so convincing that I believed her over the course of all four years of secondary school and even later thought that people should learn math. Many years had to pass before I dared to declare that coordinate systems, geometry, and integrals were quite useless, that they did not contribute to my knowledge and did not help me in life at all. I am still sorry that I allowed that teacher to convince me.

My first math exam broke me. When the teacher called me in front of the blackboard, I was scared stiff. The teacher watched sharply and pressed her thin lips. Standing on the platform completely exposed me to the critical looks of my schoolmates. When the teacher asked me a question, I answered, but not with the same words she had taught us, which is what she expected. She tried to make me think logically (this is what she called her rude and sharp scolding that usually resulted in an unsatisfactory mark). But at the end I felt completely lost and she silently and scornfully put down an unsatisfactory mark. I asked, with tears in my eyes, if I could go home because I did not feel well, but she angrily answered that I should learn more and I would feel better. The majority of the class laughed, and it seemed that they agreed with her. When the math hour was finished, I left. That was my final defeat. Up to that moment, I could pretend that I was at least a bit self-confident, but now everybody saw that I was a poor wretch. When I walked towards the bus station, I seriously thought about leaving the secondary school.

I came home in tears, but I tried to hide them because I did not want to increase my mum's worries. She had enough troubles because my father had burst into one of his rages. He shouted so loudly that all the neighbors could hear him, and it seemed that there would be no end. That evening my mum, my brother and I did not obey my father's command to stay away from my grandmother. We went to her to find a bit of peace.

My father banged the door (and the glass broke again), locked it and cried: "Go, go to that old witch and ask her to give you the money to survive! I am not going to give you a penny until you return on your knees and beg me to take you back!"

We were left without anything. My grandmother frothed with anger, invited us into her kitchen and offered us dinner, but nobody could eat. Both grandparents said that mum should get divorced, because my brother and I were such nervous wrecks.

"I cannot divorce, because I have children. Children need a father. And how should I maintain us all, alone?"

"How much did he give you for food this month? And the previous month? How much did he give for children's shoes and clothing?"

My mum looked at her father with surprise and obviously only then recognized that she maintained us all by herself. My brother and I did not care about money, but we agreed with our grandparents that life with a person like my father was Hell, even if we had a new house and a car.

In the morning, my mum woke me up to go to school, but I told her that I could not go with such a tear-stained face. I also told her that I trembled with fear when I had oral exams. She took me to the doctor who gave me a light sedative. Then we went to the legal adviser and she put in an application for divorce.

When we came home, we quickly moved the most necessary things from our new house to the old rooms in my grandparents' house. We could take only our clothing, some kitchenware, our school supplies and the TV set. My father kept the majority of the new furniture, the house and the car.

My father did not believe that we would stay in two old rooms in my grandparents' house. During the first days, he sneered and spitefully shouted that we would soon come and beg him to take us back. When a week passed, he came to the grandparents' door and shouted that enough was enough and that we should return. My grandfather opened the door and told him that my mum wanted a divorce and that he should never come back to his door again. After some days of silence, we heard my father begging us not to leave him alone.

We were well aware that his weeping would soon be replaced by shouting, so we remained hard-hearted. Then he started to send neighbors whom he'd asked to help him get his family back. One of the richest neighbors threatened my mum that he would report her to the Center for Social Work and suggest that they give my brother and me to my father.

My mum looked at him with contempt: "Go ahead and tell them also how often I had to tell *you* that I was a married woman."

He quickly left our house, but he did go to the Center for Social Work. My mum was called to their office and had to report about the circumstances in which we lived. It took her quite some time and energy before she convinced them that my father was not a poor invalid, but a wild person who shouted and beat his family. They doubted this until my mother put on the table a couple of medical certificates that proved how my father beat her and my brother.

When I returned to school, I expected that my schoolmates would increase their contempt and I had no idea how I would manage to resist. But Janez just waved his hand and said: "Good to see you again." Luka came to me during the break and talked to me—not too much, just to show that he cared about me. Margareta gave me advice about how to increase my self-confidence. Vali, who was always ready to give someone a piece of her mind, watched over me and it seemed that she would snap at anybody who might dare to sneer. Barbara and Stela quietly looked at their notebooks and Mari and Mila were still interested just in their own marks. Margareta later told me that the class had a wild quarrel with the teacher when I left. The teacher shouted that they were a group of snobs who mocked me, although their knowledge was no better than mine. My schoolmates cried that her teaching methods were too sharp and that it was she who had broken me. It was obvious that the mocking had been replaced with empathy. I did not like that they discovered how vulnerable I was and that they felt sorry for me, but the wall between us began to break.

In the secondary school, I achieved a better status because of my English. The English teacher was known as a dragon—much more difficult than our math teacher. As soon as somebody forgot the "s" in the third person singular, she indignantly raised her voice: "What?"

If the unfortunate student did not immediately correct his mistake, he got an unsatisfactory mark. Good marks in English meant something and my schoolmates started to ask if they could copy my homework.

During the first months, I recognized that there would be many low grades in Latin. I started to drill words, declensions and conjugations and then got a good mark. My French was assessed as very good, but I was rather annoyed because it was not excellent. Eliza got excellent marks for her French, although she was, in my opinion, no better than I. I noticed that Eliza raised her hand each time the teacher asked a question and tried to answer in one or another way, but I never thought that the teacher appreciated and rewarded her cooperation.

After a few months, I managed to achieve average or very good marks in all subjects except for math. Math caused everyone trouble and we often discussed how to improve our knowledge. Mari and Mila looked down upon us and said that it was simply necessary to learn, and that math was nothing special. Luka once stepped onto the platform and dramatically asked if we really knew how to learn math. One of the schoolmates answered that he should quit his rhetorical exercises, but Luka insisted. He turned to me and repeated the question, so I said that I did not really know how to learn. I repeated things written in the notebook and completed my homework, that was all. The textbook was not used by anybody, because we did not understand it. Then Luka suggested that we should buy a special collection of math exercises and solve them. Tea, from another parallel class, had told him that this was the only way to improve one's knowledge of math. The majority mocked him, but I bought the booklet and started to solve its mathematical problems. I soon found that the exercises really did help to understand math, therefore I practiced each Saturday and Sunday afternoon. I listened to the radio and calculated. I realized that math was not as boring as I had thought. It was a real challenge, when I sat at the table and tried to solve a problem that seemed all Greek to me. I found real success only towards the end of the year. My last written exam in math was very good, which increased my grade just to the satisfactory level, but I knew that I would improve it the following year.

11
New Society

A round the middle of the first year, our teacher determined that the class beauties and some of the boys chatted too much and ordered us to change seats. I was most surprised when the teacher demanded that Barbara, Martin, Janez and I should sit together in the first row. She could not have put together more different people. Barbara was the most beautiful girl in the class, but she had no wish to look clever and often admitted that we probably all had a higher intelligence quotient than she. Janez was the vainest, and used every opportunity to quarrel with teachers because he considered his marks too low. Martin was supposed to be the most handsome boy in the class, but he spoke only about cars. Barbara found Martin as handsome as an Italian movie star and fell in love with him, but Martin pretended that he had no idea about it. When the teacher ordered that I should sit between Barbara and Martin, I was most unhappy. About what, for God's sake, should I speak with her? She was not interested in anything—neither school, nor books, nor life values, nor music. What should I speak about with both boys, who discussed only the results of football games and technical details of cars?

The teacher had, of course, placed us together so that we would not speak during the lessons, but we still had to exchange some words during the breaks, didn't we? All four of us sat, disheartened, in the front row and we had just one common thought: that we did not belong together. Barbara was disappointed because she had to sit far away from Stela and Ana, who were her best friends. She would have been most happy if she could sit beside Martin, but I was stuck between them. Janez explained that he was such a genius and so disciplined that it was a mistake to place him in the front row. He could follow teachers' explanations and work also on some other projects, if he could sit in the back row. But the teacher was stubborn and did not listen to objections.

Nothing could be changed, so we had to adapt to the situation. Barbara started to tell me which clothes were modern, how to apply good make-up, which colors were best for girls with fair or black hair, which diets helped to lose kilos, how a girl should look at a boy, how to place one's legs when sitting for a photo and the like. I could not apply all of her ideas, because I had no money, but I tried to use better color combinations, mascara and had my hair cut in a more up-to-date style.

I let her copy my homework, from time to time helped her with some English and Latin expressions, told her how to memorize study materials and spoke about the books that I'd read. She gratefully copied my homework, but she was not much interested in my tips for successful studying, because she did not care about grades. Once she got an unsatisfactory mark in biology and the teacher gave her just two days to repeat the exam. She thought that it was quite impossible to learn so many pages in just two days, but I told her to stay in the school the whole afternoon and I tried to help her remember the boring data about animals. We studied together the next day, too, and she managed to pass. She was very grateful and explained to everybody that she passed only because I helped her. That was not true. She was clever and had a good memory, although she pretended to be rather simple. When I spoke about the books that I'd read or about operas that I'd listened to, she laughed and kindly said to Martin and Janez that I had strange interests. I soon noticed that she enjoyed speaking about Martin and that she was happy if I leaned forward so that she could look at him. And she was always most grateful when I discreetly asked Martin if he intended to go to a party or a dance. I often found it funny that I had to help her with Martin—she was so beautiful and dynamic that she should have been more successful without any assistance. Once she was quite desperate and cried that she would simply tell him that she was in love with him. I seriously told her that she should slow down, as all the heroes in the books I'd read had reacted in this way and they had succeeded.

Martin and Janez surprised me. I expected that I would have to learn something about cars or sports to exchange at least some words with them. But we got involved in unbelievable discussions about life values and problems, and I found it especially interesting that they both had quite similar ideas as did I. They were clever and sensitive boys and their appearance in the class was just a façade. They were grateful, too, that they could copy my homework or that I whispered a couple of English or French words into their ears during exams. We were, of course, forbidden to cheat during exams and the best students always emphasized this point. However, I didn't know why I should not offer my friends a bit of help. The teachers sometimes saw me, and I knew that I could be punished, but I still found it normal to help. After a month or two, we were all happy to sit together.

Towards the end of the schoolyear, I felt as fit as a fiddle, although my marks were average. I understood the system of learning. I knew what to do to get good marks and I was sure that I would eventually be among the best students. I was on good terms with almost all schoolmates except Stela. Several classmates asked me if I would sit with them the following year. If Barbara heard such questions, she shouted that they should back off, because she wanted to sit with me. I could not believe that she was serious, because her main friends were still Stela and Ana. My status in the classroom still increased because the librarians announced that I was the most passionate reader at the school. I went to the library each weak and borrowed a lot of books. The literature teacher just mentioned that one or another book was good, and I'd run off to the library. I also often shared my thoughts about books.

During the first year of secondary school, when I was fifteen, I still went to the religious lessons, along with about ten other young boys and girls, some of them a bit older than I. The group was led by an old priest who had speech defect. His teaching and his sermons were hardly understandable. He had most old-fashioned opinions constructed on emotion and stereotypes. I felt a deep gap between my ex-schoolmates and myself as we sat together during religious lessons. I thought that their intelligence and knowledge was on a much lower level than mine but I didn't realize that my conceit was much higher. After the first year of secondary school, I stopped going to religious lessons. The group including the priest, just exchanged unimportant remarks and were not ready to discuss real problems and values. Why not read or learn, instead of wasting my precious time? My grandma was not very pleased with my decision but did not make a fuss. After all, I only omitted the religious lessons and still went to Mass. The religious lessons were quite late in the evening and she preferred that I was home at that hour rather than walking around.

During the holidays, I got a temporary job in a factory so I could earn some money and cover a part of the expenses for books, notebooks, clothing and shoes. It was a big factory that produced cardboard and other sorts of paper. It had several buildings and several thousand workers. The premises were in the center of Ljubljana, but they consisted of largely empty spaces. The interior was cold, flat and full of machines that produced different kinds of paper. Women in the factory quarreled all the time and the atmosphere was very unpleasant. I quickly learned how to perform the manual work, but it was very boring to repeat the same movements eight hours per day. I earned a lot of money, by my standards, and I could not only buy books, but also a new coat and a suit.

My mum soon received the legal decision that the divorce was granted. However, the paper about the divorce did not contain any word about division of the property. The decision about who would keep our new house was a matter of another legal case. My father was half-owner of the building and possessed it. My mum often suggested that she would buy him a flat if he gave the house to us, but he refused all her offers. He also did not want to pay her any money for my brother and me till she filed a complaint at the court. He had a very good lawyer and Yugoslav courts worked slowly. We had to wait for the decision of the court for nine years.

We found ourselves in a ridiculous situation: my father was alone in our brand-new house and we three were crowded in two rooms of our old house, without a bathroom. We had to get out of his sight when he was in the yard (which was not his property) or he started to scold and shout. Sometimes he washed his car for two hours in order to wait for one of us to come out, so he could voice his complaints. My mum, grandmother and I did not go out as long as he was outside, but my brother and my grandfather did not care about his remarks. He kept up this childish behavior for several years before he got tired of trying to provoke and he came home just in the evening to sleep.

I had no special space for learning at my grandparents' house, but was quite happy in the kitchen, alongside my grandmother, where I repeated my lessons while she was knitting. I think that she enjoyed my learning aloud and that she remembered a lot of what I studied. My brother learned in mum's kitchen, but he did not devote much time to school. When he came home, he quickly ate something, did his homework and then went out with his friends. They usually played football or some other games. He was not as interested in school as I and was an average student. My brother inherited a lot of my father's character. He quickly lost his temper and often had fights with other boys of his age. He was a wild boy who frequently did something wrong. However, he knew what was right and what was wrong and regretted foolish things he had done. He inherited also my mum's sense of humor and was always popular both among his schoolmates, as well as in our family. We were not confidantes but the older we got, the better friends we were. We never wasted words and never spent much time together, but we knew that we could rely on each other.

In spite of all the troubles with my father and the poor conditions in which we lived, our lives after the divorce became peaceful and comfortable, so much so that I could not believe the difference. Each time my mum received a letter from my father's lawyer, and when she had to go to the Court, she got angry and upset, but after a few days she forgot it and became happy again. She had a good job and my brother and I did well in school, and that was what was important to her.

12

Friends

In my second year of high school, when I was about sixteen, I often asked myself who was my best friend and who I should sit with.

I liked Vali. She was among the class intellectuals, but she never boasted that she did not have to study. She was not a special beauty, but her dresses and her appearance showed good taste. She played the piano and read a lot, so we always had something to talk about. She was full of empathy and understanding and had a great sense of humor. But she also had a fault—she often burst out in anger. When I got a better mark in Slovenian or in English, she could not believe that "a country girl" could be better than her. Each time, she ordered me to give her my examination paper, so she could study it carefully and compared it with hers. If she did not agree with the teacher, she took my exam and hers up to the teacher and angrily ordered him to explain why my paper got a better mark. The teachers more or less patiently answered her questions. I was rather amused and also interested in how the teacher would explain my better mark. At least two or three years had to pass before she believed that my language skills were better than hers.

I shared many interests with Margareta. Her marks were neither very good nor very bad. We both loved books and classical music, especially operas. We lent records to each other and went to opera performances together. The opera in Ljubljana was rather small and its performances nothing special, but we enjoyed sitting in the dark and listening to the music. During the breaks we walked in the hall and watched women who came in long dresses and with their best jewelry. The tickets for the worst seats were not very expensive but we still had to save money for quite some time to afford them. We were the only ones in the class interested in opera. Both our schoolmates and our relatives found us a bit strange because we preferred the opera to rock music. Margareta and I always had a lot to talk about, so I decided to sit next to her the following year, and it remained that way for the rest of our time in secondary school.

It was not an easy decision because Barbara, Martin and Janez all expected that we would still sit together. There were also others who wanted to be my neighbors. How things changed in just one year! Who would have thought that I, a "miserable country girl," would have to make a decision with whom I would sit?

The only one who did not want to be my friend was Stela. Our appearances were similar: we both had fair hair, green eyes and a few too many kilos. But we often got on each other's nerves. When I sat with her best friend, Barbara, Stela glared daggers at me or mocked me whenever she could. She taunted others, too, but the majority did not answer her remarks and only laughed. I thought that she meant what she said about me, so I started to return what she gave out, with double measure. After that, she stopped teasing me.

Luka and I became good friends, although he was very busy. During each break, he rushed to the neighboring class to see Tea. They'd become a couple during the first year, and it was pleasant to see how they loved each other. When he was in love with Tea Luka seemed even more pleasant, sensitive and mature than before. At least, I thought so—my schoolmates did not agree with me. The majority of boys did not like him, and I suspected that was because he tried to solve problems in a peaceful and positive way. Some girls were also against him, especially Vali.

Just seeing him open his mouth, she would hiss: "Here we are again! He's going to make another emotional sermon."

Luka heard those remarks, but he rarely reacted. And even when he answered, he said something like: "Peter, let's stop arguing and be friends! Are we friends or not? Say that we're friends."

And Peter would mutter with a sour look: "To Hell with your friendship!"

When I tried to convince Vali and Peter to change their behavior, they just mumbled that they had a right to their own opinion.

I once discussed this with Eliza, and she said that I should not be so sure about Luka's idealism and goodness: "You don't go to parties and haven't seen him when he was in a different mood." She did not want to explain herself.

Eliza and I became friends after an event that might have otherwise caused hard feelings. Eliza was known as a girl interested in the arts, with a special gift for music, dancing, and theater. Once, the English teacher tried to teach us an English song and we all believed that Eliza would remember it and repeat it for us during the break. She did, and all my schoolmates said how lucky we were that we had a schoolmate with a musical education. But I couldn't believe my ears. When she sang, she was out of tune. She had no musical ear at all!

The next day, when we were alone, I asked: "How long have you been taking piano lessons?"

She laughed: "Eight years. I will finish the second level this year. Do you want to know why my father made me play piano? Because I am tone deaf. He wants me to develop at least a little bit of musical skill. How interesting that you are the only one who noticed it."

I did not speak about it anymore, but we started to discuss things more often, especially when we traveled on arts excursions to Italy and Austria with our school.

The arts excursions organized by our school were something quite special. Students from other secondary schools had no such opportunities and said that our trips to Rome, Florence, Naples, Madrid and Vienna were just a sign that we were the biggest snobs in Slovenia. It was not true. We had an enthusiastic and energetic arts teacher who adored arts and convinced a number of us students that the only right subject for us was the History of Art. Arts excursions were as cheap as possible, but were still so expensive that I don't know how my mum got money to pay for even the first one. We prepared for each excursion several months ahead, with weekly meetings during which the teacher showed us photos and slides and explained the characteristics of different art historical periods. Before we left, we had to pass an exam and we had to sign that we would walk with the teacher to the museums and galleries and go to bed at nine. When we first went to Florence, we stayed in a hostel located in an old Italian castle that I loved. In the morning, we had a good breakfast, and then the teacher kept us going all day long. We were dead tired by the middle of the afternoon.

She laughed: "Now who is young and who is old? Have you got magnets on your backs that pull you down onto every seat we pass?"

The excursions always ended happily because she beat the arts into our heads all day long and then exhausted us by walking, so that we fell into our beds even before nine. When we visited Rome and Naples, I was convinced that I would become an arts teacher. But certain opinions of our teacher started to irritate me.

I once tried to take a photo of Eliza beside a statue with a cheap camera I'd gotten after finishing elementary school and the teacher sneered: "What's wrong with you, that you would place an ordinary human beside such a divine statue?"

The teacher also made me angry because she mocked everybody who stopped to admire a painting or a statue that was not in her encyclopedia, saying that we cared about unimportant things. I didn't know how to respond, though I felt that such opinions were wrong.

But I remembered them and, after some months I started thinking: "How could she nag when I wanted to take a photo of Eliza beside that statue? Aren't people something much more admirable, more unique and more interesting than all the pictures and statues in the world? And why mock those who liked works that were not the most famous?"

It was quite clear: the teacher knew a lot about art, because art was what she idolized. That made her impossibly proud and unnatural. This discovery destroyed my belief that I was born to be an art teacher.

When we were sixteen, several girls said that they had boyfriends, and there were some couples in the class, as well. Among the first were Mari and Vito. I found them a rather disharmonious pair. Outwardly they seemed pleasant: both of them tall, he was dark and always ready to say something funny, while Mari was fair and serious.

I did not like Vito very much, but Barbara, an authority on boys, said that I should develop more knowledge about men: "Take a look at how tall, dark, nice, and communicative he is. And a perfect gentleman!"

In my eyes, he was a long beanpole and his school results were average. I would rarely laugh at his remarks and he certainly did not behave like a gentleman towards me.

Towards the end of the second year, two more couples appeared: Barbara and Martin and Peter and Ana. During the holidays, both girls sent me letters that described their love adventures that consisted mainly of going to the cinema with their sweethearts. I was just happy that they remembered me, even in the moments when they did not need or miss me.

I didn't have a boyfriend and could only speak of ten pen-pals whom I found through newspaper advertisements or agencies specialized in pen-pals. I never met anyone personally. We did not have computers or typewriters, so we wrote to each other by hand. I found my first pen-pal from California in elementary school. His photo showed a handsome boy, but his handwriting was horrible, and I hardly understood him. He also did not write very often. I also made a lot of mistakes in English so our correspondence finished after a couple of years. By the time I was sixteen, I had extensive correspondence with a number of boys from South Africa, Morocco, Malaysia, Germany, Australia, Italy and India. I especially liked the Italian and the Indian boy, to whom I wrote over a span of several years.

My pen-pal from Milan, with whom I corresponded in French, was Roberto. He was five years older than I and studied electronics. He was a poet and had already written a number of poems. He translated some into French, so that I could read them. Sometimes he recommended that I read Italian poets and I immediately would do it. Once he wrote a poem for me and I proudly showed it around, although my grandmother shrugged her shoulders that one Italian poem meant nothing. Roberto's French was much better than mine and he rarely wrote fewer than twenty pages, so I had a strong inferiority complex. But he was not disturbed by my weak French. He was happy because I liked to discuss each of his remarks and thoughts (as much as I understood him). I sometimes completely misinterpreted what he wrote, but he patiently and kindly explained his thoughts to me once again. I could not believe that I could correspond with such a wonderful man. After two years, we decided to meet in person, and he said that he would come to Slovenia. But there was always something that prevented our meeting.

My second favorite pen-pal was James from India, to whom I wrote in English. He, too, was five years older than I and studied theology. He sent me one or two photos (dressed in a priest's gown) and all my friends thought that he was very handsome. He might have been, but I remember him as an analytical person who liked to preach. He was a Catholic from Kerala in South India, a region where there are still quite a few Catholics. We had similar opinions about religion and about life values. He often wrote about the difficult life in northern India. Once he mentioned that he was a normal young man and wished to have a girlfriend, but it was not allowed. He was most protective towards me and was not stingy with advice on how I should behave and what I should think. Above all, he warned me to be careful with men. When I once incautiously wrote that a married man had asked me for a drink, I received an urgent letter from India in which he scolded me, over the course of several pages, about how I should not enter into relationship with an old drunkard (there was no relationship at all, but just an invitation that I refused), that I should not even look at him, that I should tell my brother who should beat him (and James would be ready to do so, if he were in Slovenia) and so on and so on. Not even my parents gave me advice like that or kept me on such a short lead.

When I was almost seventeen, I found a temporary job at the seaside. I wrote to the Slovenian Railways, which owned a village of small cottages and a restaurant that could be used by their employees, on the Adriatic Coast. They needed a number of young girls who would work in the kitchen or serve food. My grandmother did not like that I would not be under her control for two months, but my mum said that she trusted me more than anybody else. I loved the idea that I would be able to stay at the seaside for two months, swim and earn some money.

I summoned up my courage and went to the seaside alone by train. The manager showed me which cottage I would stay in and suggested that I should start working in the kitchen. I would have preferred to serve people, rather than peeling potatoes or washing lettuce, but the kitchen work was better paid than serving in the restaurant.

I thought that I would have difficulties finding new friends, but I was immediately acquainted with many girls my age who started inviting me to dances, walks, swimming and sunbathing. When I went dancing, I was rather surprised that even plain girls like me had no trouble finding partners. If I wanted, I could have gone dancing each evening, but I had to start work at 6 a.m.

After a month at the seaside, I was rather bored and homesick. Then I met two new friends, Silva and her schoolmate, and we quickly found out that we had many common interests. Silva was a year younger than I, she read less and never went to the opera, but she was interested in everything and we became best friends. Although she was younger than I, she was very interested in boys and quickly made contacts with complete strangers. Once we were sunbathing when two soldiers started chatting us up. Silva kindly asked them where they were from and what it was like in the army while I kept silent. I found soldiers rather annoying. In Slovenia, there were many soldiers from other Yugoslav republics, and they behaved differently than Slovenian boys. When they passed a girl or a group of girls, they started to greet them, wave their hands and shout how beautiful and wonderful we were. My grandmother taught me that I should pretend that I did not hear or see anything, and I obeyed, because I was really not happy if a whole truck of boys waved their hands and shouted. But Silva taught me that it was possible to look at these young men also from another standpoint.

When the two young men left, she said: "I feel so sorry for them. Tomorrow they are leaving for Macedonia and they will not see Slovenia and their families for a year. Isn't that horrible?"

Silva was from a town in the northern Slovenia, so we decided that we would correspond and visit each other and that we would go to the seaside again together. We wrote to each other at least twice per week and spoke about everything that we had been through.

When I came home, I was happy. I'd managed to spend two months in a foreign place. I'd earned a lot of money, or so I felt. I could buy books, notebooks, shoes and some new material for dresses. When I came back, I was the most tanned in the class and ready to improve my school results.

13
Maks

In my third year of secondary school, I got a little bored. I was seventeen and there was no real challenge in school. The only novelties were some teachers and a new schoolmate.

The first lesson in geography caused a storm among the class beauties. The new teacher was young and tall, he had fair hair and blue eyes. The majority of girls gasped when they first saw him. They started to wear their best dresses for geography lessons, and carefully improved their make-up and their hairdo before the teacher arrived. The boys laughed at them, but the girls continued with a number of tricks. Stela often mysteriously smiled, played with her hair and slightly twisted her hips. Barbara (although she was actually Martin's girlfriend) presented several poses of fashion models when she stood in front of the teacher and Ana spoke just like Marilyn Monroe. Even some girls who belonged to the average group started to wear mini-dresses, high heels and make-up. Janez and Luka once asked me why the girls were so enthusiastic about that beanpole, but I had to admit that I had no idea either.

All of us liked our new math teacher. She was young, pretty and loved math. She never flirted with the boys, though they tried to convince her that we should discuss other points than just math. Each hour she first called one or two students to the platform and gave them some questions for an oral grade. Then she closed the assessment book, glanced at her lesson plan and told us what she was going to teach us. After that, she took a piece of chalk and started to explain, in a sweet voice and write on the board: $X1 + X2 + \ldots Xn$. Mathematics were so marvelus to her that her face became radiant and her voice soft as velvet. She wrote mathematical rules and equations with beautiful and tidy handwriting and when we listened to her, we all found math interesting. She was not as severe as our last teacher, but she never gave a satisfactory mark if we did not deserve it. Sometimes she gave us a very difficult task that we could not solve, and she made a good-natured remark that we were artistic souls and not mathematical ones. I am still convinced that she was one of the best teachers that I had ever had and that she awoke in me as much knowledge and love for mathematics as was possible.

It seemed that I was the only girl without a boyfriend so my schoolmates often wondered when I would find one. Barbara, Ana and the others always asked me to come to their parties and suggested that they would invite any boy whom I would like to meet or that they would find appropriate one for me. I refused such invitations because I was not ready to behave in the manner that was expected during parties. I preferred to use all my free hours for reading and began volunteering in one of the public libraries in Ljubljana.

When I first saw Maks, the library director enthusiastically greeted him as a regular visitor who had just returned from Great Britain.

I immediately felt a part of me whisper: "He's the one."

But I quickly denied my imagination: "Oh, come on. Why would I find him interesting? Just take a look—you know that I don't like boys with bulging blue eyes, glasses and long nose. He is not at all handsome and I am sure that he has an unpleasant voice."

In that moment, he started speaking with the director and his voice was not unpleasant. However, I still insisted that he was not handsome and that he was certainly vain, because he studied in Great Britain.

Over the next months, he became a frequent visitor to the library again and he told me that he was finishing his MA in philosophy. I convinced myself for some weeks that he was nothing special and much older than I (he was about twenty-five and I was only seventeen) but, in the end, I had to admit that I could hardly wait for his next visit. I now found him unbelievably intelligent; he had a good character, sense of humor and rather openly expressed his religious and political beliefs which was something special in those times. The majority of people did not dare to say anything against the government and were not interested in religion. Everybody liked him, and the library director, an elderly, serious, married lady, always offered him tea or coffee and asked him to sit with us to discuss one or another theme. I liked to listen to their discussions and sometimes managed to make a remark or two. I was afraid to say more, because I knew nothing about philosophy and very little about life. Maks said that I was very clever for my age and that I could study philosophy, too. He recommended some books and

I tried to read them. I did not understand everything and often asked him for explanations. He was always prepared to explain things and I sometimes forgot that I should have spoken with all the library users, and not just with one.

I carefully hid my feelings about him. I felt so inferior to him that I did not dare to show how infatuated I was. I would never flirt with boys—that would be below the dignity of the intellectual that I wanted to become. I found it odd when I observed women smiling and praising men just to catch them in a snare. I was aware that such a handsome and intelligent man could never fall in love with me. I was still in puberty and rather dumpy, I went to the hairdresser just twice per year and my clothing was still poor, although my schoolmates thought that I'd improved my appearance. Nevertheless, I decided that I would lose at least 10 kilos and invest some more time and money in dressing and thus completely change my look. I hoped that I would, in a year or two, also improve my knowledge of philosophy and thus get the skills to participate in the discussions between Maks and the main librarian.

To successfully lose weight, I had to eat less and exercise more. It was difficult to eat just carrots and cucumbers and I often broke the rule that I would eat only 600 calories per day. Exercises were much easier. I started to go to a dancing school in which there were always enough boys but never enough girls. Therefore, the teacher offered free classes for girls who were ready to come to school more often and dance with boys who would otherwise have no partner. I went to the dance lessons at least three times per week, and sometimes even every day, and I came home so tired that I went to bed without even thinking about food. My grandmother was rather annoyed because I did not eat her lunches and tried to persuade me that only girls with round faces were beautiful, not beanpoles like the majority of my friends. She prepared pies more often than usual because she knew that I liked them, but I did not want to take even a small piece. She was miserable, and I was sorry, too, because I could have eaten it all! In two or three months, I lost 15 kilos and felt much better than before.

My mum was the first to notice the results of my diet because she had to take in all my dresses. Up until that point, she always said that my appearance was nothing special. I was not really insulted by those remarks because I thought that they were true, and besides people in Slovenia preferred to say something negative rather than positive.

But now she looked at me with surprise: "My God, how pretty you have become!"

My mum suddenly found faults with my friends and none with me.

My schoolmates and other boys started to praise my appearance. Among the first who openly and in a loud voice mentioned my figure was Janez, and others agreed with him. Peter once sighed in the middle of a lesson, saying how beautiful I was and what he would do to become at least as intelligent as I, so that I would find him interesting. Martin still played the same game as he had to date: when I had an oral exam and started to speak, he hissed something to his neighbors, who giggled and became silent. I long thought that he mentioned one or another of my faults. When they once giggled again, I asked Margareta what Martin had said.

She answered: "Oh, he always says the same. You know what, don't you?"

"No, nobody has ever told me. He can't say anything good because you always start giggling."

"We laugh because Martin so adores your voice. As soon as you start speaking, he says that he wants to listen to your voice and requires that we should all be silent so that he could hear you."

I found it most amusing, but I had met people whose voices I liked without being in love with them. Barbara, his girlfriend, quite understood that Martin liked to listen to me and became silent, too.

During the dance classes, I met some boys who suggested that we go dancing on Sunday and some wanted to accompany me to the bus station. I did not want to raise vain hopes, so I told everybody that I already had a boyfriend. Of course, they asked why he did not go to the dance lessons with me, and I said that he was in the army.

Maks could express his opinion about almost everything, but he never spoke about girls. He sometimes laughed that he liked all women, but occasionally also criticised flirtatious girls with too short skirts. If the main librarian asked him if he had a girl or a fiancée in his home town, he said that he had too much work with his studies and no time to go out with girls.

Once after I came in from the hairdresser's and wore a beautiful new blue dress, Maks entered the library, stopped at the door and just watched me.

I thought to myself: "Look, he likes me. Is he in love with me? He wouldn't watch me like that if he didn't feel anything."

I looked down and blushed. After a minute he said that he had not noticed what a pretty girl I'd become. From that time on, he always praised my appearance but nothing more was heard about my intellectual abilities.

14
Deciding about the Future

I decided that I would finish the last year with excellent results. This was strategic, as the best students did not have to sit for the leaving examination. I learned Latin, Slovenian grammar, did plenty of math exercises, repeated psychology and philosophy lessons for days. In our fourth year, we luckily did not have subjects like chemistry and biology, which I did not like. I tried to achieve the best mark I could in philosophy, because Maks studied it and because we had a very interesting teacher. But while I usually got a very good grade, it was not excellent.

We had to decide what we wanted to study after secondary school. I did not know which university program I should choose. It was not because I was not interested in anything, but because I loved almost all the subjects. It would have been easiest to opt for foreign languages—not French, as I had wanted at the beginning of the secondary school, but English and German. I learned both without any troubles and my grades were excellent. Many people said that those who mastered these two languages quickly found jobs. I enjoyed writing new foreign words in my notebook and repeated them aloud and as correctly as possible.

My grandmother sometimes said: "Start learning something else, because even I remember these words."

She knew that I repeated them just because they sounded so fine and because I liked that I could pronounce them so well.

My Slovenian marks were excellent. It was my teacher's fault that I did not decide for Slovenian studies, but not because his lectures were uninteresting. Quite the opposite, he presented the most important authors so engagingly that we listened to him with our mouths open. During his lessons, one could hear a needle fall on the floor. But he was choleric and, in my opinion, often raged for no reason. He scolded students who did not give the right answers, got very angry at parents who were surprised that their children's marks in Slovenian were so low and once he became furious because the school director reproached him when his students said a prayer during a play. All the classes had to listen that the prayer was a part of the author's text, not the teacher's own contribution to the play. He was, of course, right, but I found the profession of a teacher too difficult to want to follow in his footsteps.

Towards the end of the year, our Slovenian teacher started a discussion about what we intended to study after secondary school and seemed disappointed because just one of my schoolmates decided to study Slovenian. He asked me why I did not decide for Slovenian, because I was, by far, the best student that he had ever had. My schoolmates laughed and answered that I was the best also in English and in many other subjects. He made a wry smile and suggested that I should still think about it. I would have loved to study medicine, but I was afraid that I did not have the necessary abilities. Several girls from the class decided for medicine and they spoke about difficult entrance examinations, especially in physics, math, chemistry and biology, none of which I liked. My mum often suggested that I should study law and become an attorney. In those years, she'd had so much to do with lawyers that she started to appreciate them. My father still occupied our house, although he more or less only slept in it. It seemed that the legal case about the division of property would never end, because my father's lawyer always filed new complaints. Four years after the divorce, the situation was no longer difficult, because we got used to avoiding my father. My brother and I were interested in other things and did not want to even hear about the courts and attorneys. But my mum knew how unjust it would be if we were to lose everything and she continued with the legal case. She led her fight alone and it cost a lot of money and patience.

I couldn't make a decision about my schooling, so I convinced some schoolmates to accompany me to the employment office that performed tests to help me decide. The majority of teachers and schoolmates laughed and said that psychological tests were not worth anything. The psychologist in the employment service said that I was talented in both humanistic and science studies, but I had to decide about it myself. I finally made the decision to enroll in English and German.

Many of my schoolmates decided for medicine and law. The best students picked medicine, among them Mari, Vali and Miriam. Vito enrolled in medicine, too, although his grades were average. We suspected that he did it under Mari's influence. Even Stela decided to study medicine. When she told us, we laughed. That was a good one: she had failed one or two exams each year and had to sit for re-examinations, and now she was saying she'd study medicine. We were sure that she would not even pass her entrance examinations, much less finish her studies.

She was probably hurt by our laughter, but she looked into our eyes with a serious smile and shrugged her shoulders: "If I decide to do something, I always achieve it."

Today she is a doctor and has her own practice.

When I discussed these things with Maks, he thought that I still had enough time to decide. It seemed that he liked my idea about studying foreign languages, but he did not want to influence me.

Although he clearly showed that he liked me, he never invited me to the cinema or a dance. We went together just once when the library organised an excursion for its personnel and visitors. I sometimes asked myself when he would tell me that he loved me, but it was always the same. When we were together, he seemed very happy but said nothing. Sometimes it seemed that he would start speaking but would get interrupted by someone.

15
Black Night

One night, when we were asleep, somebody knocked at my mum's window and said: "Ana, your father has just been hit by a car. He is lying near the bus station and it is looking very serious."

My mum cried out and rushed out of her bed. She quickly put on a dress, told the news to my aunt and my grandmother and ran to the bus station. My brother and I followed. We both cried and I could not believe that I would lose a person who'd been with me for eighteen years and whom I loved more than my own father. But I felt that his time had come. I heard one of the neighbors saying that he was dead. He'd been run over by a car when he crossed the road. There was no light, the car drove quickly, and my grandfather did not see it. The reason for his death and the question of guilt were not important to me, but I was terribly sorry to lose a man whom I loved. I could not imagine how I would be able to survive without speaking to him again.

I was probably the one who was most upset that my grandfather died. I was his favorite and he'd liked me more than my brother and (as my mum often reproached him) more than his own daughters.

In recent years, when I'd gotten a scholarship and earned some money during holidays, my grandfather and I used to lend money to each other. He sometimes needed a bit of money for a drink and I for a dress. His pension was taken by my grandmother and she would certainly not give him a penny for drinking, so he gardened and did housekeeping for a wealthy neighbor. If there was nothing to do, he remained without money.

I, too, sometimes spent too much money and was happy if he lent me some coins. We scrupulously returned to each other every penny. But he often said that I could keep the money, because he had enough.

Now that he was dead, I remembered thousands of small things that would never happen again that I would miss: how he'd come into the kitchen and say a couple of words about the weather, how he'd describe the books that he'd read, how things were in the old Yugoslavia and how he'd served the army. I even missed his smoking, although I did not smoke myself.

We did not sleep that night and were sad for a long time.

After the funeral, my grandmother and I spoke about his death and I said: "I have the feeling that he did not go away at all. I feel as if he has just come to my corner in the kitchen and said: 'There is nothing to worry about, Iris. I am still with you and I always will be.'"

My grandmother, such a rational woman, was not surprised at all. She said in a quiet and matter-of-fact voice: "Yes, I feel so, too."

Although my grandfather's death was one of the most difficult shocks for me and I was quite depressed, I still performed all of my duties, went to school and to the library. I even tried to smile, because I thought that my grandfather would not like me to be sad. I do not know why and how I started to beg my dead grandfather to help me when I had problems. It just happened.

I begged him very often: for good marks, for my grandmother's health, and even when I was at the dentist's, I often thought: "Please help me so that this pain ceases." All my wishes were always granted.

Maks was on one of his study trips in Great Britain at the time. Before he left, he hugged me and told me where he would stay. I asked him to write to me and, after a couple of weeks, he sent a short kind letter. I answered with a much longer letter and told him how sad I was because my grandfather had died. He tried to make me understand that everybody has to die, and that death is just a passage to a different and better state. His letter was a consolation, but I found it rather impersonal and this astonished me. How could he come to the library each time I was there, watch me and speak so sweetly but write such dry letters? I was used to long and open correspondence with my pen-pals, so I was rather disappointed at reading Maks's letter. I thought that he might not have been used to writing letters and I answered with an even longer and friendlier one, but it made no difference. His second letter was also short, contained nothing personal and he even added that he had a lot of work with his studies.

When he returned, he soon came to the library again and I had a feeling that he did not eagerly anticipate seeing me again, as I did him. I thought that I would regain his interest with kindness and by asking about his studies. He'd finished his MA and started studying for a doctorate. The main librarian once asked him when he would start thinking about a family and he answered that he was not a man for marriage. I tried to discover why not, but he quickly changed the subject. Then I asked directly why he avoided speaking about women in his life. He seemed a little embarrassed but told me that he'd had a relationship with his colleague at the School of Arts in Ljubljana and that he broke their relationship because she did not care about her appearance, because she was too bossy and was angry each time he looked at any other woman. I did not say anything, but his words gave me a real scare. I was sure that he was in love with me. I saw it in his eyes when he visited the library. It was true that he had never said it, but his glances did not mean that he was just being friendly. Dating one woman and coming to me at the same time was not fair— neither towards her nor towards me. But I did not want to believe that something similar might happen again. That woman could not have been as kind, patient and understanding as I, and I was much younger than she.

The next time he came, I was alone. We spoke about everyday matters for some time and then he sighed that he was very unhappy.

"Why, what else do you want? You have everything: you finished your MA, you started with your PhD, you have a flat and friends and we all like you."

"Love dies if two people are miles away from each other."

I wanted to answer that my love would never die. But I asked him what exactly he was speaking about.

"During my last study visit in Great Britain, I met a really interesting girl with whom I fell in love and now I think that she has already forgotten me."

His words took my breath away. Now I understood: some months ago he dated his colleague, and now he was in love with a British girl. But, he still visited me and made me feel that I meant as much to him as he meant to me. I was brought up too rigorously to start crying or making reproaches. I just asked why he came to me.

"I like you very much because you are such a beautiful and nice young woman. But I quickly fall in love with women and quickly get bored with them. I cannot help it, that's how I am."

"I did not know that. It's not right that you didn't say that before."

He looked down and did not answer.

I could not speak either. My head only thought: "How could I have such stupid illusions, how could I think that he loved me, how could I hope that he would marry me? How stupid I was to have thought that I could bear all the blows of life until he was with me!"

I did not want to show him how miserable I was so I told him that I should close the library and go home. I saw that he was unhappy because he had hurt me, but he went out without any further words.

After he left, I cried and cried and found it difficult to get home. I never explained much about him to my family and now I could not say how mistaken I was. I told my mum that I got an unsatisfactory mark at school so that she would accept that I was unhappy and not delve deeper.

The next day, I found it difficult to gather enough strength to get up and go to school. It seemed unbearable that I would sit there, listen to the teachers and be aware that Maks was in love with another woman. It was difficult to while away the time. I was so depressed that I was hardly able to follow the lessons.

Instead of learning and trying to understand what the teachers spoke about, I could think only about Maks: "How could he be like that?"

And in the next moment, I answered myself: "How could you be so stupid as to believe that he would become your husband if he'd never said a word?"

"But he must have felt something for me, if he was coming to the library so frequently and always paying me compliments."

"Perhaps he was in love with you for some time, but he told you that his feelings did not last long."

Spring came and, instead of being happy because I was young, healthy, pretty, successful, awaiting university studies and had many friends, I sat at home and mourned. My grandmother saw how sad I was and thought that it was still because of my grandfather. She cooked her best dishes, but I could not eat.

I remembered how difficult the first days of secondary school were for me and how I decided that I would never despair again. I also felt guilty towards my family members, who obviously suffered with me. My mum gave up so many things so I could study, my grandmother was so happy when she could tell her neighbors that her granddaughter would study at the university, my brother boasted about his great sister (he never said that to me, just to his friends) and now I disappointed them by losing all interest in life.

I started to repeat to myself that unrequited love was something common, that everybody faced it and that there was no reason why it shouldn't have happened to me. I made at least a rational statement that the world would be quite different in a few months and that all love problems would sooner or later disappear.

At that time, I got some low marks and it seemed that I would have to sit for the leaving examination. Margareta knew that I wanted to finish with an excellent certificate mark and she knew everything about Maks, so she tried to cheer me up.

Finally, she said: "Listen, it's not worth crying for that fool a second longer. You must start learning. If you do not get an excellent for your math examination next week, you will have to sit for the leaving examination. Learn this week and stop just staring blankly at your notebooks."

I tried to take her words as seriously as possible. Solving mathematical problems required a lot of concentration and this helped me to forget Maks, at least for a few hours. I forced myself to repeat all the exercises and got an excellent grade on the written exam. However, the teacher was still not quite convinced that I deserved the best grade, therefore she also gave me an oral examination: to solve a completely new and very difficult problem.

I didn't manage to finish it, but my schoolmates started to shout: "How can you ask her about something that we have not learned yet?"

Stane, who was an excellent mathematician, said loudly: "I could not solve this exercise and quite frankly do not understand how Iris could have brought it so far."

The teacher finally recognized that she wanted too much and mumbled that she did not give excellent marks just like that. Besides, it would do us good if we actually did some thinking before the leaving examination, she said.

After Maks told me about his girl in England, I said to the library director that I could not come and help any longer, because I had to study. She understood, praised my work and said that the library door would always be open for me, if I were interested in coming back. I did not resign because of studying, but because I did not want to meet Maks any more. However, he waited for me in front of my school one day. If I'd seen him sooner, I would have run back to my class, but then I stood in front of him and could not steal away.

"Excuse me for coming here, but you no longer come to the library and you have no phone. I would like to know how you are and what you are doing. If you tell me to be off, I will leave in a moment. If I may, I would like to invite you for a coffee."

I was happy that he came and that I saw him again. It was obvious that he cared about me and that I still meant something to him. But I was well aware that he was not forthright, therefore I refused his invitation and politely asked how he was. I also immediately said that I had to catch the bus and study. He did not expect that I would refuse him, but he did not insist. He just asked if he could call later. I shrugged my shoulders and left. I could not believe that he'd come to see me. My schoolmates, who were deliberately standing in the vicinity and eavesdropping, said that he was very handsome and that they did not understand how I could remain as cool as a cucumber. Margareta remarked that he was obviously not very much in love with that English woman and that I probably meant to him more than he had expressed.

But she still said: "Think twice before you start going out with him. I would not. There are still many other boys interested in you and they do not have two or three girls at the same time."

My happiness in seeing him again was shortlived. It was clear that his emotions were rather changeable. He would always meet new women and fall in love with them.

16
Last Days of Secondary School

The last days of secondary school, the dance party and the final class excursion to the seaside approached.

I did not go to the dance happily because I still remembered how I'd dreamt that Maks would come with me. Margareta did not want to go because she had a serious boyfriend who worked in the evenings and could not accompany her. But we decided to go, at least for a few hours, to be there with our schoolmates and teachers. My mother's cousin made me an appropriate hairdo and I put on the new dress, but I couldn't be compared with the class beauties. Margareta and I mostly sat at our table and watched our friends. After two or three hours, we left.

The next day, my schoolmates asked why we'd left so early. Barbara said that I should have told her that I was without a partner because she could have provided me with one. We discussed eveyone's dresses and mentioned how some parents got tears in their eyes when they danced with their children. This made me a bit sad, because I could not bring my parents. I asked my mum if she would come with me, but she said that she would feel uncomfortable around my elegant schoolmates and their parents.

In the last weeks of secondary school, I had no real work. I got excellent and very good grades for all subjects and the only thing I had left was homework. The math teacher still gave us difficult homework and said that we would probably not be able finish it, but she expected us to try and do at least the beginning. I worked on it all Sunday and finally got the result that I believed was correct.

On Monday morning, Stane sullenly said that he did not manage to finish his homework: "For God's sake, this woman thinks that we are geniuses. I spent four hours and asked my elder brother to help me, but he could not." Mila, Mari and Vali agreed that it was too difficult, and the teacher surely did not expect us to finish it.

"I finished it, but I am not sure if I did it right," I said. My schoolmates were quite perplexed, and Vali scornfully waved her hand to show that I was certainly wrong.

Stane asked: "Please show me."

He studied my homework and, after some minutes, said, in low spirits: "Oh, yes, I see where I made a mistake and could not proceed. May I copy it?"

Everyone started to copy my homework. In that moment, it occured to me that I finally had reached what had never seemed possible: the best students asked to copy my homework in math!

Vali laughed: "I can't believe it! When we were in our first year, none of us thought that you would ever finish school and now we are asking you to help us with math homework. Stane has asked you, and he's always been the best mathematician in the class. Even Mila and I asked, and we've also been better in math than you! I'll eat my hat if this is not injustice!"

On the last day of secondary school, the fourth-year students usually went to all the classes to say farewell and show how happy they were. I started to feel the euphoria that was typical of all students who were leaving secondary school. It was contagious. We ended up celebrating in the streets, singing "Gaudeamus". When the celebration was finished, I finally noticed that I'd managed to completely forget Maks for several hours and that I was happy again.

My grandmother prepared a pie and, when I finished, she generously suggested that I take at least a day two to rest before I started studying for the final exams. I answered that I didn't want to study any more.

"Have you gone crazy? Students prepare for their final examinations days and nights. And you haven't done anything over the last few days, you have only celebrated!"

"There are still several weeks before the final exams. We will first go on the final trip to the seaside."

"Don't be so frivolous! You said yourself that a trip before final exams was a waste of time. Do you still have some common sense or not?"

"Oh, yes, I have. I'm not going to sit for my final exams."

"What?" She trembled with indignation.

"I don't need to take my final exams, because my grades are excellent."

She gasped, turned to the window and wiped her eyes. She was beside herself with pride. This was not just my school, it was hers. She'd accompanied me all this time and knew all my grades by heart. She knew when I sat for exams and always asked how I had done. She'd suffered with me when I got a low mark and prayed that I would achieve a better one next time.

She beamed with happiness, and when my mum arrived home, she ran to the door and shouted: "Iris passed excellently, she won't have to sit for her final examinations!"

My mum was very happy, too. They couldn't help but tell everybody how well I had finished secondary school. They teased each other that they intentionally waited for their neighbors and walked around to tell everybody that "Iris finished with excellence."

I was not very interested in the final trip, but I also didn't know why I should stay at home. I got on well with all my schoolmates, even with Stela. I expected that the trip would be a bit boring but, after all, it would only last one week. We went by train to Rijeka and then by ship to Split. The journey by ship was something new for me, but I soon recognized that it was no pleasure. I, like the others, was sick all the night. When we arrived at the seaside, we were dead tired, so I slept for an entire day.

We sunbathed, swam, spoke and danced every day, but I still felt bored. I decided to pay a visit to my mum's friend, who lived in the vicinity. She was married to a Slovenian who was captain of a ship, so they lived on the Croatian coast. People on the bus were kind and one of them took me to the address I was looking for.

My mum's friend and her husband accepted me as if I were their daughter. I went with her to the market, helped her to prepare lunch and, in the evening, we took a walk, according to the habit of people on the coast. I found it pleasant as she held my hand, hugged me and presented me to dozens of friends who all said how beautiful I was. We even met the boy who'd shown me the way and we smiled at each other.

When I came back to my schoolmates, they behaved like cats and dogs. They hurried to tell me who'd quarreled with whom, they mocked Mari who'd left with Vito because she had a cold and thought that it was pneumonia. Luka had an angry fight with Vali and said some really ugly words to her, and I could hardly believe it.

On the last evening, Stela entered my room when I was reading. She was in a short red dress that she'd borrowed from Barbara: "Iris, I asked everybody, but I want your opinion because I think that you have a good sense for fashion. Can I wear this or is it too short?"

"Yes, of course, it suits you very well."

"Isn't it too short? Am I too fat for it?"

"No, it's OK, you look fine."

She left and got many compliments from boys. I liked that I could give fashion advice to a schoolmate who often reproached me for my poor dress habits.

After the trip, we promised each other that we would meet again, but that never came to be.

17
Real Holidays

When I came home, Maks waited for me in front of the school again and almost forced me to have coffee with him. He said that he was unhappy because we did not meet any more and that he'd broken all contacts with the woman in England.

"I wrote to her that we lived too far from each other, so we couldn't make it work and she understood. It was easy because I was there only two months and we didn't meet often. It actually wasn't love, but quite an imaginary and unreal matter. She doesn't mean anything to me."

"Well, you certainly forget girls very quickly. As you once said, you are not a fixed star."

"Don't speak like that. You know how much you meant to me, and you still do. If you ever felt anything for me, there's no need to stop seeing each other. Our love is something special and we can't just forget our feelings."

I thought to myself: "Oh, yes, it was something special to me, but not to you. You are not capable of loving somebody like I loved you." However, I did not mention my thoughts. I just answered:

"You are wrong. People change. I changed so much that I sometimes do not recognize myself anymore."

It was the truth and I told it without any revenge or offense meant. It took great pains to forget him, but I managed it. I never admitted how often I cried because of him and how hard I had to persuade myself that life was still beautiful without him. And when I managed to forget him, I firmly decided that no man would ever hurt me again.

His reaction surprised me. He grew pale and remained speechless. Then he left and said that he would visit me at the seaside. When he was leaving, I saw a determined expression on his face, showing that we would still discuss the matter. It dawned on me that he wanted to become my boyfriend. When I asked myself if I was still in love with him, I had to admit, clearly and frankly, that I wasn't. What should I do with a man who falls in love with a new girl every year?

Then I went to the seaside to work during the holidays. After long months of hard work and unhappiness, I had no worries anymore. Of course, I had to serve food in the morning, at noon and in the evening, but what was that if I compared it to my studies? A piece of cake. I was free enough to swim, sunbathe and chat with Silva and with other young people who worked in the holiday camp of the Slovenian Railways. That year I was in the top group of youngsters—among those who'd finished their secondary school or were already at the university. Silva and I came approximately at the same time. We shared a room, served together, had long discussions and sometimes went dancing. Our little cottage soon became the center of social life. Many girls and boys came to us and we sometimes chatted, had an ice cream together or sat at the seaside singing while one of the boys was playing the guitar.

Silva was still my best friend and I thought that we really trusted each other. Once she put on a new ring and I asked if it was gold because it was so beautiful.

She rolled her eyes: "You are a real specialist, aren't you? Of course, it's gold, and the stone is a diamond."

"Oh, how beautiful. Did your mum buy it for you for your birthday?"

She hesitated for a moment and finally admitted that she'd gotten it from her English teacher. As I gasped with surprise, she quickly said that he gave her the ring in memory. There was nothing between them except friendship because the teacher was fifty years-old and married.

"But why did he buy you a ring and why did you take it? He will expect something for it."

"No, he is not like that. And I told him that I could not bind myself to a married man. To refuse a ring would be most impolite."

I didn't think so but, after all, it was her problem.

When we were at the seaside for several weeks, a handsome dark-haired boy, who looked like a gangster, came to our cottage and asked for Silva. I thought that he was perhaps one of her brothers, so I helped him to find her at the beach.

When she saw him, she embraced and kissed him: "Dani, how happy I am that you've come."

I was rather surprised, because I did not know anything about Dani. That evening she had no time either for me or for our friends or for Mile, one of the boys who wanted to become her boyfriend. Dani left before morning. Silva cried for the rest of the night and did not want to tell what was wrong. On the next day, she finally explained that they'd been a couple for some months and then parted, because she could not bear his flirting with other girls. When he'd come to the seaside, she was most happy because she'd hoped that they would start again, but she immediately found him watching other girls and left him. I tried to cheer her up, although the event amazed me. I'd been telling her about everything that had happened to me while she was silent about the most important things in her life.

"Excuse me, but I could not speak about these things. It hurt too much."

On the next day, we were visited by one of Mile's best friends who required that Silva explain to him what she did that made Mile try to slit his wrists.

Silva cried and wanted to run to Mile, but his friend pushed her into a chair: "Leave him alone. We dressed his wound and he is sleeping now. There was no real harm because I stopped him. But I am his best friend and I want you to tell me what you did to him."

Silva continued crying, but I got irritated that this stuffed shirt who knew Mile for just a month pretended to be his best friend, so I told him to go away and never come back again.

"Your friend almost killed one of the boys and you intend to defend her?"

"You can stop blackmailing her. If he intends to cut his veins because of a girl who will not immediately do what he wants, he won't live long. Besides, I know that it has not even been a month since he first met Silva and they are not a couple. Don't you dare to pretend that Silva owes him something and don't sit here like the supreme judge."

He left sulking and once more said to Silva that she should leave his friends alone, if she had no serious intentions.

Silva dramatically cried: "What a poor soul I am. I am the cause of so many disasters. It was me who made that English teacher divorce his wife. Dani says that he cannot be with me, although he loves me, and now poor Mile!"

The next day, everybody spoke about Mile and his unhappy love, while I found the whole matter stupid. For God's sake, so much noise about nothing! Perhaps Mile did not even try to cut his wrist, but just slipped with the knife when he cut a sausage? However, these events caused me to start to see Silva with different eyes: she obviously never told the whole truth. It seemed that she looked for trouble and then enjoyed making dramatic scenes.

Soon after, another boy started to visit our cottage and discuss her unhappy love life. Their discussions lasted long into the night, so I couldn't sleep. It was also very boring to listen to the same story again and again. The fool listened to her, comforted her and told her what a wonderful person she was and did not even notice that he fell into her snare. After such visits, she usually slept too long, and I had to work without her help. I tried to excuse her for some time, but then I shrugged my shoulders. I hardly pretended that I was sorry when she had to leave.

Just three of the girls remained at the seaside in September. Everyone else was younger, and their schools began already, while the university lectures started in October.

Maks visited me a couple of times, but just for an hour or two each. Perhaps he would have stayed longer, but I always said that I had no time or that I was going out. When only the three of us stayed in the camp, he called again. I was swimming so he asked my friend where I was and had a long discussion with her. She became quite enchanted and sighed over what marvelus men visited me. Although I didn't have much company, I did not want to stay with him. We had a coffee and then I told him that I had work to do.

"Well, I can wait. Can I see you in the evening after you finish working? Would you come to supper with me?"

"If you insist, we can have a chat in the nearby sweetshop. There is a lot of work, now that we are only three girls left."

He tried everything. He explained what was happening in Ljubljana, he complained that he could not study because he thought only about me, he said that he had a serious illness and so on. However, I knew the maneuvers boys used to make girls pity them and then lead to something more, so I remained firm.

Maks stayed for another day or two, but I did not want to meet him again. He asked one of my friends to have a coffee with him and explained to her how much he loved me. He even mentioned that he would like to marry me. She felt so sorry for him that she came to our room and started to convince me that I should meet him once again.

"No, I'm not going to. I have nothing more to discuss with him."

The third girl looked through the window and quickly sat down: "He is standing below the window and waving that I should call you."

"Say that I am not here. Tell him that I went somewhere."

"Where should you go? There is nobody interesting here except some retired old couples. And he probably saw you going to the room and knows that you are here."

"You can say that my schoolmate visited me and that we went to the town."

Maks did not wait for her answer but called my name. The three of us who sat in the room just looked at each other and did not know what to do. Then we all started with a silly contagious giggle and could not have stopped, even if we wanted to. One of my friends still managed to make a serious face, quickly looked through the window and said that I wasn't in. In the next moment, she fell on us and we continued with our stupid laughing. After some minutes, the director of the camp came to Maks and told him to shut up and stop making scandal. And my first love was finished forever.

The next day, we were all called to the director's office. He said that he had just been visited by the management board that looked for stewardesses for the business train to Belgrade, Venice and some other towns. They considered us prime candidates, so they invited us to submit applications for a course that would qualify us for well-paid permanent student work. Both friends thought that there would not be enough time to study and work, but I applied. I knew that I would continue receiving my scholarship in the future, but that it would be good to have some more money. University studies in Yugoslavia were free, but we had other expenses. Excellent students from poor families could ask for small financial support and usually got it. The amount was really low, just to cover the expenses of notebooks and study materials.

When I went to our room, I saw a young man talking with the director and smiling. I don't know why and how it occurred to me that this would be my future husband. The idea was most strange, but I remembered that a rather similar thought appeared in my mind when I first met Maks. I had also the same reaction as when I'd first seen Maks: I started to convince myself that I did not find him interesting at all. Just the opposite, I tried to find as many mistakes in him as possible. During supper I had to serve him, and I remembered that I had met him before. His name was Tone and, two months prior, he and my friend had wanted to go out dancing, but then he'd fallen asleep and had not come. Now he asked me if I would go dancing that evening. Both girls had already left, so I accepted his invitation. He danced quite well and had a lot of energy to speak about everything. He was already in the last year of his studies and liked to talk about the university. He also liked to swim and ski and he knew everything about life in the Railway camp because he had spent his summers working there in the past, just like me.

While he stayed in the village, we met every day on the beach, in the dining hall and went dancing in the evenings. I was happy to have met a boy who obviously had a similar way of life as mine. I also liked that he was not a philosopher, like Maks, but wanted to become an engineer. We went home together by bus. Just before I left, he asked for my address and said that he would like to go out with me also in the future, because we'd had such interesting conversations. I quickly told him my address but had no time to put it down because I had to get out of the bus. How stupid I am, I thought. I finally meet a normal young man with whom it is possible to discuss everything, and I forget to get his phone number. It was a big question as to whether he would remember my address.

18
University

The euphoria that I'd felt since the end of secondary school continued. On my first day at the university, I danced in the kitchen and changed my clothes twice. My grandmother advised me to become serious because I was beginning the most difficult part of my life. However, I couldn't because just thinking about university studies made me smile. Although the Arts building was no more encouraging than that in secondary school, I felt the atmosphere of youth and freedom. It took my best efforts to find the right lecture room, but I'd arrived early and was not afraid to ask questions. As I was asking about the lectures and seminars, about the timetable and the library, I had the opportunity to acquaint myself with many new young people. We talked about where we were from, which secondary school we'd attended, where we'd gone on holidays and what we wanted to become. I met some of my ex-schoolmates, too. Luka enrolled in English like me and quickly waved his hand, but he was among a group of girls and had no time for his old schoolmate. I finally found my group in front of the largest lecture room which could fit 300 students. They were waiting for somebody to unlock the door.

We were packed like sardines. I asked two girls why there was such a crowd and they told me that the lecture room was too small for all the students. Students had to come about 20 minutes before the lessons started and fight for a place. If possible, they would save a seat or two for a friend. I immediately heard that these other students were not from Ljubljana. Mara was the daughter of a Slovenian mother and Serbian father who worked for the army, so the family often moved from one place to another. She had already lived in Serbia, Croatia and now they'd come to Slovenia. Eli was from the northern part of Slovenia.

Mara was very communicative and open, and she told us that she'd started to speak Slovenian a year ago, when her family arrived. I could hardly believe her because she spoke very well, except that she did not differentiate the e-vowels in Slovenian that caused trouble for all citizens of other Yugoslav republics. She told us that she actually wanted to become a pianist, because she'd studied piano for as long as she could remember. She had to sacrifice a lot of time and miss many parties so that she could practice piano. She liked it and everybody admired her playing. In the last year of her secondary school, her schoolmates often spoke about what they intended to study, but Mara just smiled—it was quite clear that she would continue with music. She had no worries about her future because she knew that her parents would take care of material things. She lived just for the world of arts, visited concerts, listened to classical music and played piano. Towards the end of her secondary school, Mara had had a solo evening concert. She'd played very well, and all the people applauded.

Her teacher praised her, saying that the concert was wonderful and added: "Once I listened to this concert in Moscow; the performer was a young boy like you or even younger. If you could hear how he played! What emotions, what understanding of the author!"

"That young boy was better than I?"

"Why, yes, of course, he was a genius. You rarely meet such pianists."

"Among what type of future artists would you place me?"

"I am sure that you will achieve a lot."

"But I will never be like the best Russians, will I?"

The teacher looked down and said in a low voice: "There are just a couple of really brilliant pianists in the world."

Only in that moment did Mara become aware that she would probably never be one of the best world's pianists. That was the last day she had played the piano. She'd told her parents that she would not study music, quickly examined other possibilities of study and decided to enroll in architecture. It was, in a way, still part of the world of arts in which she was brought up. She managed to pass the entrance exams for the University of Ljubljana (which were most demanding) and scrupulously studied one year. She'd passed all the exams but was disappointed. The study program did not offer any elements of the arts. She had to make drawings, calculate and learn theory. It was so boring that she decided not to continue. Now she hoped that English and German would be a better choice.

Eli had started with her studies a year earlier. She enrolled in pharmacy studies and found it rather boring, so she did not even try to pass the exams. She was from northern Slovenia and had learned German for 8 years, which was quite an advantage over other students who were starting German from scratch.

I liked both very much and we became close friends.

Among other students who enrolled in English and German, I immediately noticed some extremely well-dressed girls who came from Maribor, the second largest city in Slovenia. They smoked, giggled and had cosmopolitan discussions. I could not be compared with those beauties in any possible way. They were very slim, used a lot of make-up, colored their hair, plucked their eyebrows, used red lipstick, had very nice perfume, beautifully painted nails and communicated with gentle nonchalance. I once asked one of them where she had bought a short coat of a beautiful pink. She giggled that she'd made a short trip to Vienna during the weekend, but she was already fed up with it and could sell it to me. I could not afford it, even though she wanted to sell it for only half its price. When I stood in her vicinity, I could see that her figure was skeletal, her mouth too big, her chin too sharp and her feet very long. Nobody is perfect.

I was more envious when I listened to another group of schoolmates who discussed things in English. There were no student exchanges back then, so the majority of foreign students came to Slovenia because they had Slovenian relatives or a Slovenian husband or because of war in their country. One would think that at least those from the United States or from England would not need to study English, because it was their native tongue. However, each country had its own system of education and did not simply acknowledge foreign certificates. Foreign students had to pass all exams in English if they wanted to graduate in Slovenia and become teachers.

One of the students was from Texas. She was rather round, red-haired, freckled, and always wore very interesting color combinations, especially green and violet. She spoke a lot and repeated that she studied English because she did not intend to work very hard to finish university. The next one came from Lebanon. She was dark and beautiful and also spoke English quite well. The third was fair and seemed older than other students. She did not speak very much. She said that she was from London, was married to a Slovenian, that she already had one child and that she wanted to finish the university and become an English teacher. In the group there were also some Slovenian girls who tried to speak English as fluently as possible, and there was my schoolmate Luka who had no problems with communication, either with girls or with English.

When the door opened, we almost fell into the lecture room. I found a place in the third row and quickly saved seats for Mara and Eli. The hall was in the form of an amphitheater and was very large, but those who came late had to sit on the steps and on the floor just in front of the teacher. Nobody worried about it, because students were mainly in jeans. The teachers seemed to be happy just to have so many students.

The lecturers immediately served up some statistical data: in the next year, the lecture room would be rather empty, because only about 20% of the students would advance to the second year. Those who successfully passed exams would have talent, discipline, regularly come to lectures and exercises, visit the library, go abroad during summer holidays, etc. I swallowed all this nonsense as if it were the Bible, while students from Texas, Lebanon and England laughed. Easy to laugh if English or German is your mother tongue, I thought. But the majority of us were Slovenians. Perhaps I had a bit of talent and I was certainly disciplined and prepared to go at least to England. So, I needed to fulfil just two more conditions: regularly visit the lectures and study in the library. After the lectures were finished, I went to the National and University Library. I met my ex-schoolmate, Eliza, whose father was a university teacher and who had also advised her to study in the library. He suggested that she should borrow a dictionary of phrases, put them down in a special notebook and learn them by heart. The reading room was equipped with furniture that reflected respectable age, tradition and peace. I found it very beautiful but without the vivid atmosphere of the university. Everything was so quiet that I soon started to feel drowsy and had to go out for a couple of minutes.

In the afternoon, I had another lecture so I did not go home but returned to the library and tried to continue studying. After an hour, I was not just sleepy but also hungry. In the morning, I'd eaten an egg with bread and had a coffee, but now it was already three in the afternoon and I could have eaten a wolf. However, I decided not to waste money on food, so I remained hungry and enviously watched others who sat on the steps and ate big sandwiches.

At five, I came back to the university, but our lecturer did not appear. A student in the third year came by and laughed: "Oh, you must be first year students, because you expect serious lectures already at the beginning of the academic year. Go home, babies, and remember that lectures slowly start in the second half of October."

The next morning, I came to the lectures again and many other students, too. The first two hours were cancelled. Then an old teacher began to lecture about old English literature. When he started speaking, my neighbors and I exchanged looks. His pronunciation was so poor, and he spoke English with such a horrible Slavic accent that we could not imagine how he'd become a university teacher. Of course, he had a PhD in English literature, but how did this justify such poor pronunciation? His lectures were boring, and he spoke so quickly that we could not write down his words. When we argued that we could not put down his words, he said that we could study old English literature in the library. The loudest student, the one from Texas, asked if we could borrow or buy one of his books, but he said that there weren't any.

"So, we have to take down notes, don't you think so?"

"You can, if you can't remember what I say," and he looked at her as if it was obvious that her intelligence quotient was under average. "But do not write everything, put down just what is essential. Only perfect fools put down every word that the teacher says."

Some students tried to show that they were intelligent, so they stopped writing, but the majority of us silently admitted that we were simpletons and that we could not differentiate which of the teacher's words were important, and which were not. All those who did not write notes and learn them by heart failed their exams. Then they borrowed our notes and some managed to pass.

This approach to teaching was the norm in Yugoslavia and has continued at the university level in Slovenia, with few exceptions until now. Even now, many people are not aware that students deserve fair treatment and respect. If one starts to say that teachers should focus upon students, he often hears that only really strict teaching, as was used in the previous century, forms really good professionals. What brainwashing we endured!

19
Too Much Good

O n my first day of university, I received a letter from Tone, who suggested that we should meet in the hall of the Arts building and then go somewhere to have tea or coffee. I was so happy that I started to cry. Tone's letter meant that he liked me and that he hadn't forgotten me. I also received a letter from the Slovenian Railways informing me that they found me suitable as a stewardess and that I could soon begin with the training. The invitation to the course for stewardesses suggested that I might get a good student job. I knew that a boyfriend and a part-time job would take up quite a bit of my time, but I could not disregard either.

The following day Tone waited for me where he'd suggested. I was a bit embarrassed and thought that he might be, too, but he showed only happiness when he saw me again. He invited me to lunch, and we spoke for two hours. I was so happy that I could explain to someone all that had happened, what kind of schoolmates and teachers I had, that I had the opportunity to start with a temporary job and so on. He was sure that I would be able to to study and work and encouraged me to start studying immediately. When I complained that I would have to miss some lectures because of the training for stewardesses, he said that I would be able to copy the notes of my schoolmates.

This strong support was the very opposite of the fears my grandmother presented at home:

"You do not even know if you are capable of finishing university and now you intend to start with a job? How will you study if you work? You should first finish one thing and then start with another and not try to participate in everything!"

My mum did not tell me what to do. She knew that I would continue to receive the scholarship and she was also ready to give me some money, but additional salary would come in very handy. So, I decided to start with it—after all, I could leave if it took up too much time.

I became a rather busy young woman. We had lectures in the morning and in the afternoon. My grandmother could never understand that our lectures were not from 8 a.m. until 1 or 2 p.m. like those in the secondary school. I often told her that students had to consider the timetable that was adapted to the university teachers' schedules, but she continued scolding me over coming home so late. She was annoyed that she could no longer prepare me warm, healthy lunches and that she did not know where I was all day.

Almost every month she started: "I really don't understand that you could have lectures from eight in the morning until seven in the evening on Mondays, Tuesdays and Wednesdays, but just two hours on Friday." I showed her a small notebook with my timetable several times and it seemed that she understood it for a moment or two, but after some days she forgot my explanations and began grumbling again.

It was even more difficult when I started the training to be a stewardess. The organizer tried to adapt it to our lectures, but the afternoon hours did not suit everybody. I decided to miss some lectures at the university and for some hours of training. I soon noticed that the training did not offer any special knowledge aside from searching for international connections for trains. After one month, we sat for exams in polite communication, serving the food, giving information to the passengers and so on. We also had to take a practical exam and show our knowledge in action on a business train. I knew that I could behave properly, but I could not imagine how I could bring coffee to passengers without spilling it because the train was bending and shaking all the time. I did not understand how one could carry a tray, put it on the small table in front of the passenger (if the table was not full of other things) and write a bill. I was also rather afraid that I would not be able to find the best possible route for a passenger who wanted to travel to other European countries.

During the test trip, we walked from one end of the train to the other with a difficult tray in our hands and learned how to carefully balance the tray in one hand, grasp at the seats with the other hand and stand firmly on our feet, especially when the train took a turn. We noticed that stewardesses who had worked there for several months or years did not give passengers any bills.

When the boss asked why, one explained: "When you bring a coffee, you put it on the table in front of the passenger. There is no place to put down the tray. Should we go to the next passenger, put down the tray with ten other coffees on his table and go back to the first one to write a bill? And please mind that ten other passengers are also waiting for their coffees."

One of the supervisors quickly interfered: "Well, you can first serve everybody and bring bills at the end of the journey."

The stewardess smiled: "You might, if there were only a couple of passengers. But that doesn't work on any train that is full. On such trains, there are so many orders that you immediately forget to whom you brought something. You have to work like mad for at least four hours. And the girls who prepare coffee, food and drink want us to deliver the money immediately." The supervisor seemed still in doubt, so the stewardess added: "Look, all the girls would throw money away if they brought the bills at the end of the journey. After an hour, you have no idea to whom you brought one hundred coffees. Go and try yourself, if you do not believe it." Today it is difficult to understand that the stewardesses did not give out any bills.

When she left, he mumbled: "I still think that it is necessary to write bills and that it is polite to bring them at the end of the journey."

When I had to serve coffee to one of the supervisors, my hands and legs shaked but I somehow managed to produce a smile, greet him, fix the small table in front of him, put the coffee on it and give him a bill that I'd written a minute earlier. I got a good mark. Then I had to find information on how to travel from Ljubljana to Brussels as quickly as possible. I examined the big book of timetables for quite a long time and finally found the best connection. I could not believe my ears when they praised me again.

My next challenge regarded my personal travel. The business train for Belgrade left Ljubljana at 2:45 a.m. and returned at 10:30 p.m. I told one of the supervisors that I was not from Ljubljana and that there were no buses during the night. However, he said that this was not a problem. The Slovenian Railways had several pleasant rooms for stewardesses in the vicinity of the railway station. Almost all the stewardesses came there in the evening, before they left for Belgrade, and the night receptionist would wake them up.

Now it really seemed that it might work out. Of course, I still did not know the circumstances on the trains to different towns (some stewardesses said that journeys to Belgrade were the most tiring). I also did not know on which days I would work. It would have been a disaster if I had journeys on Mondays or Tuesdays, when we had about 10 hours of lectures, but ideal if I could work on Friday, Saturday or Sunday.

I left out of this equation how much time I would need to meet Tone. I first thought that we would meet once per week, perhaps go to the cinema on Saturday or Sunday and then we would see how things would develop. However, the hours of our meetings soon expanded. In the autumn, Tone still worked on his diploma thesis, so he had a lot of time. If the weather was nice he would come to the Arts building and we would go for a walk or have lunch. On Saturdays, we went to the cinema, to the theater or to the opera. Tone did not like the opera, but I tried to show him that classical music could be beautiful. After the performance, he did not say that the opera was boring, but that it was interesting.

20
My Boyfriend

My mum observed me with a bit of suspicion for quite some time and she finally asked if I had lectures also on Saturday and Sunday, so I had to tell her that I went out with a boy whom I'd met at the seaside.

She had seen photos of the young boys and girls with whom I'd worked at the seaside and frowned: "With one of those youngsters on the photo?"

I told her that Tone had almost graduated, emphasized how difficult his studies were and said that he already had an employment agreement with a big firm in which he would start working as soon as he graduated.

"Does he intend to come and present himself? Honest boys usually come and show themselves."

I said that he would, but I didn't know how best to make it happen. How should I ask somebody who was not yet my boyfriend to come to the house because my mum wanted to see him? After all we had just gone on a couple of dates and had not yet discussed love. I could ask him to come see my mum because she was polite and kind towards everybody, but my grandmother was a dragon and would eat him alive! I felt sick when I thought of how she would look at him, decide that he was absolutely not suitable for her granddaughter and throw him out of the house. And besides, I was embarrassed to invite him into our poor house in which there was not even a bathroom. No, I couldn't, I decided. There was no chance. It would be too embarrassing.

But then, I was shocked when I heard Tone's voice outside the house, asking my grandmother if Iris lived in there and if he could see her.

My grandmother seemed amazed, but she answered: "Yes, of course. Who are you and what do you want?"

"I am Tone and would like to ask if Iris would go to the cinema with me and my friends."

I wanted to hide so that nobody would find me, but I had to enter the doorway and greet him. My mother came out of her kitchen and asked him and his friends to have coffee, while my grandmother disappeared in her kitchen. I quickly washed and changed so my grandmother had no time to oppose.

When I came back after the cinema, I expected a storm, but my grandmother was already asleep. The next morning, she only mumbled that I should study and not think just about boys. My mum later told me that my grandmother had really wanted to make a scene and forbid me from even thinking about boys during my studies. However, my mum had sharply opposed:

"You drove away all my boyfriends, although some of them are now among the most respected and hard-working men in this village. If you had given me a little more freedom, I would have chosen one or another good man and my life would have been much happier. But you will not repeat this mistake with my daughter. Just try to discourage him, and we will find a flat in the city and move away. Can't you see that the young man is honest, because he came to us and introduced himself? And besides, he will very soon become an electrical engineer and already has a job."

I knew that my mum had to employ all her weapons to win the battle. However, I also noticed that Tone made a very good impression on my grandmother, because he was an engineer. Later, I found out that she simply liked Tone. As long as I could remember, she was telling me that all men were tramps, but now it was clear that she was able to make very pleasant and thoughtful conversations with Tone. What inconsistency.

However, my grandmother could still be difficult from time to time. It was a scandal when Tone suggested that I should go with him and with his two friends to the mountains. In past years, I'd often enviously observed people whose rucksacks, strong mountain shoes, sports shirts and jackets showed that they were going to the mountains. But I did not dare to even think that I could one day become one of them. When I was in secondary school, I had no time and no money for mountaineering and no one who would take me. Tone enthusiastically explained which mountains he had already climbed and said that he and his two best friends (Ana and Franc, who were a couple) suggested that we should go to Komna and the Triglav lakes. I sadly answered that I could not go with them because I had no equipment and because I was probably not fit for such a difficult expedition. But he insisted. He offered to borrow a rucksack from one of his friends, suggested that I put on my usual jeans and said that I could take a pair of old strong shoes, because the route was not among the most difficult ones. He spoke with such enthusiasm and for such a long time that I finally told my mum that I would like to go to the mountains with Tone and his two friends. The main obstacle was, of course, not my fitness or mountain shoes but my grandmother and my mum, who opposed my going with Tone for a longer time. However, my mum changed her mind and, after two days, bought me a new rucksack. I had just enough money to buy the cheapest suede shoes that seemed comfortable. Such shoes were really the worst thing that I could choose for mountaineering, but they were rather cheap. My mum quickly sewed trousers from a piece of brown jersey, and I took a jacket that wasn't exactly sports clothing.

We agreed to meet at the bus station, where all the mountaineers gathered. When I came and looked around, Tone was nowhere to be seen. I saw a boy and a girl with perfect outfits for the mountains, so I went towards them.

The boy said: "Why don't you stay with us and we'll go to Triglav together?"

We'd never met and did not know each other, but I thought they could be Ana and Franc, so I smiled: "Tone probably told you that I'm Iris?"

They both laughed because Franc, who liked to address strangers, successfully recruited an unknown girl.

He then found a new source of amusement. "Do you think that we are going for a walk or to the mountains? Have you got new shoes? And this jacket is, in my opinion, more appropriate for a Mass."

I shrugged my shoulders and said that I did not have anything better and that I had not used my shoes until then. Luckily, Tone and I later had seats in the other part of the bus, so I did not need to think about how I should answer Franc's obnoxious remarks.

At the beginning of our climb, things did not look good. Franc thought that I walked too slowly. I was saved by Ana, who said that she liked my tempo. Tone helped me because he often stopped and admired nature, gave us pieces of chocolate and guessed at what the weather would be like. The route to the top of Komna was quite long but luckily the cottage at the top could be seen a good two hours before one arrives there, so it encouraged us to move faster. I thought that we would reach it any moment and persistently walked, although I was tired. Towards the end it started to rain, and my shoes were wet through.

Franc did not skip the chance to tease: "How are you doing?"

He laughed, when we climbed the steepest parts and I understood that he did not think just about my heavy breathing and wet shoes, but also considered me a bit too heavy because he and Ana were as thin as toothpicks. Towards the evening, we finally arrived at the cottage, washed, changed our clothes and had dinner. I was very happy because I'd managed to make it to the top, because I found it so beautiful and because I was with Tone, whom I liked more and more. I could have danced.

The next morning was sunny and we went down to the lake of Krn. My despised shoes were now dry again, while Franc was angry because he had to put on his heavy mountain shoes that did not dry overnight.

He enviously said: "Well, your shoes are dry but don't think that they are good. You will have troubles today because we are going down. Your ankles have no support and you will be lucky if you come home without hurting your feet. The way down is much more difficult than climbing up the mountain.

I was quiet, because I did not want to oppose an experienced climber, but I knew that my real difficulty was climbing up the mountain. I could descend for days without troubles. Franc and Ana slid on the sand and were afraid that they might catch a cold because of their wet shoes. After two hours, they began to complain that their knees hurt.

When Franc continued with his complaints, Tone maliciously said: "You have been to the mountains so often and have been mocking Iris all the time, but she walks much better than you."

Franc stopped for some time, but as soon as he felt better, he tried to pull my leg again. I recognized that this was his way of communication with everybody, because he believed that it was amusing. It took some time before I got used to it.

By the end of our trip, I was quite excited by the mountains and because I recognized that I was as fit to climb as others, so I promised Tone that we would go to the mountains again. Tone was happy, too, and suggested that I should become his girlfriend. It was innocent and childlike and nowadays almost hard to believe, but that's how it was.

21
Student Work

Before my first train trip to Belgrade, Tone accompanied me to the house where the stewardesses and others who worked for the Railways slept before their journeys. When we entered the door, the receptionist shouted at Tone.

"Get out! These are our girls, and don't you dare to think that you will accompany her to her room."

He meant it rather seriously, although he laughed. Tone came with me just to encourage me before my first working day. He was sure that everything would be all right. In the evening, he would wait for me so that I would be able to tell him how it had gone.

I asked the receptionist to press the bell several times, because I slept soundly and knew that waking up at two in the morning might be a problem. He only waved his hand and said that I should not worry. The room was pleasant: it had four beds, with clean bed linen and a bathroom. After half an hour, another stewardess arrived, and we really did wake up at two. The bell was very loud and the receptionist rang it several times, so that he was sure that we did not fall asleep again. Today, it is dangerous if people, especially young girls, walk alone at two in the morning, but in those days it was nothing special. Ljubljana was a safe town and even though we were at the railway station, which in some countries is considered a troublesome spot, we never experienced any troubles. Of course, there were always men who were not happy if they did not try to start a conversation with a young girl, but at the railway station there were also police and we could call them if necessary. When we put our small bags in our compartment, we stood in front of the train and I introduced myself to the railway guard who walked up and down. A stewardess, who worked on the business trains for several years, gave us some instructions, introduced us to a young woman who prepared food and drinks and then decided that the two of us would sleep until Zagreb, while she would be on duty. I was very grateful and immediately fell asleep.

In Zagreb, the stewardess on duty ran up to us: "Get up immediately, the train is full, and everybody wants to eat and drink."

The train was a very fast connection with the capital of Yugoslavia, Belgrade, and it was used mostly by politicians and businessmen. The train was new and clean, with every possible comfort. It even had special compartments for conferences and meetings. It arrived in Belgrade in what was then the record time of about 7 hours and was always on time. The passengers could sleep, study their documents or buy a compartment to discuss political or business matters. We served food and drinks. The woman behind the counter prepared everything fresh, put the food on a plate made of porcelain and added a napkin and metal cutlery. She prepared fresh coffee all the time—real Turkish coffee, because the majority of the passengers were from the Balkans and they would be most insulted if they were offered an instant brown liquid of the sort that is nowadays served on aircraft. Although each of the stewardesses served passengers in just two coaches, it was sometimes hard to manage all the work. It was usually not so difficult when we drove to Belgrade because several passengers slept, but in the afternoon, we were always very busy.

I usually worked on Fridays, Saturdays and Sundays, when I did not have lectures. It was always possible to successfully organize our availability. We had a special list on which we put down when we had time and we also exchanged our addresses and phone numbers, if we might need to change a shift. We made an effort to step in for each other when it was needed, because we knew that we could expect others to return the favor. It was very rare that a stewardess would miss her journey. We were aware that this would be considered very irresponsible.

I still remember the first two guests whom I served. They were two old gentlemen from Zagreb. They drank several coffees with cognac and became rather cheerful. I had to bring coffee and cognac again and again and later they ordered breakfast. They asked me different questions all that time and observed my hair.

When we'd almost arrived in Belgrade, they called me and one of them said: "Miss Iris, I am probably most unpolite, but my friend and I took bets on something and you are the only one who can decide about the winner. May I kindly ask that you answer me? If I am asking too much, just say so and I will shut up."

I said that I would be happy to answer, although I was a bit unsure about what I could expect.

He made a pause and cleared his throat: "Miss Iris. All our girls have dark hair, but you are fair, your hair is straight, and you have quite a unique hairdo. My friend thinks that you have a wig, but I am convinced that this is your hair. My God, I am so embarrassed that I should ask about such things. If my wife hears it, she will strip the skin off me!"

I laughed. A pageboy hairstyle was not very popular in those times. I pulled my hair and raised it so they could see that it was mine. They were happy as children and the one who lost immediately paid what he owed to his friend. The other, who got the money, gave half to me. It was more than the salary that I received for the journey. Other passengers also gave me very high tips. In the morning, I left Ljubljana with some coins in my pocket and came to Belgrade with several bank notes, and I could expect a good salary at the end of the month.

When we arrived in Belgrade, we went to a nearby hotel, slept until 2 p.m., took a shower and at 3 left for Ljubljana again. Such were the rules that we signed on for when we began working for the Railways— they wanted fresh and kind girls.

Passengers were mostly very polite and very kind. Nobody complained if a stewardess poured coffee on him (which sometimes happened, because the train changed velocity or direction). Nobody complained if stewardesses spoke Slovenian, while they spoke Serbian or Croatian. I had troubles just once, because one of the passengers stubbornly expected that I would tell him the price in his language. I could have done so, but I was stubborn, too. I insisted on Slovenian because it was a Slovenian train, and I knew that he understood me— all he wanted was to bully me.

When he started to complain in a loud voice, the conductor, a small, angry man, came up to us and asked: "What is going on?"

The neighbors of the complaining passenger said that he drank too much and that he should shut up.

His neighbor made a comment: "We have been establishing good relations among Yugoslav republics, but you know that it can sometimes be difficult."

In the afternoon, there was so much work that I forgot everything. I tried to serve coffees and beer and sausages quickly enough and I kindly asked for payment each time I brought something. I didn't even have time to count. I simply put the money into the wallet and hoped that it was enough. After Zagreb, the circumstances calmed down. We could finally go to the toilet and eat something. We were usually very hungry and tired, because we'd run up and down the train for more than four hours and carried difficult trays with bottles. When I checked the payments, I saw that I'd received big tips again and I considered myself incredibly rich.

When we arrived in Ljubljana, Tone was waiting for me.

I came out with a smile and he smiled, too: "Well, didn't I say that everything would be OK? Why were you so nervous?"

He accompanied me to the bus, which was to leave in a couple of minutes. I knew that he had to work the next day, so I found it sweet that he waited for me. However, I was not fully aware that it was a sign of serious love: he took a bus to come from his home to Ljubljana, waited for my train, met me for just a couple of minutes and then went home by bus again. He did it every time I had a trip to Belgrade!

My mum was still awake when I got home, although she had to get up at half past four the next day. She prepared me dinner and, with a voice full of worry, asked how it was. I enthusiastically started to speak about my first working day and pulled my wallet out of the bag and showed her how much money I'd earned just in tips. She was pleased, and I knew that it was not because of the additional money, but because she saw that I would manage the work.

I consoled my mum, but she was still a bit worried: "I am happy, but I will only stop worrying at the end of the year, when I see that you've managed to pass all your exams."

My grandmother loudly snarled that children should not be overburdened by studying and by work and that both would completely exhaust me. I never took such remarks as a sign of controlling and authoritarian behavior but as a sign of love. She often appeared as a dragon just because she loved me so much and wanted to protect me. Such love could only be returned by love.

22
Student Life

S ome months after Tone and I became a couple, he invited me to his home and introduced me to his mother, father and brother. He said that he was embarrassed because they had an old poor house and he did not know if his parents would behave appropriately. The house was quite a big, decent suburban house and his family had nothing against their son's girlfriend, but they were common workers, and were uneducated in etiquette. I put on my longest skirt, came almost without make-up and tried to be as kind and polite as possible.

His mother was the first to come to the door. She was very kind and said that she was glad to finally meet her son's girlfriend. His father seemed nice, although he did not speak much. Tone's brother came from his room, wearing bellbottom jeans and a wild blue Indian embroidered shirt. It suited his long red curly hair. His father eyed him from head to foot and asked if he did not have anything else to put on. The young man answered that he'd put on his best clothes. Tone's mother prepared biscuits and tea, asked me about my studies and work, said several times what a good student Tone was and complained that the younger brother, Sandi, did not show any enthusiasm for studying. Sandi had troubles, especially with the Slovenian language, so I offered that I would help him with homework and my suggestion was accepted with the greatest pleasure. We were all very pleased when I left. Tone said that his family liked me and after that I was invited to lunch almost every Sunday.

Although I had a boyfriend and a part-time job, I tried to give priority to regular and efficient studying. I knew that the majority of students studied just at the end of the year before the exams, but I decided that I would also study during the year. Mara, Eli and I passed the first exams with top marks.

Some of my new schoolmates, especially those who wore the most modern clothes, mocked us and whispered that we had no social life because we only studied, never went to discos or to student parties. But I never felt deprived, because I had a lot of work. I did not like dancing in discos because they were filled with people, cigarette smoke, overly-loud music and it was so packed that you just had one square meter of dance space. It was also impossible to speak.

Tone and I often went dancing in a big dance hall in Ljubljana, to the cinema and made excursions to the mountains. Franc, Ana, Tone and I decided to go to the mountains for the New Year's holidays. The mountain that we wanted to climb was supposed to be a bit steep, but not too difficult, though one could expect at least one or two meters of snow at the top. We did not go together because everybody was busy until the last day before the holidays. Tone and I took an afternoon bus to Bohinj and then started to walk. I was now quite fit—not so much because I'd climbed several mountains, but more because I ran on the business trains. I had to have firm and stable legs if I wanted to keep balance on the train that was tilting to the left and to the right. However, the route to the mountain felt very steep and I soon breathed hard. Our rucksacks were very heavy, because we had lots of unnecessary clothes, food and who knows what else. I was afraid that we might get lost, but Tone assured me that he knew the way and that he had a lamp, so I should not worry. After half an hour, it was dark, and we really had to seek the signs to the cottage with his lamp. We advanced very slowly, because it snowed and once even Tone was afraid that we'd lost our way. Finally, we managed to find the warm and pleasant cottage. Ana, Franc and the rest of the guests were already there, and the keeper of the refuge said that it was stupid to climb during the night because we could get lost and freeze.

We spent the evening with Ana, Franc, and other guests of the cottage. We first ate what we'd brought with us and then tried to organize entertainment. Everybody wanted to be witty and make the atmosphere cheerful. Ana was a quiet girl and said something funny only from time to time. Franc, just the opposite, mocked other people all the time and only sometimes produced a really funny joke. I tried to laugh and participate, so that Tone and his friends would not say that he had a boring girlfriend. Quite frankly, I much more liked the difficult, steep path to the cottage than the loud party after dinner.

The following days passed similarly. We ate, walked through a lot of snow, threw snowballs and laughed. Everybody seemed to enjoy themselves, but I could hardly wait to come home and start studying and travelling again.

I thought to myself: "I am obviously very unsocial. I must try hard so the others will not see what I really think."

I was convinced that I was a rather intellectual person, but I did not notice that I practically had no opinions of my own since I'd started dating Tone. Everything he said seemed so clever. I got used to reporting to him what happened since we'd last met and asking him for advice. He was ready to discuss problems for hours until we thought that we'd found a solution. These discussions were sometimes so long that I got bored, because Tone analysed quite unimportant things. When he started thinking about a problem, he did not finish in the middle but insisted until he cleared it up. He was most happy to help me with everything that caused me difficulties and he encouraged me to solve them. His encouragement was welcome because my family always tried to supress all the ambitions I had.

Once, when we were at the seaside, I mentioned that I was afraid to swim underwater and he enthusiastically decided that he would teach me. He first explained that he had his eyes open all the time when he was under water because there were so many interesting things. And, no, it did not hurt at all. Then he asked me if I really loved him and when I said yes, he wanted me to promise that I would start diving, to prove my love. This was rather manipulative, but I did not notice it then. He slowly and carefully convinced me to put my head under water, open my eyes and tell him how many fingers I saw. Then he overwhelmed me with praise and admiration. But I somehow did not feel so happy, though I'd mastered the new skill of diving. Things above the water were more interesting and, if I did not dive, my hairdo remained as it should be.

Tone often told me how he'd once traveled to Spain and that he liked Spanish towns, food, wine and the language. He generally admired foreign languages and people who spoke them. My school organized a course in Spanish, so I suggested that we enroll in it together. He accepted my suggestion with great enthusiasm and invited one of his best friends, Vita, whom he'd mentioned several times. When he introduced me, I immediately noticed that she was a beautiful and serious girl—exactly what I wanted to be. Her appearance was unique: she had dark brown hair and eyes, she was slim and appropriately dressed. She was already employed but still looked like a young student. She was interested in everything, especially in travelling. I felt that I was meeting a person who surpassed me in everything and was a bit depressed when I compared her beautiful face and figure to mine. I did not have even half of her high spirits and interest in everything. She used to radiantly greet everybody and immediately started a conversation, while I could be silent for an hour. Why did Tone choose me, if he knew this beautiful woman? I once asked him and he said that he'd known her and her family for a long time, but he never felt anything for her except friendship. Soon after we met, Vita invited us to her home, where I met her boyfriend. Bernard was taller than we were, his skin was pale, he moved quickly, and he seemed a bit clumsy. During our visit, he did not say a word at first, and then suddenly interrupted us and explained his opinion in a rather loud voice. From time to time, he simply disappeared and did not say a word about why he left. Later I learned that he had to smoke a cigarette.

The Spanish teacher came from a Slovenian family who lived in Argentina and spoke fluent Spanish, but his teaching methods were poor. His smile showed his embarrassment and it was obvious that he wondered how he'd come before 30 people whom he should teach basic Spanish. Spanish was not difficult for me because I'd studied French for four years and grammar rules were similar. Vita advanced well, too, but I noticed that Tone had difficulties with foreign languages. He came to the lectures regularly and devoted himself to Spanish lessons during free hours, but he did not progress. When the teacher asked him a question, he tried hard to give a correct answer, but he rarely managed it. His homework was full of mistakes and during grammar exercises he glanced at my notebook. I was happy that I could help him and secretly smiled because of his embarrassment. I did not mind that his knowledge of foreign languages was so poor—quite the opposite, I was glad that I was better than him in at least one thing. Up to then it seemed that he was far above me in everything: technological questions, sports, social skills and so on. It was interesting that Tone did not at all admit that he was not good in foreign languages. He wondered why foreign languages contained so many illogical things and sometimes he even remarked that the teacher probably did not know Spanish as well as we thought.

Before one of the Spanish classes, Tone said that he'd visited Vita while I drove to Belgrade, that she'd lent him her textbook and explained him some grammatical rules. He said that Vita was a really good teacher and that she should teach instead of working on research at the School of Electronics.

How could he go and ask Vita for help? He couldn't wait for me?

"I couldn't: you were in Belgrade. I had a lot of time, so I finally paid a visit to Vita's family and used the time for studying." He watched innocently and obviously expected that I would praise him, but I coldly looked at my notebook and was very angry. Instead of doing exercises with me, his girlfriend, he went to his beautiful old friend. No, I didn't believe that he felt nothing for her. He used the first opportunity to visit her, didn't he?

During Spanish class, I was quite passive and didn't want to speak to him or help him with unknown words. Studying with Vita was obviously not very successful because he made a lot of mistakes. He looked at me several times and could not believe that I did not help him.

At the end Vita smiled and said: "Well, Tone, it seems that I am not a very good teacher. It would be better if Iris helped you next time. I have to go; Bernard is waiting for me."

Tone sullenly said that it was not nice that I did not help him.

"Why, you studied all yesterday afternoon with Vita and even said that she taught very well. I expected that you would know everything."

He looked at me with astonishment: "Well… I am not good at languages at all. Why are you so angry?"

"I can't understand that somebody whose girlfriend is a linguist would go to another girl and study with her."

"I just wanted to make a good impression on you."

"Sure. Why don't you start dating her?"

It took his breath away: "What's wrong with you? Are you jealous?"

"How would you feel if I went to your friend David and asked him something about electronics?"

When he understood why I was so angry, he swore that he never thought about Vita as a beautiful girl. In the end, I felt a bit better, but I still worried and carefully watched how he behaved around her.

At the end of the academic year, it was time to sit for examinations. All the first sittings of exams were in June and the next ones in September. I'd studied during the year, so I felt prepared. I passed well and had mostly excellent marks, but I faced a problem with modern German. In June, there were no more lectures, so we only came to the building occasionally, to check the messages about exam sittings. When I looked for the date of the modern German exam, I found a notice that the exam for non-philologists was the next morning at 10.

I came at 9 and caught sight of my schoolmates who were leaving the examination room. They were all low-spirited, because the exam had been so difficult. When I asked them where they found the information that the exam was at 8, they told me that the notice was on the board for several days, but then somebody removed it. I went to the teacher, told her that the notice with the exam date was removed and asked if I could write my exam at 10 with the non-philologists.

She hesitated for a moment and then asked the main lecturer if he allowed it, but he flatly refused: "If you are so ignorant that you did not ask about the date and time of exam, then it is your fault and you will have to come again in autumn."

I tried to explain that the notice was not on the board, but he didn't want to listen. It seemed that he felt insulted if students dared to open their mouth. I had to reconcile myself to the fact that I would not have a summer free of worries. When I heard that only Mara and a few girls who had studied German in the secondary school had passed the exam, I was even more depressed. What if I failed in September? How would I be able to advance to the second year? Would I have to return my scholarship? I drilled modern German the whole summer, learned words and phrases and checked the notice board every week.

The exam was at the beginning of September and I passed with with a top mark. My schoolmates started to observe me with respect because at the time, exam results were posted with the names of the students on the notice board and everyone knew if you failed or passed and what your grade was. Today, the exams are private information that only the teacher and the student know.

The teacher who refused my exam in June taught me something that I have remembered all my life: that it is most inhumane if teachers think that students do not deserve a bit of understanding. I still find it pure evil that he did not allow me to sit for the exam an hour later. I now know why I had to go through this experience, but at that time it reinforced my intention not to become a teacher.

23
Military Service in Yugoslavia

When I was in my second year of university, Tone had to serve in the army. Back then, young men had to stay in the army for a bit more than one year. Since there was no possibility of doing something else instead of military service, he tried to stay as close to Slovenia as possible. He decided to go to the school for officers in nearby Zagreb.

Before he left, we got engaged. We knew a lot of couples who were in love with each other, but when the young men had to go to the army, their girls abandoned them and quickly found new boyfriends. Tone asked me several times if I would really wait for him and I was so sure about it that I did not want to even discuss it. I forgot who of us suggested engagement, but I still remember that we suddenly discussed how we should celebrate it and what kind of rings we should exchange. We went to a jeweller's and decided that we would buy engagement rings with our names engraved upon them and that we would later use them as wedding rings. We did not invite anybody and did not tell even our closest relatives. After a supper, we exchanged rings, and then I accompanied him to the train for Zagreb. I was very sorry that he had to leave, but I immediately started to plan when I could visit him.

The next day, I showed the engagement ring to my mum and to my grandmother. By then, they had already accepted Tone and they seemed pleasantly surprised. My mum gave the enagagement ring a good look and said that it looked like a wedding ring: "Is it engagement or a wedding ring? Do you intend to marry already during your studies? Isn't it too soon?"

"No, it is just an engagement ring, but we are certain that we will one day marry and use these rings also for a wedding."

"Is there any reason that you should marry before you finish your studies?"

"Of course not, don't be silly."

The engagement was really just an expression of our love and a sign that nothing would break it. We both found our love so strong that one's year distance would not mean anything to us. However, we did not yet think what life would be like after marriage.

I decided to find some additional work and go to Great Britain to improve my conversation skills. I took more drives with the business train than usual, started to teach a rather lazy, though very smart, son of a Slovenian politician and found an agency that organized short summer employment opportunities in England. After two or three months, I received a letter from an English housewife, asking that I send her some more information about me and inform her when I could come. She told me also a couple of things about her family, children, house, and the salary that I could expect. They lived in northern London and had two small children that I would take care of.

The young man whom I taught English was communicative, smart and intelligent; his mother was nice and their apartment was always organized and clean. His father was never at home and I never met him. My pupil's mother was about 45 years-old and she was always very kind and interested in everything. Sometimes she sighed about how unhappy she was because her eldest son had died and I quickly changed the subject, because I did not want her to be sad. Years had to pass before I understood that she wanted to speak about her dead child and that it was wrong for me to try to avoid the topic.

My pupil was interested in everything except English. He was only about 12 years-old but asked rather intelligent and tactful questions about my boyfriend, about his profession (he admired engineers and said that they were geniuses) and about the military service. I tried to convince him that we should speak English, but he said that conversation in English was not genuine. He liked English grammar even less. I borrowed books from the library and sought interesting stories in magazines, but they did not help. His mother was pleased with my teaching and asked me to teach her, too. She was a good, hard-working student, but her son was so boring that I almost fell asleep beside him.

When Tone came home from the army, I told them that I would not be able to teach them anymore, because I would have to devote more time to my fiancé. My young pupil agreed with me, said that he was very sorry, but his eyes shined because he hoped that there would be no more English lessons. His mother was very sorry and offered me more money. I found a schoolmate who was happy to take on the teaching hours. I was pleased that I did not have to teach the young man anymore. However, I thought that it was mainly my fault, because I did not provide more interesting lessons—I was obviously not born to be a teacher. I would have to find a job as a translator in a company, I imagined.

Yugoslav soldiers were allowed to accept visitors after they had been in the army for one month. During the first weeks, Tone and I just wrote to each other. Before he left, I thought that two letters per week would be enough. I wrote to him on the very first day—sent him a picture postcard from Belgrade with some words in Spanish. But after two days, I received a serious complaint that he expected more than just a couple of words. He was especially disappointed, because he knew that I liked writing and he'd even given me his typewriter to use to write to him and to learn typing. So, I started learning touch typing and I wrote a letter to him each evening, sometimes just two pages long, sometimes four. And almost every day, I received a letter from him, as well. That was moving, because I knew that writing was never his good point. When Tone finished his military service, I had several boxes of letters and I had become a very good touch typist.

I once asked him if any of his friends received visits in the first month and he answered that this was rare. The visitors were usually invited to the reception office, the receptionist called the soldier and he could speak with the visitor for an hour or two, but the soldier could not go out. I decided to surprise him. I told Tone's mother about my intentions and she prepared a cake. Poor woman, she wept when she said that I should greet him. My mum helped me to make a cake of my own. It was not very beautiful, but it tasted good, and I filled it with walnuts.

I had his address and I knew how to travel to Zagreb. I got off the train at the station that I believed to be in the vicinity of the barracks. I asked and asked, and everybody tried to help me, but in Zagreb there were many barracks. Finally, an older man told me which tram to take and where to get out.

When I came to the entrance, a number of soldiers were leaning against the wire fence, all of them kindly smiling and asking: "Did you come to visit your boyfriend?"

"Yes, his name is Tone. Is he here?"

"Yes, of course, we'll find him immediately." I hardly had time to shout that they should not tell him that it was I, because I wanted to surprise him. Some ran across the courtyard to find him, but the majority stayed with me. They watched me like it was a miracle, especially those who were from Slovenia. "Where are you from in Slovenia? What's your name? What do you do? What do you study? What a pity that you are his fiancée, you could be mine."

They seemed so lonely and so homesick that I felt sorry for them.

Tone had lost weight and seemed a real wretch. I offered him the cake, but he said that he could not eat because he was so happy to see me. He would take it to the barracks and eat it with his friends. He told me how boring it was, what a nightmare it was to know that he could not go out and how he wished to go at least to the cinema. The school for officers was not very difficult and he had no special problems. There was just one unpleasant recurring event—he fell asleep during the lectures. The lectures were after lunch and rather boring. He woke up only when the teacher pounded on the table.

After two hours, I had to leave. Tone held my hand and we slowly went to the door and a big group of soldiers followed us. I knew that it was not because they wanted to interfere with the private life of their friend and also not because I was such a beauty. Some of them had not seen their girls or relatives for months, so they wished to at least take a look at, or speak a word or two with a girl from the normal world.

24
Au-Pair in England

In the summer, I went to England for two months. I found it intolerable that I studied English but was afraid to speak because I might make a mistake. A longer stay in England should improve my skills in conversation and help me with my further studies. And I was also interested in the country whose language I studied and about whose inhabitants I learned so much. My mum warned me that the ladies of the house could be real witches, or so she heard from one of her colleagues. My grandmother frowned and said that such travels were dangerous. Tone completely understood my wish to learn English properly and supported my plans, although we would not see each other for two months. A neighbor who worked in a bank, and to whom my grandmother usually sold fresh eggs, changed my Yugoslav dinars into pounds and told my grandmother that all students of foreign languages should go abroad and stay there for some time. Still, she wept when I was leaving and said that I should return as soon as possible. I tried to explain to her that England was in the vicinity and that my staying abroad would take just a couple of weeks.

I, too, felt a bit sorry when I was leaving. Everybody and everything that I loved was at home. My wishes to travel were never so strong that I would want to leave my home for a longer time, and I was no adventurous spirit. I still can't understand how some people can leave their home forever or travel for months on end. I have always thought that all the best and the most beautiful things were at home.

At the airport in London, I immediately noticed a man standing in the hall and carrying a big piece of paper with my name. I considered him quite old. He was some centimeters shorter than I, fat, bald and wore glasses—in short, he was one of the least attractive men I had ever met. However, he soon showed his sense of humor and, after an hour, I never thought about him as ugly anymore.

When we rang the bell at a pretty semi-detached house in the northern part of London, the door was opened by a beautiful dark-haired woman of my age. She was more than 10 centimeters taller than her husband, had an angelic face and a sweet smile.

I was surprised: "You can't be the lady of the house. You are so young and as beautiful as a film star."

She obviously liked my remark, because she smiled again. She held her son, a six-month-old baby, in her arms. The baby was happy to see his father, who took him in his hands and threw him into the air. Then I met their three-year old daughter, who had some questions for me, especially regarding whether I would read to her and I promised that I would.

To tell the truth, I had no idea how to take care of babies and children. I remembered that I took care of my neighbor's daughter a couple of times, but I did not know how to hold a baby or change nappies, so I asked the housewife to show it to me several times. When I first changed the baby, its cotton nappy soon slipped to his feet and his mother told me to adjust it firmly and fix it with a safety pin. She looked at her husband and they obviously waited for my question.

"What if the safety pin opens and stings his belly? I don't know much about babies, but I am sure that Slovenian mothers do not use safety pins. Isn't that dangerous?"

Both parents started to laugh: "We expected that question. Every girl from the continent asks it. But that's how we do it in England and we can assure you that it is perfectly safe."

I still did not believe them and often checked that the safety pin was not undone.

My bed was in a room that had one wall covered with books, and a private bathroom. That was a real luxury! I was free one full day and two afternoons, so I visited all the sights of London, its beautiful parks and shops that were so rich, large and could not be compared to ours. I thought that I would be expected to also do some cleaning, but they had a special cleaner for the house, for the silverware, and they had a gardener. All I had to do was take care of the children, tidy up the toys and sweep or vacuum the places where the children played. The housewife did all the cooking herself. She went to the kitchen at about three in the afternoon and started to create something kosher, good and interesting that contained as few calories as possible. I often offered her help, but she always refused, saying that she preferred to be alone in the kitchen, because it was so small.

I was very interested in their way of life because they were both English and Jewish, so I asked a lot of questions. They liked my interest and explained a lot about their habits. They also taught me what was decent and what was not in their eyes. Among the most important things were not eating pork, not using the same knife to cut butter and meat, and not eating things that were sold in the street. Because of them, I stopped eating pork. I also tried to get used to drinking tea instead of coffee, but the famous English tea disappointed me. I still think that coffee is much better.

The children usually ate their dinner at about six and then went to bed. We had dinner at about seven, when the husband came home. Each of those dinners could have been something special, because the housewife really took every effort to create a piece of art that no one had eaten before and it was always very good. I am still sorry that all those carefully prepared dinners were so lifeless. We almost did not speak. When I came to the house, the husband tried to develop some conversation, but he stopped after a day or two because his wife suggested that we should be silent when we were eating. On Fridays, the dinners were even more solemn because they put candles on the table, red wine and sweets (it was expected that you would take just one).

I had never seen a better organized home, marriage and family. However, the house was emotionally cold, because the housewife hardly showed any emotions and almost did not speak.

She said every morning: "Good morning, Iris, how did you sleep?"

Then she kissed her children, took the baby into her arms, asked her daughter what she would eat for breakfast and prepared it. After we finished eating, she started reading or went shopping or did some tidying. She was silent all the time. When her husband arrived home in the evening, she again uttered a couple of sentences about what she'd done during the day, what she'd read, what the children had done, and then asked her husband about his day. He sometimes tried to describe his work or discuss politics, but then closed his mouth and we silently ate our wonderful dinner, went to our rooms and read. This defeated the main point of my being in England to develop my conversation skills.

At the beginning, they often took me to their relatives and friends. By contrast, they were talkative, their children shouted and ran around, but my beautiful housewife sat on her chair, drank tea, smiled and remained silent. I was most happy when I found an evening course in advanced English in which I participated twice a week, because it finally offered me some opportunity to speak. It seemed that my housewife was happy because she knew that I came to England to improve my conversation and she was aware that she could not help me.

After a month, I could hardly wait to go home, although London was always full of interesting things. I did a lot of sightseeing, explored many shops, watched a lot of theater performances and regularly visited my course in English. After testing my knowledge, they put me in the top class and the teacher sometimes joked that he was afraid of my knowledge. He was a big young man who always said exactly what had just entered his mind and also expected spontaneous answers. The group consisted of a nice and coquettish French girl, a charming Spanish boy, two Japanese girls who had considerable troubles with English, a Malaysian boy who was, in my opinion, even more frivolous than our teacher, and a Portuguese boy who quietly and humbly sat beside me and answered only when somebody asked him a question. We had to do role-playing all the time, but we also went for drinks and visited theater performances together. Once, we had to write a letter to a newspaper editor and ask for advice about our problems. I wrote that I felt very lonely, because the housewife hardly uttered a word. Then I had to role-play with the Malaysian boy, so I first read my letter and he gave me advice and then he read his letter and I counseled him. He did not find my problem worth mentioning. If you are lonely in a boring British family, you should go to a park or to a bar and start speaking and you will immediately get as many friends as you want. And you ought to start immediately, he said. There is no sense in staying in one's room, even if it is so beautiful and full of books. His problem was that he was in love with two girls and he did not know what to do. I suggested that he should wait to become more mature. I do not think that he liked my advice. But I still remember his words and still find them reasonable and useful. My English teacher often said that I should, for God's sake, stop speaking in such correct English, that my moral norms were too stiff and that I should at least sometimes say something stupid.

The relationship between my housewife and me did not become any better, but worse. She started to complain that I did not close all the windows on the first floor before I took the children for a walk. Once, she almost shouted that somebody might break in and take all her silverware and jewelery. Even if Yugoslavs did not lock the doors and windows, I should be aware that England was full of criminals, and I challenged fate if I did not close the windows. I still think that she exaggerated. England had, of course, more criminal activity than Yugoslavia, but not in the peaceful area where we lived. Besides, I always walked near our house.

I once said that she was too scared, and that made her really angry. And, being so furious, she said that I had never cleaned a cupboard in the kitchen, although she expected it. And I ate one of the beautiful red apples which she'd bought for the dinner with her husband's friend. She trembled with rage, so I immediately promised her that I would take special care to always close the windows, clean the cupboard and apologized because I ate the apple. I told her that, in my village, there were so many apples that nobody cared if you took one and ate it. She went to her bedroom and stayed there for two hours. I took the children to the kitchen and started to clean the cupboard. When she came down, I showed her the cupboard and some changes that I introduced in its organization. She thanked me, apologized and started to prepare dinner. I offered her help again, but she said that she preferred if I played with the children in the sitting room.

The next evening her husband's best friend and co-owner of the company in which they worked, joined us, so she wanted to make a good impression on him. The dinner was excellent and the atmosphere quite pleasant. The guest and the husband spoke all the time and were very interested in Yugoslav politics. They laughed, when I said that Yugoslavia had only one party and that Comrade Tito and the Communist Party were always of the same opinion. Even the housewife uttered some sentences. After the dinner, she changed into a beautiful silk kimono, took a book in her hand and sat in the sitting room. They watched TV, read, discussed things and seemed a real image of happy family life. They asked me to stay with them, but I apologized that I had some homework to do for my course in English.

I couldn't forget the housewife's nagging and was quite sullen the next day, even when I joined my schoolmates. The Portuguese boy noticed that something was wrong and asked what had happened. I did not intend to explain, but I started to cry. Everybody patted me on my shoulder, one of the girls offered me her handkerchief and I was forced to describe the quarrel. Some boys suggested that I should find another family, while my cheeky teacher said that I should try to provoke my housewife with some insolent sentences and perhaps that would make her speak.

At the end of the month, the husband invited the whole family and me to a very modern, expensive and good self-service restaurant at Heathrow. I had a feeling that his wife did not like that he invited me, but she could not simply take back her husband's words. The food was really good and even the housewife did not stick to her diet (she always repeated that she wanted to lose four pounds). At home, she usually stopped eating in the middle of the dinner, threw the rest of the low-calorie meal into a basket and went to her bedroom. Her husband never said anything, but it seemed that he was happy because at least I sat with him and ate.

Although we appeared to be an organized, happy and polite family, I felt more and more unhappy and, on my free days, I stayed in the city until ten o'clock in the evening. Sometimes I went to the theater, had coffee or tea or just walked. I once came to my station in northern London at eleven and, when I started to walk home, I noticed the silver Mercedes of the husband. He waved for me to enter the car and I asked him what he was doing out at that time of the night.

"I heard that you were going to the opera and I was afraid that you might have gone to Covent Garden."

I answered that Covent Garden was too expensive for me and wondered why I should not go there.

"I heard that The Irish Republican Army placed a bomb there today. We worried about you."

I thanked him and went to bed as soon as I got back.

About one week later, the housewife invited me to have tea with her. She told me that her friend expected a baby in a week or two and that her au pair had to leave for France. Would I be so kind and help her? She already had two small children and really needed an au pair. Of course, I was so kind, although I was sorry that I had to leave both of her children, whom I liked. Besides I really did not feel good in that cold atmosphere. The housewife assured me that I could come back if I wasn't happy in the new milieu.

My new family had moved into their big house with a large garden just a year earlier. The house was still under construction so some rooms were locked. There were holes in the floor and the housewife always waited for one or another worker and cursed when they did not appear. This housewife was five years older than I, she had a big belly and her eyes flashed with high spirits.

She spoke all the time: sometimes she praised or scolded her children, complained about her mother-in-law, laughed at her husband, spoke ill of her neighbors or gave me advice. When I first came to her, she asked me to change the nappy of her daughter, who was a real small devil. The two-year old Leah immediately opposed with all her body and started to cry and kick. I prepared a fresh nappy and everything necessary to wash her, quickly and unexpectedly caught her, slightly leaned against her legs so that she could not kick, successfully changed a nappy and turned her round so that she started laughing.

"Well, you are really a pearl, aren't you? I could not believe that Jane had such a good au pair and she was prepared to offer your services to me. Why did she let you go? Did you quarrel?"

I could see that my new housewife did not sugarcoat her words, but I didn't mind. I actually liked it.

"She didn't really need me. Her two children are so good that there wasn't anything to do. She also has a lady for cleaning, a special cleaner for windows, for silverware, a gardener and she does a lot of work herself. I felt quite useless sometimes. I was free two afternoons, one whole day and on Sundays."

"Well, to be frank, you will not be so free in our house. I will need you, especially when I go to the maternity hospital."

"I don't need so much free time. When you are in the hospital, I will not move from here. I already saw everything in London. I will be happy if I can do something useful and help you."

"As you can see, our family is much less organized than Jane's. We just started our house renovations and those damned workers never come when they say. And also, I am afraid that we are a much louder family. You've seen how Leah cries if she doesn't like something. Johnny uses bad language and my husband shouts if he doesn't find something he needs. We don't want to scare you, but I must tell you what you can expect."

"I am very glad that you are not as peaceful as my former family."

"Oh, yes, I suppose you are. Does Jane speak more with her family members than in society?"

I had to admit that she didn't. She was very interested if they quarreled and how the atmosphere was in the house and I told her that they never quarreled, but I always felt cold.

"Yes, I thought you would. They are both very pleasant and honest people, but something is wrong."

The new family was really loud.

The husband shouted because he could not find his socks or his glasses, my housewife yelled that she was not his slave and that he should find them himself, little four year-old Johnny lifted up women's skirts and sang: "I can see your panties, I can see your panties." Leah could not speak yet, but she ran very quickly, and it was necessary to catch her all the time. She enjoyed if she could run outside or open the cupboard and pull everything out on the floor.

When the housewife had to go to the hospital, her mother came to check on how we were doing. Before leaving, the housewife said: "Take care of my children, my husband (but not too much, she laughed) and my plants. Jack always forgets to water them."

I scrupulously did everything and, when she brought the new baby home, I enthusiastically reported that everything was OK.

Some days later, we noticed that things weren't. Both her husband and I watered her flowers and they died.

When she showed me the baby, I made a mistake. I was used to seeing Leah and Johnny, who were really beautiful, dark children with brown eyes. The baby was small, red, bald and pimpled. I tried to be polite and said that it was quite an interesting creature.

"Come on, tell me the truth. What do you really think about my baby girl?"

"Well, if you want the truth—I think that Leah is much more beautiful. What is so special about a baby? Babies are actually ugly."

She started laughing, told all her friends what I said about her beautiful baby and added: "The girl is frank."

They hired a nurse for the baby, and she lived in the house for about a month, took care of it, fed it and changed her nappies during the night. Women in reasonably wealthy families did not breastfeed. I knew that from my former housewife, who answered my question with such a face that one would've thought that I'd asked her if she had to pee.

The nurse was an old, annoying lady who pretended to be loyal and humble if the housewife was in the vicinity. As soon as we were alone, she started to gossip. The baby cried a lot and Leah often joined her.

All that crying got on my nerves and I thought to myself: "Oh, Lord, I would like to wake up at least one morning by myself and not because a baby's crying."

I believed that I had no real sense for children and once I told this to my housewife. She said that she, too, did not like the crying of other children, but her own did not disturb her: "You are quite normal, don't worry."

When I left England, I beamed with joy that I would see my family and Tone again. I thought that I'd improved my English. I had no idea that I'd learned plenty of other things: how to keep a household, take care of children and understand relationships in a family. Such things seemed quite unimportant to me at the time. I was sure that Tone and I would not have any troubles, that we would not quarrel because of unimportant trivialities and that my new cooking skills were quite useless. Why should one know how to cook? You take a cookery book, put into the pot what is suggested, and you produce something to eat.

When I arrived at the airport, I was told that the company that had sold me the ticket went bankrupt, so they could only accept me if one of the seats was free. I was desperate because I longed to come home and because I knew that my family would worry if did not come. However, there ended up being one seat free. I did not expect that my whole family, with my grandmother and my brother, would come and wait for me at the airport. Tone was also there, which quite surprised me. He'd left the army without permission just to see me. He had to go back to Zagreb immediately, so that they would not miss him.

25
Accelerating Studies

When the academic year started again, it seemed that my knowledge from England was of no use. We continued studying Shakespeare and a couple of other old writers and poets. We had modern English courses, but the teachers expected that we would speak without mistakes and use phrases that we read in the textbook. I really missed the amusing English courses in London.

I continued to get good marks and started to accelerate my studies. I knew that it would be easy to study and sit for an exam without listening to the lectures, so I asked if the the school would allow acceleration. They were amazed and wanted to know why I wished to finish my studies faster than other students. I explained that I would like to get employment as soon as possible. They did not quite understand why somebody who was a regular student with good marks would want to finish earlier, but I got permission. I asked Mara if she would join me and she agreed. After sitting for an exam, we usually went to a nearby coffeehouse, had coffee and a cigarette and discussed the exam questions. We were successful, but we slowly lost contact with the other students.

Tone and I often said that we would live a simple life near nature, never have a car, climb the mountains as frequently as possible, spend summer holidays at the seaside—in short, we did not wish for any special material goods. My mum secretly mocked our words but did not say anything. After Tone returned from the army, he was convinced that it was not possible to live without a car. He could afford one, because he was employed and had a good salary.

"Come on, you don't even have a driver's license."

"I can get one soon. My brother also wants a driver's license. And you can join us, too. It will be easier for you."

I sharply opposed. Back then, it was considered difficult to learn to drive. I heard that women had to sit for the examination several times.

Besides, I was not gifted with technical things and he knew it.

"Think about it. Wouldn't it be nice to have driving lessons together? Sandi and I will help you. This is a unique opportunity to learn how to drive."

During the first days, I refused, especially because my brother had said that I was as capable of driving a car as riding a cow, and my mum indulgently smiled. However, Tone was insistent and at last he convinced me. I started the course with him and his brother. During the first hour, I reluctantly listened to the teacher, who explained the inner part of the engine. When real driving lessons started, I found them interesting and I could hardly wait for the next one. Of course, I made mistakes, but so did Tone and his brother. We had to cover quite a lot of hours with the teacher, because we had nobody who would lend us a car or teach us driving outside of the course. Other young drivers usually trained by driving the cars of their fathers, who accompanied them.

We had the exam on the same day and at the same hour. My mum and my brother, who suddenly stopped teasing me, said that I should not worry too much if I failed:

"You must be aware that you had no car to practice with, and you are not very gifted when it comes to technology, so you may fail several times. Never mind it, you will be able to repeat the exam. The majority of people do not manage to get their driver's license immediately. Tone and Sandi are boys and they have technology in their blood."

It seemed that Tone and Sandi thought the same.

At the beginning of the exam, I trembled, so the teacher took me by the hand and told me to relax. Some examiners walked by and I wished that my examiner would be at least a nice person. The last who came by seemed extremely unpleasant and my teacher said that he was the most demanding.

I said to myself: "Oh, Lord, I am sure I will fail if this one assesses me."

After a minute, he called my name. He unkindly asked if I wanted to drive through the town and follow his directions or choose my own way. I answered that I would prefer his guidance. When I had to mind the traffic, I soon forgot both my teacher and examiner and concentrated upon driving. I was rather awkward when parking, but I passed.

I danced with joy and thought: "If I passed this exam, I can pass anything!"

Tone and Sandi both failed and had to do some additional hours and then repeat it. Tone, Sandi and my brother were very surprised, but they did not envy me. After all, at least somebody from the family managed to get their driver's license on the first try.

I was fed up with my work travels to Belgrade, so I started to look for a permanent job. I did not find it difficult to stay up in the middle of the night, but everything was so monotonous: always the same work and the same problems that I could solve with my little finger. Seldom did something interesting happen and even such events were more unpleasant than amusing. Once, I had to serve one of the best-known Slovenian politicians. Two strong young men stood in front of his compartment and seemed to observe nature through the window. All the stewardesses were annoyed if passengers stood while we ran around. The train was narrow and such passengers presented an obstacle. We always tried to convince them to take a seat. So, I started to tell them that they should sit down because the train might make quick turn or stop and they would fall and break their noses. They seemed amused but said that they would stay where they were. I complained to the conductor, who told me that they were bodyguards and could not go away. I should be happy if they would let me enter the compartment at all. They did, but I had to leave the door open and one of them stood right behind my back. The politicians were most kind and gave me big tips.

Much less pleasant was a middle manager of Slovenian Railways, who traveled with his friends and acted as if this was his personal train. The conductor allowed him to use the special compartment without payment, but I had to ask him and his colleagues to pay for what they ate and drank. He seemed rather annoyed because he had to pay and asked why I did not wear my official uniform. I had the uniform on, as wee had two models, so I politely and coldly answered that it was my official uniform. He got really angry and said that he would report my behavior to the general manager. I never received any reminder or punishment, so he must have forgotten to report me.

26
Permanent Employment

had no idea how to look for a job. I thought that I had poor teaching
abilities, so I decided that I would first try to find something
appropriate in international business. Many of my friends said
that companies in international business were among the richest and
most appreciated in the country. I would surely find a translating job,
get a great salary and have a lot of opportunities to travel around the
world in international trade. So, I started to read daily magazines and
examine employment advertisements. I noticed that several companies
looked for people who graduated in English and German and I sent
some applications. In one of the firms, I was told that I should first
graduate and then start applying for a job; in the second enterprise,
there were several applicants and one had many more skills than I. The
third company invited me to come for an interview. I spoke with the
general manager for a long time and he seemed very pleased when I
told him that I was taught how to behave. He also liked that I'd worked
in England as an au pair and as a stewardess on the business train.

Thus, I quickly got a permanent job during my fourth university
year when the majority of students studied for five or six years. The
general manager suggested that I should start immediately, but I asked
him for two more weeks, so that I could finish one or two exams.

On my first day of employment, I felt uneasy. The strong smell
of coffee that spread up to the third floor of the business building
caused unpleasant feelings in my stomach. I was aware that I'd started
something quite new and was afraid that it would not end well. I saw it
in the eyes of my future coworkers, who seemed to have been informed
that the new general manager's secretary was coming, and they eyed me
up and down.

When I introduced myself to the receptionist, he gave me the keys
to my office and said that the administration people had not arrived yet.
He suggested that I should unlock my room and wait until somebody

arrived. I was looking for the switch in the darkness until an old lady heard me, helped me turn the light on and showed me which desk I should sit at.

After some minutes, a big and strong man about ten years older than I entered the room and told me that he was the manager's driver, Tomo. He knew that I was the secretary, and he also knew my name because I lived in the vicinity of his village. He did not have his own office because he spent most of his time in the car. In the mornings, he was used to sitting with the ladies from administration and they always brought him his morning coffee. I immediately liked him, so I obediently offered to bring him a coffee.

"Good. Order a double short coffee without sugar and with cream. The intern number of the coffee room is 20, but you will have to pick it up yourself. They will not bring it just for us two. Go to the second floor to the left and explain to the woman there exactly what I want, because she has two left hands. When the general manager arrives, you will order the same for him just without cream."

I ran to the coffee room and quickly brought what the driver required. He first checked if the cup was clean, tried what I'd brought and then nodded that the coffee was all right. I asked him when my mentor would arrive, and he answered that the lady was on holiday somewhere in China and that she would not be back for at least two weeks.

I anxiously asked who would tell me what to do, but he carelessly waved his hand: "The lady in the next room is the personnel manager and should be able to help you. Also, Flora who sits here will come soon. Flora has no special education, but she might be able to tell you a thing or two. Don't be so worried. You should be happy that your mentor has not arrived yet. Try to enjoy these fourteen days. When she comes, you will see a devil."

Another coworker entered the room. He was rather small, had a handsome face and introduced himself almost too politely. His name was Denis and he said that he was president of the company Trade Union and the clerk for personnel issues. He mentioned that he would also like a coffee.

The driver growled: "Go and fetch it yourself. The secretary is not here to bring you coffee. She will also have no time to chat with you, because she will have too much work."

The young man's face became dark, but he shrugged his shoulders, smiled and left.

Tomo said: "Be careful not to serve everybody who will sponge off you, especially not to such a hypocritical ass as this one. You will learn what he's like: he sticks his nose into everybody's business and then forwards his observations to the general manager and who knows to whom else. You can be kind, but do not trust him."

In that moment, the door swung open with a bang and the general manager, Mr. Herman, said in a loud voice: "Tomo, there is something wrong with my car. When I shift up—oh, look at her, that's my new colleague! How are you—did you pass those exams? Of course, you did, I knew that you were a clever girl. Why are you standing here? Has nobody told you what to start with? Oh, yes, Mrs. Belak is on vacation. Nothing to worry about, I would say. It is better that you get used to the new environment slowly and in peace. However, the personnel manager should explain to you how to sort the letters and order coffee."

When the personnel manager arrived, the director asked her why she had not come earlier and gave me some basic information about work. She frowned and said that she'd managed to sleep for just an hour, because her baby had a fever.

"Well, acquaint her with her tasks, at least. I must discuss some matters with Tomo." The director and Tomo disappeared into the director's office and I quickly brought a coffee also for the director. I wanted to bring one to the personnel manager, but she refused.

After five minutes, I entered her room with a notebook and pencil and enthusiastically said that I was looking forward to her information about the company. She sighed, rather tired and in a low mood, that she had too much of her own work and that she did not understand why she should perform the job of that old witch, who either caused troubles in the company or traveled around the world. Then she quickly described international trading and the main departments of the company. They imported most different things: tools, machines, office equipment and other technical products from Germany, computers from the United States, tools and machines from Italy, Switzerland and Great Britain. I already knew those things because I had read the company brochure. She also mentioned a couple of laws and suggested that I should take a closer look at the archives in my office.

Since the other coworker was still not in the room, I started to examine big cabinets in the office to find the laws and the meeting minutes of different committees that the personnel manager had spoken about. When I opened the first, one of the folders fell onto my head and a pile of papers ended up on the floor. I could soon see that the cabinets were in horrible disorder and that their organization would be hard work. For the time being, I had no idea what all those papers were about and how to file them.

The manager and the driver finished their discussion and entered my office. "Well, I see that you already started to work on the most critical point of our office, the archives. I would like you to organize the documents so that you would be able to bring me a document immediately if I need it. Please be different from other women in this company. No one, not even your future mentor, wants to deal with the records, so we are always looking for the missing papers. I claim, again and again, that a good secretary has well-organized documentation, but nobody listens to me. So, I will be back at about one and then I will tell you more about your duties. And I will also need you to help me with a special task."

When I started to pull difficult folders out of the cabinets, I noticed that one contained mainly minutes of the Workers' Council; another of the Committee for Personnel Issues, in the third there were letters in foreign languages and so on. If I were to offer the manager a document that he might need, and if he could tell me which committee or council dealt with it, I could perhaps organize documents according to individual organs and consider the dates, I thought to myself and started to read the minutes.

Flora, a young administrator, arrived at about ten. Her main duty was typing. Her face was swollen and red. "I bumped against the door," she mentioned, as I observed her a bit too long.

I brought her coffee, and this made her happy. She started to explain what had happened in the company and described the character of their employees. She asked if the director had grumbled when he saw that she had not come on time and then embarked upon a long description of his despotic management. The general manager scolded sector directors because their departments didn't bring in enough money; he reproached salespeople for spending too much money on business dinners; secretaries got on his nerves because they flirted and women in the accounting department didn't work on anything worthwhile at all. He often changed secretaries though the last one remained a bit longer. The last secretary fluently spoke four languages, typed very quickly and was exquisitely dressed. She was always invited to business dinners and knew how to speak with representatives of foreign firms. This sent me into a cold sweat. I was aware that I had no such abilities. I could speak only two foreign languages, and even those not as well as I wanted to. I was not pretty, I had no money for elegant clothes, and I was rather antisocial and dull.

One of our coworkers came to the office, introduced himself and asked if the post was sorted. I had no idea what he was talking about. Flora answered that he would get the post in about an hour. He should be aware that I was new and could not do everything immediately. Then she showed me a pile of letters on the desk and told me to sort them, put the main data into a book and then call the courier lady to take them to individual departments. I did not know which departments dealt with the many products that were mentioned in the letters. I tried to use the company brochure and asked Flora if my sorting was all right. When I finished, I was worried that the letters might not come to the right people, but Flora said that the courier lady had been in the company for thirty years and that she would correct my mistakes.

Then I continued to organize the documentation. The work was boring, and I was not sure if I worked in the right way. From time to time, I asked Flora about one thing or another, but she did not know much about the documents. I went to the personnel manager, but her answers were so abstract that they did not help.

When the general manager came back, he frowned at Flora but did not say anything, because she was two hours late and brought her a short letter to type.

"Just look at how he treats me—he keeps giving me tasks."

Quite frankly, I didn't think that Flora had done anything that morning except to chat with people who came to the office. I offered to type the letter, which was only about ten sentences long. She refused, saying that she should do it herself, otherwise the director would complain again. She typed and typed, the director loudly asked twice when the letter would be written, but the document was finished late. Flora put it on director's desk and went home.

After a few minutes, he came to me and growled: "Excuse me—I know that you are a beginner, but I must send this off today. Take a look at some other letters and type this without mistakes, even if you sit here until the evening."

I quickly found the folder with the correspondence and typed the letter in a similar way. I was very happy because I had a big modern typewriter. Flora said that it was all mine and even showed me a liquid with which I could erase mistakes. I had no idea that such a thing existed. So, I enjoyed typing and the director was happy when he received the letter. He signed it and asked me to post it, because the courier lady already left. Then I should come back so that we could discuss some things.

I returned in fifteen minutes and he waved for me to come to his office. He had a lamp on his small desk, a piece of paper and an English textbook.

"Dear girl, my English teacher will be here in half an hour and I still haven't written my homework. Will you help me?"

27

First Impressions about International Business

When Flora came the next day, her eyes were shining: "Have you seen him?"

"Do you mean the young man who has just entered the neighboring office?"

"Of course. That's the new lawyer. Isn't he handsome? So tall, fair-haired and blue eyes! And how clever he must be, he graduated already at 28!"

"Well, I am even cleverer. I'm 22 and will graduate soon."

"I bet that all the women in the company are already making plans about how to get to him. But our position is certainly the best. We must convince him to have coffee with us."

"Didn't you say that you were dating the receptionist? What will he say if you flirt with the lawyer?"

"Oh, come on, a bit of flirting has never hurt anybody. And my relationship with the receptionist is not ideal, you know. I did not bump against the door yesterday. Dani beat me so that I am black-and-blue. Take a look."

I shuddered when I saw red and blue spots on her shoulders and her arms and asked how it happened.

"He is so jealous. I dare not even look at another man. He beats me just if I speak to somebody."

I didn't know what to say, but Flora did not care about past events anymore. She started to make a strategic plan as to how she would win the lawyer. After some minutes she got up, went to his office and asked if he would like to have coffee with us. The lawyer accepted her invitation and we introduced ourselves to each other. During our conversation it was so obvious that Flora flirted with him that I became embarassed and started to ask him about his law studies. After a few minutes, the general manager loudly opened the door and frowned. Then he said that it was right that we get acquainted and that he would like to speak to both the new lawyer and to me. The director and the lawyer spoke for two hours and, in the end, the young man came out with a red face, a forced smile and the smell of smoke. The lawyer did not stay in our office, although Flora tried to keep him.

Then it was my turn. "Well, Miss or rather Comrade Iris, I will now give you some basic instructions on how to behave as my secretary. You will get more information about your secretarial work from Mrs. Belak when she returns from China. She has been in the company since its beginning and knows how to perform your job. You must be aware that being a secretary means being the right hand of the director. Everybody who will want something from me will first try to convince you that you should sell their idea to me. Be careful that you stay objective and that you keep a distance from everybody. Do you know what a distance is?"

I mumbled that I was taught about it already on the business train because the book of rules for stewardesses contained the sentence: "stewardesses should keep passengers at a distance and politely refuse their invitations with the excuse that they are tired and have to get rest."

"Good, so I recommend that you try to be as official as possible, don't address people in the informal tense, don't have personal discussions with your coworkers either during work or after. Be careful not to be too kind to anybody, try to dress as conservatively as possible and, in front of all, don't participate in the birthday and other parties that you will be invited to. Don't be like this poor thing, Flora, who can think of nothing but men. Don't be like my former secretary, who had affairs with several men in the company. Remember what I am going to tell you now because it is true: men go just as far as women let them go. Don't you ever try to make excuses that somebody persuaded you."

The instructions surprised me, but I obediently nodded that I absolutely agreed with him and that I never thought of making closer contacts with anybody, because I was sure that my fiancé would not like it: "You don't need to worry, because I am exactly the person that you want."

"OK, I am pleased to hear that. I hope that I will never have problems with you of the sort I had with my former secretary. She organized a birthday party when I was absent, invited half of the employees who got dead drunk and then she danced on a table. Can you imagine a general manager's secretary dancing on a table?"

When I assured him, once again, that I was not like that, he calmed down.

"I would like to start with serious work, but nobody told me what exactly I should do from seven until three o'clock. Will you teach me, so that I will not waste my time?"

"No, I actually don't know what a secretary should do. Wait until Mrs. Belak arrives. But I noticed that you manage very well, you immediately started to check the documentation."

"What shall I do until my mentor arrives? You will think that I am lazy and incapable."

"Do what you think is the best. You can even bring a book and study. Just be careful that nobody finds you studying. I am sure that you won't be able to be lazy under the mentorship of Mrs. Belak. You will work like a slave."

The small young man from yesterday knocked and asked if the director would have time to accept him. But the general manager frowned and snorted that he would call him if he might need him.

"That hypocrite. If we were not in this idiotic system, he would have never become a personnel clerk. Do you think that he has any schooling? He finished a one-year political course which is recognized as a four-year secondary school. Just because he is in the Communist Party. What about you, are you in the Party? No? Even better. I am, because a director should be. But my work is to provide that the business functions well and that 350 employees have salaries."

Somebody knocked again and one of the sector directors entered the office. The general manager introduced me, said that we would continue our conversation next time and closed the door behind me.

In the afternoon, I asked the general manager if I could leave when I finished my work. He liked the question and said that there was no need to ask him every day. He told me that I should be careful to work my quota of 42 hours per week, but I could leave at two if I wanted to. If there was something urgent, he would ask me to stay. When foreign business leaders arrived, I would have to accompany them to lunches, dinners, show them around Slovenia and, on those occasions, I would be busy all day long.

On the next morning, I continued reading the minutes of different committees and councils. One document was obviously written by a joker. It said: "Then Comrade Bolton said to the Comrade General manager that the latter was an old washout and Comrade director pushed him out of the room."

I was laughing, when a tall young man entered the room: "Am I the first one? Isn't the meeting of directors at 8.00?"

I did not know anything about a meeting and just stared at him. Flora was late again so I had to ask what the meeting of directors was.

"For God's sake, don't they intend to give you a mentor? You can't become a good employee if nobody tells you anything. If they don't appoint you mentor, require one of them. The law gives you the right to a mentor. Well, I put it down that the sectors' directors should meet today at 800. Also, directors of the financial and legal sector will be present."

"Which sector do you lead?"

"I am the Secretary of the Communist Party and it is my duty to participate in all meetings. My name is Jan Glaser. If you ever need me, just give me a call."

"Thank you," I mumbled and was pleased when I saw that others started to come.

I was not very happy that the young man stood so close to me, and I was afraid that he might ask me when I intended to enter the Communist Party. Many people think that everybody in Yugoslavia was a member of the Party, but this was not so. Just those who wanted to make a career usually had to enter it. There were many reasons why we did not like it: members had to follow rather strict rules of behavior, they were forbidden to go to church, and they had to pay membership fee.

The directors sat down in the office of the general manager and closed the door. I started to think about what I could do so that my working day would pass a bit faster, when the door opened and the director shouted: "Quickly, Iris. Take some paper and a pencil and put down the minutes."

The general manager first introduced the new lawyer and me and then started with a discussion that I hardly understood. I put down almost everything they said, from time to time ordered coffee and opened the windows. The directors often started a loud quarrel and were so offensive that I did not understand how they could continue the conversation as if nothing had happened. The meeting lasted until twelve. In the next two hours, I wrote the minutes and showed them to the general manager. He seemed pleased, because I wrote them quickly and independently, but he crossed out a number of sentences, saying that it was not necessary to write what one or another stupid fellow said.

"I have decided that you and the lawyer will go to all the departments over the next few days so that you will get acquainted with the program and with the people. You will start tomorrow at nine. Then write a report for me so you can better remember things. Don't write while you speak to the sector directors, but when you return to your office."

The next morning, the lawyer and I went to the director of the third sector, Doler. He was sitting in a small office with glass walls, his legs were on the table and he was taking a long phone conversation in German. Other employees, whom we could see through the glass, were either on the phone or studying their papers. The director's phone discussion lasted almost half an hour. Then he kindly, but in a rather patronizing way, greeted us and started to explain which products were imported by his sector. I first heard expressions like CIF and FOB and tried to remember them to break through the secrets of foreign trade. I asked question after question, and Doler was happy to answer. In the end, he mentioned that his sector earned so much money that they financed practically all the company, including the administration department, like the general manager and his employees, while other sectors did not bring in much profit. He invited us to come to him if we had any further questions.

Then we went to the second sector that imported tools, microfilms and other technical things that did not mean much to me. The director of this sector, Fatur, looked a bit older than Doler, but his behavior was similar and he was very dynamic. Fatur let us know that his sector made big profits and that it financed even the administrators, like the two of us, who actually just spent money and did not contribute to the company income.

The next sector, which imported computers, seemed a bit more pleasant, perhaps because we were accepted by the assistant director and the secretary, who were both kind and less competitive than others. As it was 1976, up to then I'd only heard about computers in science-fiction, so I was looking forward to seeing one. They showed me some brochures with photos of boxes with a keyboard, each about one meter high. When they imported a computer, they sent it directly to the bank or some other institution that could afford the purchase. The assistant director, who explained the history of imports, mentioned that they once made a deal that could have caused bankruptcy, if Mrs. Belak, with her charm and language knowledge, had not have managed to improve the contract conditions.

After getting acquainted with the main sectors of the company, I wrote a report about everything I'd been told. The general manager seemed very pleased and suggested that we should go to the accounting and finances sectors the next day. Then he called the assistant director of the first sector and asked if he could come to his office. I heard them shouting at each other. After half an hour, the general manager opened the door, took his coat and hat and angrily ran out.

I watched him with surprise and then asked the assistant director what had happened.

"Your report contained my statement that the company made a mistake when it bought the first series of computers. He wants me to stop speaking like that. But I don't want to because I know that I'm right."

It took my breath away and, in a moment, I looked at my acquiring knowledge about the company from a different angle. Was Herman sending me around to spy?

I shuddered and apologized that I did not know what reaction my notes would cause, but Jakob waved his hand: "Both you and I told just what was true. Besides, the matter is not as horrible as you might think. Herman is a man who must break out when somebody makes him angry. He will forget all about it tomorrow and so will I."

"I could never forget if somebody shouted at me like that."

"Then try to learn to do so as soon as possible. I used to foam with rage, but I learned how to deliberately forget negative events. I am much happier now and have many more friends. I will get a visitor from a German firm in an hour, then I will have to take him to lunch and dinner and this will occupy me so much that I will probably forget everything about the quarrel with the general manager."

This standpoint seemed interesting, although I knew that I was not capable of using it in practice. I was touchy and remembered ugly remarks and even dirty looks forever.

I could not fall asleep that evening. Even when I did, I started to dream that one of my coworkers was shouting about what a bad worker I was.

The general manager did not mention the quarrel with his employee the next morning. He quietly drank coffee, read the newspaper and then asked me to call Doler. I did and then went to the financial sector alone, because the lawyer settled some matters in the court. In the accounting and finances departments, there were many women, and all accepted me with cold looks. The financial director explained some basic facts about their work.

When I asked a few questions, just to show interest, not because I really cared about finances, the women watched me even more coldly and one of them said: "Why do you ask so many questions? If the general manager is so interested in our work, tell him to come himself and not send you."

I did not know what to say. I saw no need to apologize, but I could also not give any tactful reasons for my questions. I made a wry face, thanked them for the presentation of the sector and left.

In the afternoon, I brought the general manager some letters to sign. He noticed that I was unhappy and asked what was wrong. Then I told him that I had a bad feeling because everybody thought that he sent me around spying. He did not say anything and shrugged his shoulders that such things happened.

Over the next days, the atmosphere got better. Herman had to go for a business trip to Belgrade and we stayed alone with Flora. The lawyer apologized that he could no longer drink coffee with us and Flora whispered that the general manager forbade him from further contact with us. She decided to introduce me to some other nice coworkers. She used informal language with everybody and introductions were made very simply. She called one person after another and suggested that they should come to the office and get acquainted with the general manager's secretary.

A day before the general manager returned, Flora told me that we were both invited to the birthday party of director Doler.

I never liked such parties, so I tried to avoid it: "But Comrade Herman forbade such parties. He told me at least five times that he did not want me to participate. I believe that I should listen to him."

"For God's sake, Doler's invitation is an honor and we have to go. Otherwise he will resent it. Such parties develop a better atmosphere in the company. And Doler knows how to organize a party. Last year, he made such a good feast that some of the most arrogant women from the finance department had to be driven home because they got so drunk. You must come and put on plenty of make-up, so that you will not look so pale."

I felt more and more dislike rising inside me, and slowly developed avoidance tactics: "Who will answer the phones?"

"Why is it necessary to always anwer the phones? They can call again tomorrow."

"No, that's not right. Let me tell you that Herman not only forbade me from participating, but I don't like such parties. I am rather shy. I think that I should stay in the office, answer the phone and type your letters, while you go."

"Do you intend to accuse me tomorrow when Herman returns?"

"No, I won't. I really won't. But please try to understand that I don't enjoy parties."

"Well, do as you like. But be careful not to say anything tomorrow. We will know if you accuse us and then you will not be popular anymore."

She put on some make-up and went downstairs. I could hear the music, the clanking of glasses, loud discussions and laughter. After a few minutes, Doler called and repeated his invitation. I first wished him all the best for his birthday and then apologized that Herman forbade me to participate. I also mentioned that I was not a very social girl. He insisted for a minute or two, but then stopped.

When it was two o'clock, I immediately went home.

The next morning, I was the first to arrive at the company. When I heard the general manager coming upstairs, I felt that he was very angry and that he knew everything about the party. When I brought him coffee, he snorted: "So, it was a pleasant party yesterday?"

I blushed and said that I did not participate in any party.

"I know you didn't. I got a very detailed report on who participated, that the noise lasted until ten in the evening, that the neighbors complained and that many glasses were broken. Are you aware how much money was lost because nobody worked for hours? Do you know how many clients called and got no answer? You can be convinced that they will not phone again but will go to the competition. And I am sure that many women made fools of themselves because they drank too much. I've had enough of this Doler! He does not only put a monkeywrench in other people's wheels but deliberately and arrogantly breaks my explicit orders. Tell him to come to my office today at eleven. I will make him wait and suffer for a couple of hours. Now start calling the other directors who also participated so that I can tell them what I think about such stupid events."

While I was calling, he angrily opened the door to the next office, said to the lawyer that nobody cared about his orders and kicked Denis's door open: "Comrade President of the Trade Union, is it your duty to remove harmful elements from the company or do you intend to just purchase and sell potatoes this autumn?" As an aside, this was also one of the Trade Union's tasks.

"Comrade director, I just wanted to come to your office and ask for your advice…"

"I don't intend to waste time with words. You should have stopped yesterday's folly. The Trade Union should start appropriate action agains such shenanigans."

When Herman spoke with the other directors, he did not shout anymore, but I could hear him saying that I had the strongest character in the company, although I was quite green.

Doler entered at eleven, with a cosmopolitan though slightly nervous smile, and winked: "Well, I will learn my lesson now. But we had such a good time that it was worth it."

I weakly answered that the director was very angry, that he gave the others a good ticking off and mumbled that I did not say a word about the party. He already knew it.

"Oh, yes, of course not. The information was sent by the Secretary of the Communist Party. Never mind, we are used to Herman's outbursts."

They spoke for two hours. Doler came out with a red face and ears and again tried to make a casual wink, but I noticed that director had given him a good lesson.

At twelve, the company worked at full speed and the general manager rubbed his hands when he went out. He said that he would take a walk and that I was a good girl who knew how to behave.

28
Mentor

I wanted my mentor to be pleased with me, although everybody considered her a dragon. I cleaned the room, once again read a book on manners and swore to myself that I would not take offense at the remarks about my ignorance of foreign trade, weak knowledge of foreign languages or anything else.

The director's door was open all morning. When he heard that she'd come, he ran to her, helped her to take off her coat and led a pleasant conversation about her travel. Her descriptions of the architecture, culture, landscape and shopping were most interesting. I ordered coffee for her and offered her my chair because I knew that it was hers before I arrived. She liked my gesture, but she laughed: "Dear girl, keep your chair. I will now sit on the other side of the table." The general manager invited her to his room to discuss things that happened while she was away and then I experienced the first lessons of mentorship.

"Come on, we will examine the letters." Her voice was no more kind and cheerful as it had been just a few minutes ago but became severe and official. She carefully explained what each letter meant and sometimes also described certain words which she thought I did not understand. She stated the differences between personal and business correspondence and she told me how to enter data into the book of letters, what to do in case something was not clear, what to inform the general manager about, and so on. In the end, I did not know which way to turn. It was not just because I saw how little knowledge I had, but also because my mentor started to ascertain that the university should have taught me at least a couple of basic things that it did not. She thought that I should know how to write business letters and be acquainted with basic business expressions in English and German, but it was obviously not so. She asked about my marks and I told her that I passed almost all exams with ten, the maximum grade. She shrugged her shoulders: "Well, the School of Arts seems to give good marks even when somebody does not know anything. When I was a student at the School of Economics, this was not so."

I humbly apologized and said that we mainly studied literature. I thanked her for everything that she taught me. She showed a good mood again and asked me to bring her a good book, because she liked reading.

Then we continued with the outgoing post. I had no idea if the letters were well-written or not, but I could see that they contained a lot of grammatical mistakes. My mentor stopped at each wrong word and explained what was wrong: the content, form, terms and translations. She mentioned that her German was fluent because she spoke it at home and, besides, she had taken at least ten courses in English so that she had enough knowledge to see my mistakes, although I had studied English.

I quickly agreed and admired her because I was aware that I didn't know anything about business English. I knew a lot of Shakespeare and Heine by heart, but that did not help.

We were interrupted by a salesman from the second sector who shouted that he would go to Zürich that evening and that he needed a plane ticket. Mrs. Belak told me to go out to the nearby tourist agencies and walk around until I got a ticket for the evening flight. We had two couriers, but they were not trained for such tasks.

"Quite frankly you are probably not much better, but you must start and now there is an opportunity for you to show what you can do."

It was snowing heavily, but I went to two or three agencies and got the ticket. I came back all wet and my shoes were dirty. As soon as I gave the ticket to the salesman, the general manager called Mrs. Belak and me to his office, so that I could see how to give short summaries of the letters that he had to sign. Mrs. Belak handed him the letters, repeated all her strict remarks about salesmen and suggested that the director should send the letters back and require corrections. He did not, signing almost all of them.

During our checking of the post, they both looked at my dirty boots and the director put on a wry smile: "What boots you've got."

Mrs. Belak made a remark that we would bring another pair of shoes to the office so that we would be able to change if necessary.

The following days were similar. Mrs. Belak fanatically taught me everything that a good secretary should know. I started to hate the word "secretary," while my colleagues used it more and more often. On one day, so many people told me what the duties of a good secretary were that I began to cry. Hang it, the company hired me as a correspondent and I was promised that I would be able to translate letters and contracts and now I have to buy plane tickets, stamp documents, check letters and some coworkers were so shameless that they thought I should prepare coffee! The general manager saw that I had cried and asked what happened. When I bitterly explained the situation, he paced around the office and said that nobody considered me just a secretary. I should not worry. I would have a lot of translations in the future. But I should try to listen to Mrs. Belak because she would really teach me everything about international business.

The next day, the general manager suggested that all the contracts should be brought to me, so that I would get more practice in translation.

I was happy, but the director of the second sector mumbled: "Well, of course…but our translations are made by Mr. Matos and Mrs. Belak. Do you think that a young girl will be able to translate contracts?"

"Mrs. Belak will soon have some other work to do and Comrade Iris will do her best to translate the documents."

After a day or two, Mrs. Belak said sweetly: "Well, now you will try to translate this contract. Be careful to translate it accurately, and mind the legal expressions, because you can ruin the whole contract if you use a wrong word. You must be aware that the contract is essential for international business. If it is not well-translated, this can cause quarrels during negotiations and thus reduce the possibilities for successful business. And, of course, it is necessary to translate quickly. It should have been translated already two days ago."

I immediately started to translate and decided to continue at home to show my competence. Since my mentor said that I could ask her for advice, I asked her about two or three expressions. Each time she raised her eyebrows, was astonished that I was not acquainted with everyday words and disapprovingly smacked her lips, so I soon stopped with my questions. I tried to find the right words in the dictionaries and in the already-translated contracts.

I finished the translation exactly at the agreed time. Mrs. Belak thought that some sentences sounded strange, but perhaps I would slowly learn to improve my style. I was furious, but I shut my mouth because I knew that I had better not make her my enemy. I was happy that I finally got some translation works, but I was well aware that my mentor was right. My translation was not at all eloquent, and one of the expressions was wrong. However, the worst was my awareness that I did not enjoy translating. I sat at the table for two days, consulted dictionaries, looked for the right expressions and then typed everything. It was not pleasant. I found translating painfully boring work. I tried to cheer up by thinking that I would get used to it and that it would not always be necessary to look for unknown words.

On the same day, Mr. Matos angrily arrived at my office because I corrected one of his translations and he accused me that I did not know basics of German. To avoid repetition, I used two different verbs for the German "must." He was no linguist and did not know that there were different verbs to express obligation. I patiently took the German grammar book and showed him grammatical rules, but he still shouted that he had never heard about that.

The general manager and Mrs. Belak quietly listened to our quarrel and did not interfere. After he left, Mrs. Belak murmured: "Well, I told you that we needed a translator and not a peasant with only an elementary school level education. He feels that Miss Iris knows more than him. Don't think that he will now be silent. He has just started."

On that day, my mentor took the folder with letters and stayed in Herman's office for almost two hours. Flora whispered that something was brewing in the accounting sector. The situation was similar over the next days: the general director and Mrs. Belak remained in his office for hours and then invited the lawyer and the director of accounting and finance to join them.

The latter first came to the general manager's office calm and with a raised head but, later, she furiously threw a paper on my table: "Give this to the general manager and to that damned old witch. I intend to leave very quickly."

I showed her notice first to Mrs. Belak, who remained quite cool: "We will find another financial manager, don't worry. She is not the only one in the world. If you work in a company, you should be flexible and not stick to every small regulation. If salesmen worked like her, the company would have gone broke long ago."

I knew that it would soon be necessary to produce the balance which could be made and signed only by the financial director, so I asked her if we were able to find another person quickly enough. Seeking personnel was a long and difficult procedure. However, Mrs.

Belak was confident that it was possible to find somebody appropriate within the company itself.

29
Changes in the Company

Since the financial manager gave notice, it was necessary to find somebody to replace her. The director didn't lift a finger to settle the situation until the sector directors started to press him that it was urgent. He made faint excuses that he tried to find an appropriate person in some other business firms, but it didn't work. There were very few financial directors. They required high salaries and had to stay in their companies until the balance was over.

Finally, he suggested that we should try to find someone within the company who could be moved to the place of the financial manager in a week or two, sign the balance and save the crisis. Everybody said that there was no such person.

The general manager turned to the director of the first sector: "Your assistant is a young economist with perspective. Why not ask her if she wants to become the financial manager?"

The director of the first sector flushed with anger and shouted that he needed a whole year before he introduced her to the business. He would not stand that the general manager would steal his staff. If such a stupid conversation continued, he would leave immediately.

The general manager then suggested a salesman from the third sector, but Doler reacted with even more anger.

"What should we do, comrades? Is there any other economist in the house?"

The general manager looked at me. I answered that only Mrs. Belak was an economist. The majority thought that she was a capable woman, but she was employed only part-time, her health was poor, and she also didn't know much about accounting and finances. The general manager nonchalantly said that the lady was, according to his opinion, quite healthy and that she knew a lot about finances. She can still learn something about accounting—after all, the company can pay somebody to instruct her. She can start working immediately and sign the balance. The directors started a lively discussion and then suggested that the general manager should ask her if she might be interested in a full-time position.

When they left, the general manager tapped on my shoulder with satisfaction: "We did that well, didn't we?"

Mrs. Belak seemed like a cat on hot bricks, when I called her to the general manager. After a long discussion, she came out of his office and told me that she'd accepted the position of financial director, so she would not be able to teach me anymore. I made a sad face, though her words made my heart thrill.

"Thank you, dear God, for saving me from my over-eager mentor!"

But it was not as easy as I thought. She ordered me to write some business letters and when I brought them to her, she found mistakes in each of them. She sharply said that she had no intention to be as indulgent as Herman and that I should put down things as was expected in the business world.

I corrected the letters and, on the next day, asked the general manager if I would be also Mrs. Belak's secretary.

"Don't be silly, she has lots of women in accounting and finance and they have plenty of time to type letters for her."

"Well, she said that I would have to also be her secretary."

"Don't worry, we will discuss that soon."

I thought that he did not intend to do anything. In the evening, I told Tone about it and wept. He listened to me, tried to cheer me up and gave me a number of suggestions on how to solve the problem. He was helpful, but I knew that I should not follow his advice word for word. He often said that I should answer teasing with irony or sarcasm and dictated words that I should use when solving conflicts. I thought that cynicism would only make things worse.

My mum was very helpful. She was always ready to listen and when she did not know how to advise me, she said: "Wait a little and things will settle down. Let some days pass and the right idea will occur to you. You've always found solution for each problem and I am sure that it will be so this time."

I cleaned the house all Sunday, went to Mass, and on Monday I felt a bit better. The general manager and I were examining the post when Mrs. Belak entered the office and brought a letter that the general manager should sign immediately.

"Please take a seat, dear Mrs. Belak. I have two or three letters to read and then I will devote myself entirely to you."

I saw that she was most impatient because she was in a hurry, but she sat down. The general manager slowly finished with the post, then discussed the weather and events in the company and finally started to read her letter. He turned it in his hands, already wanted to sign it, but again put it on the table, sighed, lit another cigarette and seemed to be lost in deep thought.

"Well, what? What's wrong? Didn't we agree that I write a letter in this way?"

"Why, yes, of course, dear lady. But please be a little more tactful… You are not yet officially director of accounting and finances. You should sign as a deputy."

"To Hell with the administration! Well, Iris, type this letter again and please make no mistakes."

I blushed with anger, but the general manager said sweetly: "Oh, no, dear Mrs. Belak, Iris is my secretary and she will type only for me. You should find your own secretary. God is my witness that your women don't have much to do."

She looked at him as if she wanted to kill him, but he answered with an innocent smile: "You know that your women don't have much to do. How often we spoke about it."

She took the letter and stormed out of the office. The letter was typed the next day and I found three mistakes in it. Mrs. Belak obviously had to become more tolerant. In the next days and weeks, she was no longer sharp and superior. She kindly asked me to help her move her things to her new office and I did it with great pleasure. I suggested to Tone that we should make a pilgrimage because God had saved me from my mentor.

When Mrs. Belak enthusiastically and devotedly took over management of the finance and accounting sector, life became peaceful and pleasant. My working days passed quickly because several salesmen asked me to make translations for them. I wished that I could find at least one or two good friends at work, but I didn't. Everybody in the company was cautious and emphasized that it was necessary to respect distance. I had a more personal relationship only with Flora, but I had to be very careful, because she immediately spread everything I told her. She was a simple soul and didn't do it intentionally. I could discuss more openly with the driver, but he came just in the morning. The Secretary of the Communist Party came rather frequently. He often spoke about his first wife, whom he divorced, and mentioned that she was quite unable to take care of his child. Sometimes he spoke of how he met his second wife and discussed the education of his two daughters. Once he asked if I was religious and I said yes, although I was not much of a believer in those times. He opened his mouth and, in the next weeks, very often spoke about the mistakes that the Church had made in the past. I persistently answered that priests were sinners, just like all other people, and that I was not interested in hearing it. He sometimes said that he had nothing against religion and that he liked to take a seat in the cathedral of Ljubljana and listen to the quiet steps of people passing by. It made no impression on me, because I did not appreciate religious feelings and emotions. But even if that was not so, I would quickly be placed on firm ground by Tomo, the driver, who liked to sit on Flora's table and make merciless comments:

"Tell me, my dear secretary of the Communist Party, do you really go to the church to listen to people's steps or do you try to find out who among the Party members takes part in religious ceremonies?"

The secretary started to cough, but he had to be patient with the driver. Tomo was helpful when people needed a professional to repair their cars. He knew a lot about them and had good connections, so he quickly found the right person to help, if he could not do it himself. And, of course, he had already helped the Party secretary. Tomo was more careful only when speaking with the general manager and with Mr. Belic. I did not meet the latter for a long time, although I'd heard of him, and I thought that he was an old man with grey hair.

The general manager once told me that Belic would come and said that I should offer him a glass of whiskey and a cigar: "Here is the key to open the cabinet with whiskey. And be careful to call me immediately when he comes."

I was amazed. I knew that there was a cabinet in our office in which the general manager kept strong drinks and cigars, but Flora told me that only he had the key and that he opened it very rarely. I was even more surprised when Mr. Belic arrived. He was a handsome young man with whom it was most pleasant to discuss things. When I jumped up to call the general manager, he smiled and said that he could wait. When we spoke, I noticed that he was able to discuss everything, even poetry, so I was quite charmed.

I forgot that I should have called the general manager, but he came out of his office, greeted him and then reproached me: "How could you let Mr. Belic wait? You know that I have nothing important to do today."

He had a meeting with the director of the third sector and I knew that it was important, but I just apologized.

Mr. Belic remarked: "Please don't blame Miss Iris. She wanted to call you, but I did not let her. I am so happy when I can speak with a nice, young girl."

Director Doler came out of the manager's office and produced a pleasant smile: "Well, I am happy that we arranged everything, Mr. Herman. Have a pleasant day and see you tomorrow."

I was even more surprised. Doler never came out of the general manager's office with a happy face and they never arranged everything. They usually quarreled and shouted at each other.

When the general manager and Belic took a seat, Herman asked me to bring whiskey and some personnel folders. I quickly fulfilled his wishes, smiled at the nice young man and closed the door.

Their discussion lasted for two hours. Then Belic left and the general manager gave me the bottle. "All right, now you lock the cabinet and return the key to me."

"Do you think that I will drink it?"

"No, of course not. But before you came, whiskey often disappeared. If I have the key, this can't happen. Now repeat exactly what you discussed with Mr. Belic before I entered your office. That devil Doler made me angry again and I forgot to take care when Belic arrived. He immediately started to make inquiries, didn't he? Did he ask which foreigners were here last time?"

I had to give him a precise recounting of the conversation with Belic. It was quite innocent, because the guest just asked how I liked the university, which courses I'd taken, which was my favorite and how I felt at the company.

"When he comes again, remember that you should speak with him as little as possible. Bring him to me immediately."

I had enough of the secrets and asked who, under the open sky, this young man was and why he did not want me to speak with him.

"Oh, Lord, how green we are. You have no idea about politics, do you?"

"No, I am not interested in politics. Even when my schoolmates made protests against who-knows-what I preferred to study."

"I hope you will continue to behave like this. The young man belongs to the secret police, if you must know. And now enough about that."

I was even more interested, and my eyes sparkled with curiosity. I had always liked criminal and spy stories. "Why does the secret police come to the company? We respect laws, don't we? Is there anything wrong?"

"Nothing is wrong. But we work in foreign trade and have a lot to do with foreigners from around the world."

He turned around to leave, but I seized his arm and enthusiastically continued: "I would never have thought that a detective from the secret police could be so nice. Do you know that this is the first person in the company with whom I could discuss poetry?"

The general manager frowned: "Of course, he is nice and can speak about everything. Now forget about him and start working."

The general manager intended to spend a month in Great Britain that year because he wanted to improve his English. He looked forward to it because he adored foreign languages. His German was good, but his true love was English. He studied it for several years, but his brain functioned too analytically and technically to accept it with ease. He thought about each sentence at least ten times before saying it, looked for logical connections, tried to find associations between German and English words and did everything possible except repeating words and phrases. I sometimes tried to convince him that it would be better to relax, learn words and sentences by heart and let them come out of his mouth when necessary, but he did not believe me.

"They would come out of your mouth because you are talented with languages. But other people must invest a lot of work and energy. I don't know how you can say that I should relax—all the pedagogues recommend learning by association and logical thinking."

I laughed at his eager efforts: when I explained something to him, he enthusiastically raised his shoulders, put his hands between his knees and looked like a young boy who was going to learn something marvelus. But I did not dare to laugh too much, because he could be quickly hurt if it concerned English. Before he left, I asked him to write to us in English every week.

30
Getting Married

When the general manager left for England, I had some more time and decided to devote it to my studies and to graduate as soon as possible. I knew that my colleagues would not like my studying during working hours, so I hid the notes from English literature below dictionaries and contracts. I studied in the afternoon, during weekends and on holidays too. In my opinion, it would have been best if Tone and I met just once or twice a week, so that I could devote the rest of my time to studying. Tone agreed that I should accelerate and graduate as soon as possible. But he did not like the idea that I should study even during weekends and holidays. He enjoyed it if we sat in his car on a Friday afternoon, or at least on a Saturday morning, and drove either to the seaside or to the mountains. I liked it, too, but I thought that it was a real waste of time. When I once suggested that we should stay at home for the weekend, he frowned and resentfully drove away. He did not call for several days, but in the end, he waited for me in front of my company. He hardly spoke a word, and, after a long silent walk, he asked if I would go to the seaside the next weekend. I didn't want to make him angry, so I said yes, and his face became a bit friendlier. During the weekend, he said several times that I should not neglect our relationship. I agreed with him and, after some time, it seemed that he forgave me. I was surprised that he could sulk for such a long time.

But this did not make me question whether I wanted to marry him. Such small annoyances did not disturb me very much and it never occurred to me that I should investigate them. Quite the opposite, I thought that I should learn how to be patient and maintain a good relationship because we'd started to think about marriage. We had been together for almost four years and were engaged. Tone was 27 and I was 23. I had a job and would graduate in a month or two.

The main question was where we would live. Tone's house had a small room, a kitchen and a bathroom in the mansard. The place could be enlarged with one or two more rooms. But the staircase was very narrow and Tone had to bow when he went up. There were also other reasons why I did not like the idea of living in Tone's house. On one side, I was strongly attached to my home and I did not know how I would survive without watching the moor in front of our house and the fog floating above it. On the other side, I was aware that my mother-in-law was not a person whom I would like to meet every day. I knew that it might come to a serious quarrel between us. My mum often said that she would give us the house in which we'd lived for such a short time, but my father still refused to leave the house that we had built nine years ago and the legal process about its division was still going on.

One day, my mum visited me at my company. It had never happened before, and I ran to her in fear: "What happened? Did you have to call the ambulance for my grandmother again?"

She smiled: "No, I have good news. I could not wait to tell you, so I came here. Your father agreed to move out of the house, but we have to pay him his part. Do you know what that means? We will finally feel free and I will give the house to you."

I was surprised. It seemed impossible that my father would yield and sell his part of the house. Besides, it was the house that my mum had built with her own hands. Why didn't she decide to live in it with my younger brother?

"No, I want to give the house to you. I am sure that you and Tone will make the necessary improvements and change it into a small villa. Your brother will have his flat on the first floor of our old house and two rooms are enough for me. This way, you will each have your home."

Poor soul, she'd hardly collected the money for our studies and now she already wanted to help us with our home. Where would she get the money to reorganize the attic of our old house?

"I will ask for a loan and we will work. Besides, your brother is not in a hurry. He is only twenty and you can see that he only thinks about friends. He will need many years before he starts thinking about his own family. For now, I just want to show him that I intend to give something to him, too."

We were happy that things began to develop in the right way, but where would we get the money to pay off my father? My mum saved some money, but she did not have enough. Finally, Tone and I decided to take out a loan, and the house was ours. My father left and, from that time on, lived with his second or perhaps his third wife. I never saw him again.

We could not believe that we were now free, that we could walk on the lawn whenever we wanted, and that the house was ours. But the building was in awful shape. During the long and cold winters, the plumbing installations had broken, and the floor was partly demolished. My father also had not kept the house clean. We had to renovate the floors, decorate the walls, furnish the bathroom and buy necessary pieces of furniture.

Tone groaned about how much work we would have to do and repeated that he hated construction work. But he was aware that we would solve our housing problems forever. Tone was much happier when we discussed our honeymoon. He collected a number of tourist brochures and finally found a nice trip to England and France.

My brother, who participated in wedding organization in our village, tried to persuade me to have a big traditional wedding, but I didn't want to hear about it. I found all the ceremonies connected with the wedding showy and irrelevant. However, we had to consider some rules, if we wanted to marry. It was clear that it would be a church wedding, which meant that we should go to the priest and to the registry office. The registry office required only some papers and two witnesses. The priest said that we should first have lessons about married life, go to confession, to the registry office and finally to the church. The wedding should be during a Mass. I hated all these arrangements, but I had to accept them.

We first started with the lessons that should teach us how to live as good Catholic man and wife. We were not taught by the main priest, but by his young assistant, who was very popular among the people, especially women. When I saw him, I asked myself why they liked him so much. He was nothing special and I immediately discovered that he had no idea about literature or business. When we started, Tone was in a good mood and participated. I was reserved, dull and spoke just when I could oppose the priest's teachings. The priest's assistant did not seem to notice that. During the second meeting, I found him more interesting and became friendlier. Then we could hardly wait for further lessons and began to explain to our friends what a nice priest we had.

When the lessons finished, we asked about when we should go to Confession and the chaplain said: "Why should we speak about another time? I can hear your Confessions now and then we can have a glass of wine."

I looked at him, quite perplexed: "Yes, but we should prepare for Confession. Do you think that I can simply kneel and list my sins? One needs to repeat the prayers, think about all possible sins, there should be a system…"

He started to laugh: "Oh, dear, I have never heard that people might need a system for Confession. We have been speaking about values in life and marriage for several weeks, you attended religious lessons for eight years, you know what is right and what is wrong and that's it. The prayers are in this booklet and you can read them."

Tone quickly agreed while I gazed forward uncertainly. There was no time to resist because they sent me out of the room. Tone decided to make his Confession first. I found it careless and irresponsible, but if they insisted, I had to adapt. I quickly started to think about sins and tried to remember the prayer of regret. Tone came out after ten minutes and whispered: "Don't worry, he knows his business."

All right, so I began with my Confession. I thought that he would interrupt me already when I said that I had not gone to Confession for two years, but he didn't. When I admitted that I also didn't go to Mass, he smiled and said that I obviously did not have time because I studied and worked. And so on. During the whole Confession, he did not utter even one judgement but showed only understanding. The Confession was actually not so much discussion of what I'd done wrong in the past, but how I should live in the future.

When we left, we thanked him, and he waved his hand: "See you at the wedding."

Now I thoroughly understood why all the women were so enthusiastic about him.

Before we married, Tone's mother said that we should visit her sister, who lived in a far away village and was dying. Tone often spent holidays in her house and also found it his duty to pay her a visit. We went to a village near the Sava River and then crossed it in a vehicle that seemed like a gondola that was operated manually. One of us sat in the gondola and the other wound up the rope and the gondola slowly slid across the river. Then the gondola had to be brought back and the person on the other side of the river repeated the procedure. Then we had to walk for two hours to see his aunt.

When we arrived, nobody waited in front of the house. We entered the kitchen, which was black and smelled of smoke. Tone's cousin whispered, with tears in her eyes, that the priest was in the room of the dying aunt, giving her Last Rites. We waited until the ceremony finished and then entered the room. Tone's aunt was pale, and she could only speak slowly. But we still exchanged some kind words and greetings. Then she asked that Tone and the others would wait outside the room, because she wanted to speak to me. We thought that the poor soul was no longer aware of what she was doing, and Tone obediently left the room while I sat beside her and listened.

"So, I understand that you will soon get married?"

"Oh, yes in a couple of days."

"Will it work? Do you love him?"

"Yes, I do. And he loves me, too."

"Have you thought about it well? Marriage is not just love, you know. It means that you have to be patient with the mistakes of your husband."

"Oh, I know that, and I am ready to do it. But Tone is a wonderful man and hasn't made any mistakes."

"Did you ask yourself what your future husband was like? Is he ready to work for the family, go through the troubles, will he support you? Or will he prefer to stay in pubs, hotels, go to trips and parties? If you marry such a man, it will be difficult for you."

"No, Auntie, Tone is a hard worker, he finished his studies in time, has a good job and we have similar ideas about married life."

"Well, then I wish you a successful marriage."

I told Tone what we spoke about and he indugently smiled and said that his aunt was already half in the other world. I smiled, but I was aware that his aunt actually spoke truth. I just didn't know how she'd learned that Tone liked to go to hotels and parties, while I enjoyed hard work. Later, I often heard that people, who were going to the other world, as I don't believe that they cease to exist, had much better insight into everything than others.

Anyway, I did not take her words seriously and did not think about them.

Our wedding was very simple, with just our family members. My mum started to prepare everything for the wedding lunch a week ahead of time. Tone and I settled the last formalities. There was no need to buy wedding rings, because we already had appropriate engagement rings and the goldsmith just added the date of wedding. The witnesses were our brothers, who first took us to the registry office and then to the church. In the church there were just the four of us and the chaplain. But it was moving. The chaplain quickly read the Mass, said some cheerful words, we exchanged the rings and our brothers congratulated us. They were young boys, around twenty, and thought only about cars and girls, but they still felt that this was an important event and wished us luck.

I was sure that our marriage would be happy and good. Of course, we had some quarrels, but we knew that it was necessary to discuss each problem, to clarify things, to form a common opinion and everything would be all right. I prayed with all my heart that I would be a good wife. Tone meant everything to me. He was my strength, hope, comfort and happiness. I decided to do all I could to make our marriage successful. In communist Yugoslavia, all women had to work. If one stayed at home, she was deemed lazy, even if she had three or four children. We planned to continue with our jobs, work at home in the afternoon, go to the cinema, visit our friends and during weekends make excursions around Slovenia. Tone knew that I would need two more months to finish my studies, that it was necessary to make some repairs to the house and that we would, sooner or later, get a baby for whom we would have to care, but he said that we would manage it. The most important thing was that we had each other.

When we returned from the church everybody congratulated us. Tone's mother wept: "Oh, my son, now you don't belong to me anymore."

The remark seemed strange and my brother-in-law said that she should be grateful, because her precious first son got a good wife. His mother didn't say anything, and she also didn't seem happy when I started to call her "mother."

The next morning, we had a flight from Zagreb to Paris and, after a week, from Paris to London. We looked forward to traveling. But our honeymoon was not as wonderful as we expected. When we arrived in Paris, I was sick and tired. I found it difficult to visit museums, Montmartre, the Paris Opera House and other places that we wished to see. I suspected that I was pregnant, so I did not worry. Actually, I was happy because I very much wished to get a baby. Tone wanted it too, but he was a bit disappointed: "I thought that we would visit all the places in Paris and London, but you walk so slowly and feel sick."

When we returned home, all our family members were in panic. A couple of hours before, two planes crashed over Zagreb and they were afraid that we were in one of them. I was very sad when I learned that two of my schoolmates who worked as stewardesses were in one of the aircrafts and died.

31
First Days of Marriage

I was a young married woman. I had more than I'd ever dared to dream about: a husband whom I loved, a house of our own. We had good jobs in very successful companies, and we expected our first child. Long gone was the time when I'd thought of myself as a silly ugly duckling, convinced that I would never achieve anything. I sometimes said to myself that I could reach the moon, if I really wanted to. Had I been more reasonable or religious, I should have known that such ideas were conceited. But I had almost no time for serious thinking or for religion. I hardly managed to complete the most necessary everyday errands.

It was amazing that my main source of work and troubles was my married life, although I had expected that it would be my strongest pillar. Before we got married and during the honeymoon, Tone and I made plans about how we would organize our life, to understand and love each other and never to become like other couples who always quarreled. When discussing such questions, Tone usually spoke about going to the mountains, to the seaside, to the cinema and traveling, while I was more interested in everyday routine: in the morning, we would have coffee together, drive to our work, in the afternoon Tone would pick me up, then we would cook lunch, I would study for an hour or two to graduate as soon as possible, in the evening we would read, go to the cinema or pay a visit to our friends. At the end of the week, we would clean the house and organize it so that we could invite friends and relatives for lunch or dinner.

When I said that we should put the rest of the rooms in order, he frowned: "We have a sitting room with a kitchen, a bedroom and a bathroom, why should we furnish the whole house if there is no need?"

I tried to convince him that we should not be so lazy and leave half of the house a mess, especially because we would soon get a baby. He waved his hand and said that we would discuss that when the baby was born.

Things did not develop as I planned. It was all wrong starting first thing in the morning. Tone woke up early and made a lot of noise. He was full of energy and eagerly prepared all sorts of things while I was mostly tired and sick. There was hardly an hour when I did not feel that I would vomit. I told myself that this would cease after three months and that I would then feel well again. I was aware that it was worth suffering for the new human being who grew in my body. But I still felt so sick that I barely made it through each day. I also noticed that Tone had an unbearable habit: he needed at least twenty minutes to get himself organized to leave for work. He often forgot where he had left his keys or his bag, he had to clean the car, check if he locked the door, he forgot to brush his teeth, sometimes he noticed that he should put on a warmer coat. If it was raining, he looked for his umbrella, if it was sunny, he had to find his cap, he had to go to the toilet…dear God!

After the first week, his morning errands got so on my nerves that I wanted to throw myself onto the floor and cry. I was so sick, but I still managed to take a shower, put on a dress and make-up and prepare breakfast. Then, I had to wait for him in the car. Sometimes I waited just ten minutes, sometimes half an hour. I tried to convince him that he should prepare everything for the next day the evening before, even though he got up two hours before me and could have easily arranged everything before I woke up. Once or twice he decided to get more organized, but his good decisions did not last long. If we'd had two cars, I would have used my own, but we didn't, so I had to wait for him. Of course, I could have taken a bus, but I was too sick to stand in a crowded vehicle for half an hour. So, I had to adapt to my husband's impossibly slow tempo. Sometimes I fell asleep in the car. Tone usually arrived out of breath and then he quickly drove to Ljubljana.

From time to time, he frowned: "I don't understand how one can sit in the car without worries and think about nothing except sleeping."

In the afternoon, when he was supposed to pick me up, it was even worse. We agreed to stay at work until about three and work also on Saturdays. Our working hours were measured by a timekeeper. You could start working between six and eight and leave between two and five, but it was necessary to cover 42 hours per week. In the afternoon, Tone had no better feeling for time. Sometimes he came at three, as he said, but usually this time was prolonged by an hour or two. If I scolded him for being late, he said that I had no reason to complain. I was in my office where I could work, couldn't I? So why did I quarrel if he had something to do? He could not simply leave everything and pick up his wife exactly when she wanted to go home. That was, of course, true, but I still hated his inaccuracy. Once, I waited for two hours and then went home by bus. He was very hurt, and it took some days before he spoke with me again.

When I got married, I was sure that I would have no troubles with cooking because I loved to prepare different dishes. Even at thirteen, I'd convinced my mother that she should allow me to cook lunch during holidays. I always tried to prepare something new and exotic. Sometimes I invented a recipe myself and I was very proud, because I was so creative. My mum usually ate what I prepared. Sometimes she said that she could not eat, because the hotel cook had brought her something just before she'd gone home, and she could not refuse him. My grandmother liked when she saw me cooking, but she often said that it would be better if I cooked classic dishes, like soups, potatoes or salad, and not Indian chapatis. I always told her that I was an international girl. Later, I learned a lot about cooking from my Jewish housewives in England and often prepared a lunch or dinner at home or in Tone's house and everybody praised me. Tone was proud of my cooking skills.

On the first day of our married life, he showed a strange rudeness. I prepared crackers with butter as a starter, then spinach with egg and rice, some leaves of salad with mayonnaise and baked apples.

When I put the crackers on the table, he looked at me as if I'd fallen from the clouds: "Are you joking?"

Offended, I answered that I prepared a sophisticated lunch and that crackers were only a starter. He shrugged his shoulders and quickly ate them all, even mine. He said that he found them rather dry and that he preferred soup as a starter. In his home, they always began lunch with a soup. When he saw the spinach with rice, he mixed rice and the egg and said he was used to eating spinach with potatoes and meat and that his family always had a big bowl of salad, not just a couple of leaves. If I'd forgotten to buy some more, I couldn't put on the table more than a few leaves, could I?

When he tried the baked apple, he shamelessly made a wry face and said: "Was this apple baked in margarine? It has a horrible taste."

"We always bake apples in margarine."

"I can't eat it. I can't stand margarine. Give me some bread, I'm still hungry."

I'd worked so hard to produce the lunch, and I was sick and then he said that it was worth nothing! I started to cry, ran to the bedroom and cheered up only when he, at least ten times, said that I was a good cook, but this time I'd put together things that he didn't like.

The next day, I prepared mushroom soup. I thought that every soup should boil for just a few minutes. When I cooked, Tone was reading the newspaper and observed what I was doing. He asked if five minutes boiling was enough for mushroom soup.

"Of course, why should I cook it for half an hour?"

"I don't know, but I think that my mother cooks it longer."

Soon after lunch, he felt pains in his stomach and had to go to the toilet for the whole night. On Sunday, when we visited his parents, he joked that I'd tried to poison him with mushrooms.

My mother-in-law wanted to know exactly how I cooked the soup and then raised her arms: "Dear Lord, what did you think? The mushroom soup should boil at least twenty minutes. And besides, it would be better to prepare beef or vegetable soup. Mushroom soup could contain a poisonous mushroom. Be aware that you will be guilty if something happens."

Members of Tone's family had a nasty habit of accusing each other of being guilty of various transgressions, and they used to remember each others' guilt for years. My mother-in-law repeated at least ten times how I should cook mushroom soup.

In those days, every responsible and good housewife had a freezer in which she put bags with vegetables, fish, meat, mushrooms and other food that she prepared for the winter. Both my mum and Tone's mother often gave me vegetables and meat and I put them in the freezer. Once we had almost nothing in the fridge, so I decided to take a chicken from the freezer and prepare chicken soup. I consulted a cookbook and it said that it was possible to put frozen meat into water and just prolong the time of cooking. I took our biggest pot, poured water and put the frozen chicken inside. I added some vegetables and let it boil.

I was pleased with my economic use of time: "So, the chicken soup will now boil for two hours and I will be able to study in the meantime."

The soup boiled and boiled, but the chicken remained frozen. Tone said that he had never heard about cooking soup from frozen chicken, but I showed him the cookbook. He grumbled about wasting gas and about a late lunch, but what could I do? Should I go to my mum's and ask her for some food?

After four hours, the chicken was still not cooked, and the kitchen smelled funny. I abandoned all hope and told my mum to give it to the dog. Tone had left already two hours ago and had lunch with his family. In the evening, he told me that his mother always defrosted the chicken first and then cooked it, but I didn't want to listen. Instructions from my mother-in-law were not what I needed.

When Tone and I were married for fourteen days, my mum came to have a coffee with me. She looked around and asked if I was still sick all day, because the dishes were not done and the house was disordered.

"Well, today I have had no time to tidy up, but I will certainy wash the dishes by evening."

"It would be good for you to introduce a routine of tidying up the whole house. You could do it every Saturday. You know that your grandmother, although she is a bit careless, washes her kitchen and dusts the furniture every Saturday. And I tidy up all the cupboards, wash the floor, change the bed linens, wipe the lights, and so on."

"I would like to make it a routine, but I am too sick now."

On Saturday, Tone and I intended to drive to the coast, but it was raining so I suggested that Tone wash the floor and change the bed linens, while I would wash the clothes, dust the furniture and prepare lunch. He did not seem very enthusiastic, but he nodded. After an hour, he said that he would go home and ask his father how many tiles he should buy for our bathroom. He would wash the floor and do other things in the afternoon. I thought that he would come back for lunch and cooked, but he returned only in the evening. I sullenly asked where he'd been, and he said that he was at home. He and his father made a plan to reorganize the bathroom and the children's room.

"Where did you eat?"

"At home, where else? So, you didn't need to cook and could rest."

"You did not say that you wouldn't come, so I prepared lunch. Now it is not fresh anymore and all my work was for nothing."

"I can eat it now. What did you make?"

"Roasted potatoes, chicken with peaches and salad."

"Well, that can really not be eaten now. Never mind, we'll give it to the dog. Anyway, I am not hungry. My mum prepared dinner and she is sending you her apple pie, here you are."

I wanted to proudly refuse it, but she made really excellent pies, so I ate it.

Since Tone showed no intentions of fulfilling his share of the weekly cleaning, I told him that I'd done mine and that he should also do as we'd agreed upon that morning.

"I am so tired today. I will do it tomorrow."

On the next day, the weather was fine, and we drove to the seaside. While we were absent, my mum came and cleaned everything, so that the house shone like the sun.

I looked at her in amazement and she said: "Look, I cannot abide such an untidy house. I know that you have a lot of work and that you are sick, so I did the cleaning today. When your sickness is over, you will have to roll up your sleeves yourself."

"Yes, but I think that Tone should participate in cleaning. He promised as much, but now he doesn't even think about cleaning."

"You can't expect men to clean the house. You can count yourself lucky that he is a kind man and that he is ready to help with construction work. Don't have illusions that he will help you with cleaning and cooking."

Tone liked our clean house, but he still claimed that we should be independent and that he would take on his part of the housework. He spoke about it also at home and his mother nodded that his thoughts were right and that she always taught him to work hard. When Tone left the kitchen, she whispered that men liked to promise things, but that it would be better if women took care of the kitchen and cleaning themselves. In the long run, they can do everything according to their own taste and the work is finished when women want it to be. Cleaning and cooking make women independent.

After about two months of marriage, I went to the gynecologist at the students' clinic and she confirmed that I was pregnant. I was so happy that I gasped, and tears entered my eyes. The doctor frowned, looked at the nurse and whispered something to her.

The nurse said: "Do you wish to have the baby?"

What a stupid question. "What do you mean? Of course, I do. I did not get pregnant to give the baby to somebody else."

Both began to act in a friendlier way and the nurse apologized: "Quite frankly we have to ask each woman if she wishes to have the baby or if she wants to have an abortion."

"Oh, God, I have been looking forward to getting pregnant and you are asking me if I want an abortion? How can you even think about it?"

The doctor and the nurse looked down: "We did not intend to make any suggestions. But the majority of students do not wish to have babies and it is our duty to ask what they want to do."

"I certainly have no such intentions. But you can tell me what I could do to feel less sick. Perhaps you could give me a week of sick leave."

"It is already the second month and the sickness will soon cease. Sorry, but there is nothing I could give you to help. Avoid all remedies, because they might hurt the baby. I also cannot give you a sick leave if you're not sick. It's just the natural state of pregnancy. Be patient."

What strange logic. They asked me if I wanted an abortion and, if I had, I would have been offered sick leave. But they could not help me with a couple of free days if I was happily pregnant—that was against the rules.

My mum and my grandmother were happy when they heard about my pregnancy, but immediately remarked that I would probably not be able to continue my studies with the baby.

My mother-in-law softened when she heard that I was pregnant. She got tears in her eyes and did not allow me to even lift a pot of water. She'd had several miscarriages before she'd managed to carry her pregnancy, and her deliveries had been complicated. Each time I visited her she cooked me something good or baked a pie. She frequently explained what pregnant women could do and what they could not. She instructed the whole family on how to serve me, so nothing would go wrong. When Tone hesitated about equipping the room for the baby, she immediately ordered my father-in-law to help Tone. They should do everything alone and not allow me to carry anything heavy. She was annoyed that I had to study for my diploma thesis. She suggested that I should postpone my studies because stress might hurt the baby. Such an idea never occurred to me.

My female colleagues soon noticed that I'd stopped drinking coffee as I suddenly did not like it anymore, that I ate enormous quantities of pickles and they smiled, but no one said anything. When I told them that I was pregnant, they congratulated me. The general manager nervously lit his cigarette, took his coat and went out without a word.

I looked at Mrs. Belak and she raised her shoulders: "I told you how he would react. He has just gotten used to relying on you and now he will have to find another secretary."

"But don't you find it normal that a woman has a baby when she is young? He can't think that my job is more important than the baby. Do you think that he is aware that I've got a new, small human being in my body?"

She looked down and sighed: "No, in my opinion men are not aware of such things. And you, are you aware of how lucky you are to be expecting a baby?"

I certainly did not expect such a sentence from her, because she always criticized women who went on maternity-leave or sick-leave because of children. I thought that she would cause problems, but she was very kind. Sometimes I thought that she was deliberately coming to my office in order to try to live a part of life that she'd missed through me.

The general manager sulked for about fourteen days and wanted neither to greet me nor to speak to me. I heard him complaining to the director of the second sector that modern young women were irresponsible and that they simply got pregnant instead of asking their superiors if that was allowed. But nobody showed him any understanding. The director of the second sector abruptly said that the company was successful enough to bear with one or even ten pregnant women.

32
Degree

Although I was married and pregnant, I studied every afternoon. The final phase of getting my degree in foreign languages meant three examinations: in grammar, English, and American literature. During the first months of pregnancy, when I was sick, I tried to read as much obligatory literature as possible. Our teachers demanded that students read the books that were chosen by the teachers. If somebody dared to suggest another book or author, they firmly said that books were not famous because people liked to read them, but because they were written according to certain rules. My teachers were, of course, people who had PhDs in literature, but I knew that some of them had no sense for good books. However, if I wanted to graduate, I had to not only go through their brainwashing about rules, but sometimes even pretend that I liked the books and poems, although I found them boring.

When the time for graduation came, I did not feel well, but I did everything to achieve my goal. I successfully passed two examinations but failed the third. The teacher asked me about *The Great Gatsby*. At the time, the people of Ljubljana rushed to the cinema to see *The Great Gatsby* with Robert Redford, and the teacher probably thought that I'd seen it. But I hadn't. I simply did not like the book and I still don't, because it is too pessimistic and speaks just about money and wealth. So, I failed the first exam of my life.

I could not believe that it was possible. I cried, called my mum, Tone and my schoolmate, Mara. They all tried to cheer me up, saying that this was nothing terrible. After all, I could repeat the exam after two months and would certainly pass it. When I could finally speak normally, I called my office. The general manager answered. I found it a bit embarrassing, but I knew that I would, sooner or later, have to tell the office that I did not pass the exam. I thought that he would embark on a serious sermon, but he started to comfort me, just like everybody else. He softly said that this was no tragedy and that I would pass it next time.

Tone invited me to the cinema, bought sweets and cracked jokes so I forgot my misery. By the next day, I felt much better, especially since I'd heard kind words from everybody in the company. I was very grateful and decided that I should develop such compassion, too. I also became aware that my decision to graduate exactly at that time was quite an unnecessary limitation. I did not notice that my failure might be good for some other reason—that it reduced my self-conceit. Before I'd failed the exam, I thought that something like that could not happen to me. Now I realized that I did not know everything and that I should expect to weather the occasional storm, just like anyone else.

Before I failed the final exam, I thought that I'd had enough of studying and I looked forward to putting all my books away. I swore that I would then devote myself completely to my family and job, but now I had to continue studying. I discovered that it was not at all difficult. The first three months of my pregnancy passed, I was not sick anymore and I felt like a bird in the summer.

When I sat for the exam the next time around, it was an easy task. I read and studied *The Great Gatsby* thoroughly, but the second time I got very different questions. The whole family was happy that I graduated.

Both my grandmother and my mother-in-law said: "Now forget all about your books and studies and devote yourself to housekeeping and to your family."

A few hours earlier, I'd been of the same opinion, but hearing them articulate it now got me annoyed. Of course, I wanted to do everything for my family, but why did they think that I could forget the books? Did I graduate just to get the diploma and then wash dishes for the rest of my life? I frowned and answered that this would not do. If you study foreign languages, you have to renew your language skills all the time.

"So, you intend to continue with your studies? No usual worker needs to think about his work in the afternoon while you, who graduated with university education, will have to make further studies?"

"I sure will. Even Tone brings papers home and works if necessary."

"Yes, but he is a man. How do you intend to feed the baby and study?"

"I will probably hold the baby in one hand and the book in the other."

It took their breath away and my mother-in-law said that such a marriage could not work and that the poor children would be motherless.

33
New Colleagues and New Businesses

Over the next months, my company buzzed with events. Flora and I got a new colleague, Marina, who had been on maternity leave until then. She'd come to the company some years earlier. Everybody said that she had an extremely difficult character. Flora sighed that life would become unbearable, because Marina would control us all the time and hand out malicious remarks. Also Mrs. Belak claimed that Marina did nothing but cause quarrels. Tomo, the driver, thought that she was a dragon, but that it might be possible to tame her. The general manager called me and the new lawyer, who would be her director, into his office and we had a serious discussion.

"Dear comrades, our colleague Marina returns tomorrow. Please engage all your capacities to have a good influence upon her. She has much more energy than other people and performs her job most eagerly, but she can be difficult. If you try to maintain good relations with her, you will have a good colleague. If you start quarreling with her, you could not get a worse enemy. She and Mrs. Belak are mortal enemies and they sometimes fight so that one can see feathers flying in the air."

Flora and I tidied up our office on the day before the new colleague returned and I suggested that we should accept her in as friendly a way as possible. Perhaps the baby had changed her character and she'd softened or become more patient. In the middle of our cleaning, the phone rang. Flora lifted the receiver, at least ten times said "yes" and then put it down with a miserable face.

"Well, she has already started."

"What happened?"

"Marina called, and she says that she wants to sit at the table where I am sitting now. This really used to be her table, but why can't she sit at the other one? I have to move all my things to the other end of the room just because of her. This woman will be the death of me."

Flora quickly started to transfer her things to the other table.

When Mrs. Belak heard what happened, she furiously hissed at the general manager, who appeared at the door: "Well, didn't I say that she was impossible? She has not come back yet and already causes unnecessary work! If you do not want to fire her, at least place her in another office. How can you let her speak with our clients? You know that her appearance is horrible and that she has no education."

"My dear lady, you are right, at least to a certain degree. But how could a communist director fire a woman with a baby? Everybody would deem me inhuman. Besides, she can be a good worker."

"To hell with communism! But Marina is, of course, a member of the Communist Party and you have to make allowances for her, don't you?"

"Of course. She is not just a member, but also the deputy secretary. Besides, her father heads up a police department and is acquainted with a number of important politicians. You know that it would immediately cause a scandal if I said anything inappropriate. You will have to show some patience."

The next morning, Marina came to the office at six o'clock. I expected a thin, dark-haired woman speaking in Styrian dialect, but she was a fat, poorly-dressed creature who desperately tried to hide her uncertainty. I started to ask about the baby and she began to describe her little treasure so that it was not possible to stop her.

Tomo arrived soon after me: "Why did you come so early from your maternity leave? Couldn't the doctor prolong it? Now you will poke your nose into everybody's affairs, won't you? Tell your husband to make you another baby as soon as possible."

She laughed, but soon looked around herself: "It will be necessary to tidy up the room. The cleaners do not seem to do anything. Are they still always on sick leave? And these poor plants—you, Iris, are probably not interested in them, are you? You have quite a big belly, how many kilos did you put on? What, fifteen? How do you intend to deliver, if you continue like this?"

Tomo answered instead of me: "Oh, shut up, you witch. You are much bigger than Iris and you are not pregnant. Do you know that you will not be able to lead the administration department anymore? Are you aware that you will, from now on, have a boss who graduated in law, which is something quite different than your unfinished secondary school?"

"Yes, I heard that the director of the administrative department is a green young boy. However, I am sure that I know much more about the law than him. My father knows all the laws by heart and he often explains them to me. Don't speak about the unfinished secondary school. I enrolled in college and intend to finish it."

"You have been speaking about it for years but have not yet passed even one exam. Besides, I really don't know how you managed to enroll in college if you had no leaving certificate. Well, anyway, I am going to bring you coffee, girls, to show you my devotion."

Marina did not seem insulted by Tomo's words, but she immediately started to explain why she did not pass any exams: "The baby takes all the time that I have. I tell you, Iris, that a baby requires all the energy of a mother."

Such remarks always made me wonder how some mothers could take care of three or five or seven children, but I did not want to argue.

When the lawyer arrived, he greeted Marina and kindly asked her to come and have a coffee with him, so that they could get acquainted and exchange some words about the work.

"I must do something for the general manager now, wait a little."

"All right."

When the lawyer closed the door, she explained: "I must teach him on the very first day that he cannot just whistle and I will run to him, like a puppy."

After an hour, she knocked on his door and entered. They had quite a long discussion and Flora and I expected a storm of malicious remarks and complaints when she returned. However, she did not say anything, but started to examine her cabinets. She soon nervously discovered that her records were not complete and asked me if she could borrow my papers and have them photocopied. I found photocopying unnecessary because we were in the same room and she could use my documents. However, she thought that she needed her own evidence which she could rely upon. She turned everything upside down, photocopied for two weeks, made additional copies and labored like a slave so that I sometimes felt pity for her.

I once mentioned to the general manager that the administration could have just one collection of documents, but he opposed: "It is better that she works with papers than walks from one department to the other and causes quarrels."

After some time, I recognized that Marina enjoyed bringing the right document when the director required it or dramatically presenting a paper that proved somebody's mistake. However, she had no good feeling for organization of documents and often lost or mislaid something. During most meetings, she'd breathlessly run to me and ask if she could borrow my papers. I always gave them to her, and she was much friendlier towards me than to others.

We were all very surprised that she had nothing bad to say about the lawyer, her new director, with whom many people had predicted a serious battle. She did everything he asked for and did so immediately, thoroughly and reliably. And she did not only, carefully and thoughtfully, perform everything he asked for, she thought about what he might need in the future and how she could help him in advance. If somebody criticized him, she defended him, and she was often ready to quote a wise idea that the lawyer had uttered during a meeting.

The general manager found out that the lawyer and I had a good influence on the quarrelsome woman and praised us. I smiled and said that I took no special credit. The lawyer changed the topic of conversation.

In December, the directors prepared their plan for the next business year. Those who presented better possibilities to earn money received a bigger budget to realize their plans. The general manager could praise and award those who introduced new products to the market, so the sector directors and salesmen fanatically competed among themselves.

The main battle that year was between Fatur and Doler—between the second and third sector. Doler asked for a special meeting with the general manager and gave me a hint that he planned an unbelievable business that the world had not seen before. If he managed to realize it, his department would no longer be just the main source of the company's money but would make all other businesses look like drops in the ocean. The general manager accepted this and listened to his plans.

The directors' meeting the next day started at eight. All directors ran to it like racehorses. They wore suits, white shirts, ties, new shoes and everybody tried to prove that his plan would bring the company a lot of money. All tried to ruin Doler's plans, saying that he would not receive the political support for the import of the equipment that he wanted to bring to the Yugoslav market. The general manager did not speak much but smoked one cigarette after the other. In the end, it was decided that Doler's business proposal would be supported. The meeting lasted until five in the afternoon and everybody smoked so many cigarettes, drank so much coffee and said such malicious things to each other that even those who had nothing to do with the plans went home feeling quite worn out.

The battle continued the following day on an individual level. Each of the sector directors came to the general manager, they repeated their plans and tried to reduce Doler's share. The director of the second sector had to wait for almost an hour, so we had an opportunity to exchange some words. He told me that Doler was a difficult character who always tried to put a spoke in somebody else's wheel. In the last company he worked for, his workers threw him out with their own hands. However, I was more interested in how Fatur got his leading position in a business firm, because people said that he was a pilot. He told me that he enjoyed flying, but he could not prolong his certificate because he did not want to enter the Communist Party.

"Was it difficult when you could not fly anymore?"

"Each difficult situation brings you something good. When I wanted to end my life because I could not fly, I met my wife and I must say that I am absolutely satisfied with that result."

Although the directors tried to convince the general manager that Doler's business plan would not be successful and forced me to ask Herman if he was really sure that Doler would establish a good brand, the general manager thought that it would be a great business model and grounded his opinion based on a number of data points.

Doler became even more self-centered than before. If the general manager had any remarks, he used to say: "If the old man or somebody else is not pleased with my work, I suggest that he introduces a new brand to the Yugoslav market. But at present, I'm the one who maintains this company."

In those times, it was common that employees wrote up job descriptions. Everyone had to describe in detail what they did every day and how many hours and minutes were devoted to a certain task. Our company called a specialist from Zagreb who would examine all the tasks and provide for the so-called "allocation of posts." The personnel department hired a new employee, Sonja, a nice, communicative young girl who would process the job descriptions. Tomo loudly suggested that Marina should do it instead of running around the company and causing troubles or Denis, the president of the Trade Union, who also had no work other than buying provisions for the winter. However, both Marina and Denis claimed that they had too much work to accept additional tasks.

Sonja was a clever girl and we liked her. Her only weakness was being late in the morning. Sometimes she was two minutes late, sometimes five or even ten. She worked until the late afternoon and covered enough working hours. Marina told everybody who praised the new employee that she did not come on time, that she made typing errors and that she had rather student-like ideas about work and life.

Denis and the lawyer liked Sonja and they talked about her in superlatives. Denis no longer tried to drink coffee in my office but had it with Sonja. When Marina, fond of teasing, asked why he avoided our office, he mysteriously puffed tobacco smoke in the air to indicate that he was no longer interested in our poor selves.

I liked Sonja because she had sense of humor. I often exchanged some words with her, although I usually avoided the offices that belonged to the lawyer. Once, Denis remarked that Sonja had a lot to do, so I quickly apologized for troubling her during work and wanted to go to my office. But Sonja said that she was not in a hurry and started telling me how clumsy she'd been the day before when she had to speak to an Englishman.

Denis joined our discussion: "I, too, made a horrible mistake some years ago. I noticed a British woman with a perfect figure and when I tried to get acquainted with her—you know how that goes—I asked her: 'Can I invite you for a drink?' She didn't answer because I should have said 'May I invite you?'"

Denis was called to the phone, so Sonja laughed and whispered: "I don't think that this poor wretch has ever addressed a woman."

I noticed that Denis heard the remark, so I tried to settle the matter with the explanation that the mistake was not so serious.

After a week, Sonja had to quit. Marina, as the deputy secretary of the company Communist Party, and Denis, as president of the Trade Union, who were in the committee for assessment of her work, gave an extremely bad opinion of her skills and their two voices outvoted the lawyer. We all knew that Sonja had to leave because of envy and revenge, but the evidence of her late arrivals in the morning was enough that they managed to fire her.

Our driver, Tomo, had built himself a big house and he used to report to me every morning how the construction works went on. Sometimes he complained about the high prices of masons, that he could not buy cement because in those times, it was necessary to order it a year before one needed it, or that he lacked sand for the façade.

Once he spoke about it when two salespeople came to my office and they shamelessly laughed at him: "Let your wife organize such things, if you can't do them yourself."

I felt pity for Tomo and said that it was really difficult to get cement, but they were merciless: "Oh, come on, if you are ready to pay, you can get everything. It is not difficult to buy, it is difficult to sell."

In the last days before I left for maternity leave, the whole of Yugoslavia protested because Austria removed Slovenian names from signs in villages near the border. The Communist Party sent instructions that all employees had to participate in those protests and that directors had to allow this.

Our company received such a notice and the general manager grumbled: "Just look, they want me to pay for protests! They are stealing our money. To Hell with them."

"So, you are not going?"

"Of course, I am, what do you think? The general manager should set a good example. You can say that you are pregnant and avoid it, but I am in the Party and must go."

I thought that I would be able to quietly tiptoe out of the company, but Marina called me to her group of more than ten other employees. So, I was forced to say that I did not feel well and could not go because I might catch a cold, or somebody might push my belly.

"Don't seek excuses. All Slovenians will go and, besides, this is within working hours. When I was pregnant, I once had to go as far as Belgrade. Don't say that you can't take a few steps to Congress Place."

Nobody could oppose such a wave of national consciousness. The director took Marina's hand and led her towards the exit: "Marina, please take me under your umbrella, because I haven't got mine. We will show those Austrians that Carinthia is Slovenian land and that we don't intend to leave it to them."

Everybody else followed them. I was the last one and slipped away when they turned the first corner. Marina was rather suspicious the next day and asked where I'd been. I just raised my shoulders and said that the place was terribly crowded.

34
My First Baby

When my maternity leave started, I enjoyed every minute of my life. No more fears that I would not graduate, no general manager shouting at employees, no Mrs. Belak who would be shocked because modern students did not have any knowledge, no Marina who would find hundreds of mistakes in my work, no Flora who would gossip all day long, no clock that would measure if I'd come to work on time. That was heaven! I felt as free as a bird. I could sleep all morning and nobody would say anything. As always, I read a lot, but after one week I was fed up with my freedom and wished to work on something. I was full of energy, so I made a plan to tidy up the house from the garage to the attic.

I asked Tone to help me repair the floor in the garage, then I painted the walls, washed everything and asked my father-in-law if he could make me some shelves. I also threw away all the rubbish. My husband and his father said that I should not have thrown things away, but I was sure that we would never use them again. When I pressed that we should clean the attic, they said that I should leave it as it was. The attic was meant as a deposit for old bricks and boards, old baskets and containers and for old clothes that might be useful when difficult times arose. They thought that I would not be able to climb to the attic and enter through a very narrow opening. But I did and slowly brought all the old junk to the dustbin and cleaned up there. My grandmother and mother-in-law were quite horrified when I told them that I'd climbed up and down the ladder for the whole week.

I carefully prepared for the baby. At first, I attended a course for pregnant women, learned the technique of breathing during delivery, how to change nappies, how to hold the baby and so on. Tone and I bought everything, prepared the baby's room and waited for the moment when labor would begin.

When I visited the doctor, he ordered that I should go to the hospital. I had high blood pressure, too many kilos and the child was in the wrong position, so I was told to expect troubles. I was in the hospital for three days that seemed as long as three months. I had a diet without salt, the doctors were examining me all the time and I was worried because I was afraid that the baby's heart would stop beating. I finally felt weak cramps that came regularly each hour and, after some time, I was sure that the baby was coming. My mum and Tone visited me in the afternoon when I felt pains. In those times, it was not usual that men would be present during delivery. My mum was anxious, but she smiled and said that it was all normal. Tone could not hide his nervousness. Every five minutes, he asked if the pains were serious.

When a cramp came upon me, I took his hand and said: "Now, there it is." It was not so horrible, but he made a face as if I were dying. He tried to force me to call a doctor or a nurse, but I knew that they would not do anything before labor was really strong. I finally suggested that Tone and my mum leave, because I had to prepare for delivery. My mum bravely swallowed her tears and said that I should be patient while Tone, poor soul, looked at me as if I was going to die. I felt pity for him.

When they left, a nurse helped me to prepare for the delivery. The labor was strong and I could hardly follow her instructions. She soon took me to an unpleasant small room. When the difficult iron door closed, I felt as if I were in a cage. I knew that the worst pains were coming.

It was so horrible that I could not imagine anything worse. Since the baby came out with its bottom first, they suggested artificial contractions, although my own were so strong. It hurt so that I shouted, although I knew that it would not help and that shouting only disturbed the work of the doctor and of the nurses who stood around me. The doctor told me to calm down and that it had hardly begun (what bedside manner), while the nurse stroked my hair and said that I should wait just a little longer and the pains would end.

Finally, she said triumphantly: "It's a girl, push once again."

I was so worn out that I could not feel anything. If they had offered for me to sign my death sentence, I would have signed it and died happily.

Then the nurse brought me a small girl and proudly said: "Isn't she beautiful? Take a look, she is just like Snow White! If she'd come out in the normal way, she would be red and blue." Then they gave me narcosis.

I still don't understand how some women can sleep immediately after delivery. I woke up very soon and saw that I lay on a narrow bed in the corridor. There was a draught and I was afraid that I would fall and would not be able to stand up again. But I was also worried because of the baby. I was looking at the wall clock all the night and the hours never passed so slowly. Every movement caused me pain and I felt strong bleeding. There was nobody around. Oh, Lord, help me to survive this night, I thought.

I was left in the empty corridor because all the beds were full but, in the morning, one of the women went home and I got a normal bed in a room with about six other new mothers. They all got their babies to breastfeed except me. I anxiously asked what had happened with mine and one of the nurses explained that they would bring her around noon. So, I had time to enviously watch how women fed their babies. Some were more, others less successful and their children cried because they did not get enough food. Then they took the babies to another room and brought us breakfast.

I had not eaten for two days and I suddenly felt hungry. The nurses brought me coffee, bread and an egg. When I was pregnant, even thinking about eggs made me sick. I waited to feel that disgust again, but it was gone and I ate it happily. When the nurses washed us, I felt much better and decided to rise and go to the bathroom. When I started walking, my legs didn't obey me and I fell to the floor, while other women called the nurse. I quickly recovered but was not allowed to go anywhere alone.

Finally, I got my little girl. She produced a faint cry which became stronger because she was hungry, and I didn't know how to put her on my breast. An energetic and slightly rude nurse came and showed me what to do so the baby could eat. Then I could hardly wait to get her again. I was worried because she slept in a room full of babies who always cried. I asked myself if my baby could sleep with such noise, so I often rose and checked on her. Each time I came, she was asleep.

Tone and I chose the names for both a girl and a boy before I went to the hospital. When the nurses asked me if I already knew the name, I put down Lili.

After four days, I felt so well that I could hardly wait for Tone to take us home. I asked him to pick us up at ten, but he was late again. I had to leave the bed at nine, because they needed it for another woman. I had to stand and wait in the corridor with the baby in my hands for more than an hour.

When we arrived home, the house was very cold because Tone had stayed with his family while I was in the hospital. He switched on the electric heater, though it needed a few hours to warm the place. I got angry: how would I change nappies in such a cold place?

The house slowly warmed, my mum brought me soup and I managed to change the nappies and breastfeed the baby. When I was in the hospital, I thought that I would be happy and healthy immediately upon returning home. But it was not so. Feeding the baby required a lot of energy and changing the nappies was difficult, too. I was without strength and still had pains. Tone offered to change nappies during the night, but I could not wake him up. When he heard the baby crying, he grumbled that he wanted some sleep and I had to do everything myself. I tried to do my best, but it was difficult. I never knew if I would be able to stay up and change nappies or if I might faint again. When the baby started to eat, I felt as if she was taking out of me not just milk but also my life force.

The next afternoon my mum came, changed the nappies and held the baby in her hands. She suggested that I should take a short nap. I did and then felt much better. But I was still worried. Does the baby know that she should breathe? What if she forgets to breathe? What if she turns in her small bed in such a way that she cannot breathe? What if she has digestion problems? As she sneezed, I asked myself if she might have caught a cold.

My mum once watched how anxiously I changed the nappies and said: "Can't you see that the baby is big, fat and as strong as possible? Be happy and don't look so miserable." Then she took Lili, rocked her and sang something and the little girl really seemed pleased with her life.

I fully understood that I worried too much when the nurse from the home care service started to visit me. She stayed for an hour or two, explained everything, had coffee with me and encouraged me.

After a month I felt much better and became happier again. The first month had been so difficult that I lost 15 kilos.

The situation soon became even better. I learned to understand the baby's sounds and to know when she just produced vocalizations as opposed to when she needed something. She liked to take a bath, so Tone and I developed a routine of bathing, breastfeeding and speaking. Tone enjoyed speaking with Lili and such conversations consisted of his saying "aaaa" or "eeee" and then the baby repeating the vowels. Sometimes they spoke like this for ten minutes. When Lili started to smile, I felt like the happiest woman in the world. If she slept too long, I came to her bed and waited until she woke up, till she looked at me and smiled.

Then I usually thought: "My God, what have I done to deserve this wonderful, unique child?"

35
Holidays Are Not Always Holidays

Tone booked a trailer on the Croatian coast for our first holidays with the baby. In those days, almost every company had small wooden houses or trailers on the Adriatic coast and their employees could rent them at very reasonable prices for a week or two each summer. They were the cheapest possible holidays. Tone liked camping, but I was not very enthusiastic. It was quite comfortable, but there were no toilets or bathrooms, so we had to use the common bathrooms that were usually in the middle of the camp. In the morning, all the people took showers and there was often no hot water. Besides, some visitors did not tidy up either the toilets or the trailers when they left.

We could have gone to a cheap hotel, but Tone thought that it would be stupid to waste money if either he or I could book a trailer that cost practically nothing.

Tone's mother strongly agreed with him and was unpleasantly surprised when I hesitated: "I don't know what you want. To be on holiday together with your family, prepare food for your husband, swim, take a walk at the seaside, enjoy fresh sea air… Excuse me, but I think that you are rather vain and ungrateful. Tone is offering you a great holiday to get some rest, while you have wishes like a queen. If I ever had such an opportunity, I would have taken it with both hands. But Tone's father never wanted to go to the seaside. He always found it a waste of time and money."

Well, perhaps she was right.

Tone got one more good idea: namely, that we could take his mother with us: "Just look at that poor soul, how she wishes to go to the seaside. She has worked herself to death and has had nothing from life. Would you mind if she comes with us? She will be happy to take care of our baby and we will be able to go dancing."

I felt pity for her and agreed that she should go with us. I did not need a nanny, because I was happy to take care of Lili myself, but I would not mind if we went dancing again.

I regretted our decision as soon as we prepared for departure. My mother-in-law had a lot to do before we left, just like my husband. I arranged my and Lili's things in an hour, while Tone and his mother needed two days. My mother-in-law first made plans about what we would cook every day, prepared all the necessary vegetables from her own garden, and brought different pots and other equipment that she knew was already in the trailer. She carefully wrapped lettuce in newspaper so it would remain fresh; took oil, vinegar, corn, tea, nicely put them in small boxes and baskets and then she and Tone started to load everything in the car. The world never saw a more sophisticated process. They put the boxes in the car countless times, took them out and again put them in until everything was in perfect order. My mum, grandmother and brother sometimes came around and exchanged looks or even smiles, but Tone and his mother did not notice anything. On the last day, they loaded the car until two in the morning. At four, we woke up and left. My mother-in-law sat in the front seat, had a lively and happy discussion with Tone, showed him interesting things, while I sulked in the back seat. It was rather uncomfortable and lonely. As if I were a maidservant and not a wife.

When we arrived at the seaside, I immediately took a bucket of water, disinfectant and a towel and started to clean the caravan. The family that was in it before us left it clean and in order, but I was still afraid that my daughter would catch a virus. Tone and my mother-in-law found my cleaning a bit over the top. It would be better, they thought, if I helped them unload things from the car. I angrily hissed that I could not help them, clean everything and take care of the baby.

Tone's idea that his mother would take care of the baby proved wrong.

On the way to the seaside, when we stopped in a small town, my mother-in-law said: "Well, you stay here with the baby and Tone and I will take a short walk."

I got angry and answered that I would also like to go for a walk.

We met some Croatian women, who started to admire the baby: "How beautiful you are!"

My mother-in-law proudly answered: "Oh, yes, my son is handsome, isn't he?"

Tone pretended not to have heard anything and admired nature while I maliciously commented that they did not admire her precious son, but my baby. Why should women admire an adult man in the company of his wife?

"Oh, do you really think so? Be careful that another woman does not seduce him. You are no longer sixteen."

I was twenty-four, but I looked much better than ever, so I did not care about her remark. But her mischief surprised me. Such small spites continued from one day to the other. Tone sometimes supported me and opposed her, sometimes he was silent or pretended to read or sleep. We went dancing just once, and for a very short time. When we came to the trailer, my mother-in-law said that Lili had cried, and she was sure that the baby was ill.

"You should be aware that you are a mother, so you should stop dancing and take care of your child. I am convinced that something is wrong with your milk. Instead of eating nutritious things, you prefer salad and yogurt and the child is ill. Do you have any maternal feelings, or do you think just about yourself?"

I turned pale and rushed to the trailer, but Lili slept. I touched her forehead to see if she might have a fever, but she did not. Then I tickled her chin to wake her up, but she just smiled and continued sleeping.

When we cleared up and drove home, I began to feel at ease. I was much happier at home, where the rooms were not so narrow, where I had a bathroom and a toilet and nobody watched every movement that I made. My mother-in-law was happy because she'd been to the seaside again and Tone promised that we would take her with us next year. I did not like the idea, but he had his way: we spent many further holidays in trailers and we always took her with us. I still wonder how I survived.

36

Decision for a New Job and New Study

Since Lili was healthy, I had a lot of free time. I soon began to read, cook, clean and I still had too much time. I quite frankly felt like a rusty housewife who did not think about anything other than her home and family. I thought about it for a week or two, then I shared my thoughts with Tone and finally decided to start studying again. I first thought about an MA in English Literature at the School of Arts and almost decided to enroll. When I came to the students' office and wrote a letter asking the school to allow my studies, the secretary snorted that the letter should be typed and not written by hand.

"If you don't want me, I will go somewhere else. There are still many other study programs and universities."

She was so surprised that she did not know how to answer. For me, this was just a sign that I should try something else. At the School of Arts, I could enroll in an MA in Old English or German Literature, which I did not like very much. Besides I noticed that my company much more appreciated lawyers and economists than linguists. That was strange. After all, we were a firm that imported foreign products, so it should hire as many linguists as possible. Among more than 300 employees, there were only three linguists and our salaries were not much higher than those of the secretaries with only a secondary school education. The salespeople, although the majority had just secondary education, had much higher salaries than we did. The lawyer, who came to the company at the same time as I, had not only received a much higher salary than I, but also got an apartment. And everybody seemed to appreciate him. People who knew laws by heart and were able to explain them were as important as directors.

I decided to enroll in the School of Law. I explained to Tone how I intended to join my work and studies and he found it quite acceptable. The general manager expressed his appreciation and said that I would surely be successful, but it was written on his nose that he lied. The lawyer started to explain about the teachers and the courses. Mrs. Belak and Marina were at least once of the same opinion, namely that a mother should devote herself completely to her child. My mother-in-law and my grandmother also thought so.

On the first day of lectures, I felt the same or even more euphoria than I had five years ago, when I started with studies at the School of Arts. It was a wonderful autumn day. I took my bicycle, drove to the School of Law and immediately started to talk with other students who also waited for the lectures. Before coming to the school, I'd felt old and rusty and now I found myself young again. My schoolmates did not believe that I already graduated from the School of Arts and that I had a family. The loudest among the boys asked me to bring my grade report book from the School of Arts. I had it in my bag, so showed it to him. His mouth opened when he started to check and loudly read my marks, which were impressively high.

The first lectures were given by Dr. Bajt, who was an authority on economy. His small eyes flashed with malicious pleasure when he said that just about a third of us would finish our studies. I sat right in front of him and gave him a straight look that promised to be among that one-third. He did not make much of an impression on me. That class of his was the epitome of boring. I preferred Roman law—not because of its contents, but because of the lecturer. He was very intelligent and gave us unbelievable tasks to solve. We had to use all our knowledge and logical thinking, but we still did not manage to answer the majority of his questions. I tried to be present during his exercises, but I did not always manage. My grandmother and my mum liked to take care of Lili, but I still had to breastfeed her, so three hours was the most that I could devote to lectures.

I mainly studied at home. It took me a lot of time because I had to learn everything by heart. There were many laws, and teachers could ask you about any of them. I borrowed a book about memorizing by mind maps. This technique helped me a lot. I not only remembered things more quickly, but also developed better concentration. I had troubles with it, because Lili always did something interesting, new and unique and I preferred to admire her than to study.

Before I left for maternity leave, the general manager said

that I would get another job assignment when I returned, namely registering and organizing contracts with numerous foreign firms that our company represented in Yugoslavia. It demanded knowledge of languages and law and I considered it to be a post with perspective. However, when I returned, Tea, who had replaced me, firmly told me that she'd gotten the job I'd been promised, and that I would continue to be the general manager's secretary. It surprised and angered me. I had already imagined myself working in a post which was, in my opinion, much more reputable. Now I had to accept the fact that I remained the secretary. I never thought that Herman perhaps preferred me as his nearest collaborator over Tea. The only thing that struck me was that the job that had been promised to me had been given to another person who was less competent than I. It was injustice and a sign that I should seriously think about other employment. I was convinced that working in that big company, full of competition, was not the right place for me. To that point, I'd never tried to find something more convenient, because I'd had too much work, along with graduation, pregnancy and the baby.

When I started to think about another job, I first dreamt that I would become a freelance translator. If I had enough translations, I could work at home, stay with my baby and study. However, it was difficult to get translations if your husband wasn't the director of an international firm. I worked hard and found some translation projects, but I did not enjoy working on them and they were also not very good. Translating simply required more sitting at the desk and working with dictionaries than I liked, and more accuracy and knowledge than I had. So, I started to look for other institutions that needed people with knowledge of foreign languages.

Although I'd decided to find other employment, I tried to improve my work and knowledge of international business. I noticed that my colleagues were more pleased if I tried to foresee what they would need. Besides that, I pretended that everything interested me.

The general manager was very happy and often said: "Just wait and see what a good saleswoman I am going to make of you. Or a lawyer."

It became clear that Doler's business idea, in which the company invested a lot of money, would not be realized because the state forbade import of the very products they'd planned to focus on. I do not remember what products he wanted to introduce and why he and the general manager thought that it would work. Each year there were plenty of new business plans and I could not even remember all those that were realized. Sector directors came to the general manager, one after another, and complained that the company had thrown away a lot of money because he had supported Doler's project. The general manager waited until Doler boasted again how much money his department brought to the company and then shouted that he should stop telling such stories and calculate how much money he'd just thrown away. Doler defended himself that it was the fault of the state that limited the import. But now he was attacked by all the directors— they said that he should have anticipated it. They told him straight to his face everything that made them angry.

At last, Doler, low-spirited, said to the general manager: "I think that I deserve at least a bit of respect and that you should not let them walk on me like this."

I felt pity for Doler although he often said that I was a part of the unproductive administration that spent what his sector earned and I thought that the general manager would not trample him down.

But he coldly turned to him and said: "You do not deserve anything. Any other person would be a better director than you."

"If you say so, I will have to think about giving notice."

"Oh, come on, stop talking nonsense. You changed more jobs than anyone in this country and in each of them you had a fight. You cannot do anything other than stay here. Where could you get a job after this fiasco?"

"Be careful, or you will be sorry for your words."

"I won't be sorry. Such a sissy will never give notice."

"Bring me a piece of paper and a pen, Iris."

He wrote his notice on the paper and threw it in front of the general manager. The latter silently took it and finished the meeting.

It did not seem that anybody was sorry that Doler would leave. The general manager happily rubbed his hands and said: "Well, I didn't think it would go that easy. I provoked and provoked him so that I was afraid that he would throw a cup of coffee at me and I hid behind you, Iris. Thank God this passage is behind us."

"Aren't you sorry that he is leaving? He did do some good business, didn't he? Perhaps this matter was not just his fault?"

"Oh, I know that he was successful, and he still could be. But we are all sick of him because he causes so many conflicts. You will see that he'll soon recognize what a mistake he made and suggest that I throw his notice away. But I will not. It is impossible to live in the atmosphere which he cultivates."

Doler really did come back the next day, embarassed, red-faced, kind and humble. But it did not help. The general manager did not want to discuss things anymore.

37
New Job

I started to read job advertisements, and write applications, and soon received some invitations for interviews. I answered each invitation, because I was interested in all the companies and institutions that responded. I finally chose the biggest Yugoslav construction company that sought a translator. The personnel manager told us that the company received thirty appropriate applications, but just two of us reached the final phase of selection. We had to take psychological tests and prove our translating skills. My written translation was quite good, but my oral presentation was poor. The company lawyer who performed the tests asked me to tell him something in German, whatever I wanted to. I should have been able to do that with ease, because we had a lot of foreign partners, but I avoided free conversation. I did not know what to speak about and was afraid that I would make a mistake. The other candidate who competed with me was much better in conversation and she got the job.

Then I had an interview at the National and University Library of Ljubljana. I knew it well, because I'd often studied in it, but I did not know that they had so many employees and departments, among them one focused on the acquisition of foreign books. Right at the beginning, I was told that they'd chosen two appropriate candidates, myself being one of them, and that they would prefer the other one because she had teaching experience. I had almost forgotten about them by the time I heard that they'd accepted me. Later they told me that the first candidate had refused employment, so I was the second choice.

There were many reasons why I liked the library: it was in the center of the town in a very beautiful old building designed by the most famous Slovenian architect Jože Plečnik. It seemed that the library did not encourage a competitive atmosphere and that there were fewer quarrels than in my former business company. I loved the smell of old books and was intrigued by my handsome new boss and the library director. They immediately said that my salary would probably be worse than in the international business sector, because librarians were not appreciated by anybody in society. However, the salary was not my priority. I opted for the new employment as soon as my new boss told me that the time organization was rather flexible and that I could go home early if it was necessary because of the baby. So, I signed a contract for permanent employment without a trial period (what good conditions we had in Yugoslavia!) and gave my notice at my old company.

The general manager first got angry and then tried to convince me to stay. If there was anything I wanted, I should tell him, and he would think about the possibilities. He asked if I'd given notice just because I did not get the job that he had promised me before I went on maternity leave. I told him that it was not just that and that I saw no real possibilities in commerce, because I was more interested in culture.

"Oh, come on, if anybody is talented for business, it's you. And not just for business, also for administrative and legal matters. I feel that you could achieve the highest position in this company and that could happen very soon. Please forget those contracts that I promised you, they are nothing but papers without life. You could become manager of the administration department, take over some commercial matters and slowly become my deputy."

"Thank you, but no. I've decided on the library and I think that I found what I am really interested in. And besides, librarians do not seem to make such a fuss if women have children."

"But you already have a baby! You don't intend to have another?"

"Oh, I do, perhaps three or four."

"You are out of your mind. Why would one need so many children? Culture is a nice thing, but it does not bring money. Money is produced by companies like ours."

I liked that he tried to keep me in the company, because he made me feel that I was useful, but I did not understand at the time what he offered me. If he'd said that today, I would seriously think about staying in the company. He promised me a leading position and, then just a twenty-four-year-old woman, I was sure that I would be good at it.

The National and University Library had fewer employees than my first company: there were only around one hundred of us. However, the library was large and magnificent. Before you entered in the building, you could admire the wonderful harmonious architecture, beautiful gray and red stones, trees and benches in front of the building, and a wall made of glass through which you could see old furniture with lamps on the reading room tables. The most moving part of the library was the heavy main door, with its handle in the form of a horse. The first thing you saw when you entered was a big staircase made of dark marble leading to the reading room. The corridors were long, large and full of doors to many rooms, some of which I never managed to see, although I stayed there ten years.

My new boss, Frenk Vodeb, told me that the majority of employees worked from about seven to three o'clock. He mentioned that time was not something that intellectual workers should pay special attention to. We were not in a factory or in a business. On the first working day, I came at 6:30, because I wanted to make good impression. In the reception room, there was a morose old lady. She did not reply to my "good morning," but just asked if I'd been unable to sleep. She did not find the keys to my office, so I placed myself in front of my office and decided to wait for my boss. I already knew that the colleague with whom I would share the room was on holiday.

When I'd stood there for about an hour, a young, handsome boy passed by, greeted me and continued on his way to the first floor. His shoulders shook with laughter.

My boss arrived at about eight: tall, with dark hair and green eyes, about forty-years-old and with a pleasant smile: "I heard that you arrived before seven. I am sorry that you had to wait so long."

What an embarassing situation: if I confirmed that I'd come so early, it would be clear that I'd waited for a long time and perhaps he would take it as an insult. If I'd said that I'd waited for half an hour, I would have lied. So, I just smiled, answered that I'd arrived early, but the time had passed very quickly, because I'd observed the beautiful inner court with its fountain and a lime tree.

"Come to my office and I will tell you more about the library and about your work, while Monika will make coffee, won't you, Monika?" The door between the boss's and the next office was open and I could see a young, pretty woman who nodded in reply. He spoke about the history of the library for an hour and I sat, evermore upright and proud that I was employed by an institution with such a long tradition and such enormous library funds.

Then somebody brought the keys and my boss took me to my office. The whole room was filled with books and I automatically started to examine them and read the interesting titles and summaries. After a few minutes, I realized that I'd ceased speaking and forgotten all about my boss. I quickly turned around and apologized, but it was not necessary.

He smiled: "We are birds of feather, don't you see that I am doing the same as you? These books arrived yesterday. I like them, too. Perhaps book acquisition is not as important as the research department but be aware that you will be the first to see all the important books that arrive in Slovenia."

I felt as if I'd won the lottery. In those times, it meant something if you could have a survey of the most recent foreign books. Today, you open Amazon.com, but in the 70s, the import of books to Yugoslavia was limited—not just because of money, but also because the state censored publications.

"We also have a lot of books that are forbidden to the public, but the national library has to collect them because they were written by Slovenian authors. Those are in a special cabinet in the director's office. I will show it to you when I introduce you to the director of the library."

"What shall I do today?"

"You just arrived and already want to start working? OK. I will first take you around and introduce you to the heads of the most important departments, then we will go to the director, and after that you will meet the employees in our department. At noon, we have coffee together and we say a word or two about our work and culture. Then you will translate a letter for a Russian library."

I enthusiastically nodded, although I thought that he'd planned too many introductions and not enough work. Never mind, if I had some free time, I would take a look at all the books that awaited processing.

At first, he took me to the bibliography department that produced descriptions of Slovenian books. A most authoritative gentleman mumbled: "Oh, that's the young replacement for our translator. I hope that you will be as good as she was."

My boss frowned and dragged me away: "Jakob sometimes speaks without thinking."

I was used to such comparisons, so I did not worry when I learned that my predecessor was an extremely capable, beautiful and clever blonde who'd found employment in another library.

The boss of the next department, which provided the classification of books, seemed even more authoritative than the first one: a big gentleman with a loud voice, whose face reflected a good-natured person. When I mentioned my observations to my boss, he smiled that this might be so, but that I should take care of each word when speaking with him. He was touchy and if somebody made him angry, he raised his voice.

The boss of the information department was a thin, very well-dressed woman and my boss said that she was one of the best Slovenian translators from French. She translated Proust so she must have been exceptionally good. Perhaps she might give me advice on how to improve my translations, I thought. She accepted me with a polite smile and praised my dress, saying that in the library there were not many women who wore modern clothing. When we left, my boss whispered that I should be very polite and careful with her, too.

Over the next months, I tried to be very polite and I asked her for advice on how to improve my translations. She answered that she did not know much English, so she could not help me. However, when my first translations were published, she found all my mistakes, went to the library director and told everybody that my language knowledge was poor.

The boss of the research department was quite the opposite: round, with a kind, open smile. When she heard that I studied English, German and law, she said: "You see, Frenk, we would need somebody like that in our department, because none of us speaks a foreign language. Never mind, young lady, you pass the library qualifications and you will have the possibility to advance, perhaps even to our department."

My boss frowned and loudly answered that working in the acquisitions department was as reputable as research and that she was being silly: "If you need an employee like her, you find her by yourself and don't try to steal my staff as soon as I introduce somebody to you."

She laughed and smoked her cigarette, while my boss grumbled and led me to the director's office. Of course, I said that I was most interested in the acquisitons department, but I remembered that the researchers monitored the work of all the Slovenian libraries and tried to provide for their development. I doubted that I might ever be able to perform such research work, but it certainly sounded interesting.

When we came to the director, Berce, I was a bit nervous, but felt better the moment he started speaking. He was formally dressed and seemed a nice, humane, warm and wise man. He asked if I was ready to translate letters for him and I enthusiastically nodded. Wasn't I born under a lucky star: I hardly arrived, and it seemed that everybody needed me for real translations and one of them even mentioned research work! Perhaps it would not even be necessary to make coffee or perform other humiliating administrative tasks, as in my previous company.

At noon, I nervously expected that my boss would order me to make coffee for everybody, but he came just to invite me to a circle of about seven or ten employees. I cautiously asked who was so kind as to make coffee and my boss answered: "Our Monika makes the best coffee in the library."

After a few days, I recognized that making coffee in the library did not indicate an inferior task, but a friendly gesture and that the person who made it was appreciated.

I liked all my new colleagues. Monika did not speak much, but Ana was her opposite. It seemed that she knew all the books in the library. She had sound ideas about life and I even liked that she did not use any makeup, wore very simple dresses and behaved naturally. It was quite the opposite of other women in those times. I was acquainted also with an old gentleman who had been the library director for many years and was now retired. He still came to the library every day. He said he could not live without it.

After the coffee break, I translated and typed the letter that my boss gave me. My predecessor had well-organized records. I needed just to take a look at some files and I immediately found the basic words and phrases necessary for the translation. On my table were the most recently published dictionaries. The general manager in my previous company thought that a good translator did not need any dictionaries, so I'd had to bring my own. The typewriter in the library was much better than the one at the rich international business company. My new boss could not believe how quickly I translated the letter.

I had never been so pleased with a job before. I worked in a magnificent palace, among wonderful, good, educated people, surrounded by the most popular new foreign books. I could translate—there was nothing else that I could wish for.

38

Tina

On one of the following days, I met Tina, with whom I was to share the office over the next years. My boss mentioned that Tina and my predecessor had a horrible fight and that Tina reacted quickly and spontaneously, therefore I should not be surprised if she suddenly jumped or cried or protested against something: "That's just her way of expressing opinions and emotions. But she is very open and honest."

I was a bit surprised when a woman between thirty and forty years of age quickly entered, ran to the window and closed it: "My God, why are you airing the room so early in the morning? It is so cold, and you are almost naked."

It came to my mind that this was probably Tina, so I replied with a kind smile and told her that I overheated because I worked so hard.

"Well, let's hope that we will have better cohabitation than I had with Brigita, who was here before you."

"What was wrong?"

"I don't know how to explain it. She did not like my rhythm of work and thought that I was sloppy. And I didn't like that she was so perfect and precise. I know that you translators must be precise, but to organize your life so that you have no freedom is, in my opinion, stupid."

"Don't worry, I am not perfect. Actually everybody, including my husband, accuses me of not being perfect."

"Thank God and I hope that you will remain like that. There are too many perfectionists in the world."

I did not quite believe her, but Tina immediately won my heart.

The young boy who'd laughed at me on the first morning, when I was standing in front of my office, entered the room. Tina introduced us and I learned that he was a photographer and that his name was Miro. The old texts in the library had to be photographed, not copied, and the library needed him because they organized a lot of public events and he had to take photos.

When he looked at me, he began to laugh again: "You were as silly as I on the first day—you came in before seven!"

"Well, if I come to the library at eight, I should stay in the office until four or five in the afternoon. I can't do that because I have a small child and want to spend some time with her."

Both Tina and Miro rolled their eyes. Tina taught me that people should come to the office at about eight and go home at about three.

"Oh. But this does not make forty-two hours per week."

"On Wednesdays we work in the afternoon and the library is open also on Saturdays, so we have enough hours at the end of the month."

My brain calculated whether these additional hours were sufficient, but our boss entered the office and I did not find it reasonable to continue with questions. I knew that the library had no timekeeper, so I asked if the employees registered their arrivals and departures in a book or if the receptionist did it. My boss nobly answered that every department had a boss who took care that the employees were in their offices when it was necessary, and that intellectual work could not be measured by a technical instrument. That would be humiliating, wouldn't it? I quickly nodded and hoped that it was true.

After a week or two, Tina determined that I was trustworthy enough that she would introduce me to her circle of the most traditional librarians. On Friday, towards the end of the working hours, she took a box of the cheapest biscuits from her bag and told me to follow her to the third floor. We came to a very small room, now in disuse, that was equipped with some chairs and tables. In the room sat a few employees from our department, the photographer, and some other employees whom I hadn't met so far. We each got a small glass of wine and a biscuit and we spoke about anything and everything. This circle did not discuss educated cultural matters, but everyday problems. I liked it very much, although I knew that the library management would think that we were wasting time that should be devoted to work and that employees should not drink wine during work hours.

After a few weeks, I noticed that there were tensions within the library, but they were not nearly as sharp as in the international business world. The first to quarrel were Tina and our boss. Our boss told me that the library had just finished with the allocation of posts, defined new salaries and that there was a lot of bad blood around it.

Tina attacked the boss and reproached him that her salary was too low.

"Tina, you made your own job description and I told you to be precise. You laughed at me and said that it was just stupid administration. I added some of your tasks myself, because you forgot to describe them. I made your salary as high as possible and you should be grateful. Mind that you did not finish university and that you simply cannot have the same salary as those who graduated."

"Oh, really? I can't have the salary, but I can work in a place that requires university education! And don't you say how much you did for me. You are the boss, and this is your duty."

I hoped that they would not include me in their conversation, but Tina suddenly asked if my business company, too, provided for job descriptions.

"Yes, and it caused a lot of anger."

"And who implemented the descriptions? Wasn't it your director?"

"Everybody had to describe their tasks for two months; then we gave our descriptions to a specialist from Zagreb and he compiled them. But I think that those who did not make good job descriptions got lower salaries."

The boss smiled victoriously, but too soon.

"I think that everybody has to do his work. My work is to send books and magazines to foreign libraries, while department managers should take care of work organization."

She repeated this several times then, and later she continued during the coffee break. Our boss did not argue but he left the room annoyed.

Tina told me that I would probably have quite a decent salary, because my job description was made by my ambitious and precise predecessor. And she was right. Although everybody thought that library salaries were poor, I got more than I had in the business world. I was thankful for my decision to switch to this job, as well as thankful for the woman who'd worked in my place before I'd come.

I noticed that Tina started to look at the phone and through the window around ten each morning, as if she were waiting for something or somebody. If the phone rang, I usually heard a man's voice and she spoke with him in a sweet, soft tone. Then she hurried out to take a break and came back quite euphoric.

"Why are you batting your eyes, as if you just met Robert Redford?"

"You are so prosaic. Have you ever been in love?"

"Of course. Why?"

"But it was finished when you got married, right? You see, I am not married but I am still in love. Marriages ruin love. Each time Janez calls, I feel as if I'm on my first date."

"So, this is your son's father."

"Yes."

"Does he, too, think that marriage ruins love?"

"Of course. He knows that much better than I do because he is married."

"What if his wife hears about you, comes to the library and pulls a gun out of her bag…?"

"Ha ha, that would be fun. Quite frankly, I often imagine that she would come and that we would fight. She might at least start to think about divorce. I can't understand why she still lives with him as if they were happily married. She must know that he comes to me every day. The whole town speaks about it, but she covers her eyes. Oh, those married women."

"What about him, do you think that he does not love her?"

"He is only with her because of their children. His present wife brings up both their child and two children that he had in his first marriage."

"She must be a generous woman."

"I never said she wasn't. If you ever meet her in the street, you would ask yourself why Janez fell in love with me. His wife is good, beautiful, well-dressed, and well-organized. In short, she is perfect. And I think that Janez doesn't like her perfection."

Quite frankly I also liked Tina much more than other perfect women whom I'd met in my life.

"Why do you think that all Ljubljana speaks about you?"

"Because Janez is one of the best Slovenian writers."

"Well, I heard his name, but so far I haven't read anything written by him."

She looked down on me: "Yes, I always say that girls who enroll in foreign languages are beautiful and those who study comparative literature are wise. How can you admit that you did not read anything he wrote? I would be ashamed to say so."

I was not ashamed because I'd not read something. I knew she only said that because comparative literature was what she studied. But whenever I heard that an author was good, I immediately borrowed one of his books. So, I took one or two books written by Tina's lover.

But he drove me to dispair. He was as pessimistic as Dostoyevsky and his language was full of strange phrases and sentences which critics found beautiful and original. I am not sure if I ever dared to express my opinion to Tina, but I know that I mentioned it to my boss. He laughed and said that I should not speak like that if I did not want to be characterized as a stupid blonde who was completely without a sense for literature.

"I don't care. Everybody can say that one or another author is important, but I believe it when his book convinces me about it. What do critics know about literature? What they were taught in school. But I feel good literature in my mind and blood and soul. Good books can transport me to another place."

"Yes, I noticed. But Janez is at present the most popular author in Slovenia and you'd better not announce your sinful thoughts aloud."

Once I explained Tina's idea that marriage meant the end of love to Tone, because I was interested in what he would say. He furiously snorted that a man who loved a woman married her and that I would do better to avoid people who obviously taught me heresy.

Tina's opinions about love and marriage were most extraordinary and I often poked my nose into her affairs. Once she was in rather low mood and fed up with my questions: "Shut up, you fool! (That was our way of communication—we called each other fools in one moment and forgot all about our anger in the next). Of course, I'd like to marry him. But what shall I do—he is married! I fell in love with him and I love him more than I've ever loved a man. I am happy if I can meet him at least during the coffee break and I am in heaven if he comes to me and to our son in the evening. Then I feel as if I have a family. Are you happy with my answers? Did I answer you well?" She was red with rage and gasped for breath.

"Please excuse me. I didn't want to hurt you. But how can you be in love for ten years? It usually runs out in a year or two. I am certainly not in love anymore, but you purr with satisfaction when he calls you."

"Shut up and work instead of questioning me like an inquisitor." She looked through the window: "Oh, dear, I forgot that I have a date because you are so provocative. I will be out a bit longer today. Leave the window open."

I stared when I saw her take her bag, take her shoes off, jump through the window, put her shoes back on and then run to a rather old and thin man. She looked into his eyes, took his hand and left.

I quickly turned to the door because our boss just entered the room and asked: "Where is Tina?"

"Oooh, she can't be far away."

"Did she jump through the window and go for a coffee with her lover?"

My face became red, but our boss just laughed and left.

39
Some Librarians Could Be Annoying

After a few months, I noticed that not all the librarians were pleasant. The old gentleman who was once director of the library and who sat with us during the coffee break was a horrible nuisance. As soon as we sat down and wanted to start a discussion, he began to speak and would not finish if somebody did not interrupt him. He knew everything, or so he thought. We had to listen, again and again, to how he joined the Partisan army—and not with a gun like my grandmother. He just wrote graffiti against German soldiers on walls. He knew everything about Slovenian culture and could immediately provide an opinion about any artist. He had been in many foreign countries and knew the national characteristics of individual nations. According to his words, he also had an ideal family.

Tina once made a joke that many of his female colleagues were charmed by him and he waved his hand with contempt: "Yes, as a director I was always supposed to have relationships with different women, but such thoughts were wrong. Of course, it happened that one or the other woman expressed her admiration, but I never had affairs because I was married." Tina was not quite pleased with that explanation, but she did not oppose.

I first found him rather irritating, when my boss returned from from the Soviet Union where he visited some of the largest libraries. I was interested in what he would tell us because I had never been to any Eastern European countries. As soon as my boss mentioned a couple of things, the old gentleman interrupted him and started to describe his visits to the libraries in Moscow, Saint Petersburg and other cities in Russia and Poland. We tried to encourage our boss to continue speaking, but it was in vain.

When Tina and I returned to our office, I firmly said that the old director exceeded all limits of polite behavior: "For God's sake, we were interested in the experiences of our boss and had to listen to those old stories that we had heard ten times."

Tina shrugged her shoulders: "Yes, he speaks too much, but he is definitely the most educated man in Slovenia."

"Oh, come on, you can't be serious! Why should he be the most educated? Has he got a master's degree or PhD? The present library director is certainly more educated because he has a PhD."

"Well, yes, but a PhD means somebody who is specialized in certain scientific field and does not have large, general knowledge. The old director has broad knowledge and world perspective. And you know how many foreign languages he speaks."

"Just stop admiring his knowledge of foreign languages. He probably speaks German because he went to German schools, but he doesn't know a number of German expressions from librarianship. His English is horrible. We all more or less speak Serbo-Croatian and we all understand Russian. You can't say that this means knowledge of many foreign languages."

"Come on, you cannot speak like that about a man whom everybody knows as the most intellectual person that ever worked in this library. Of course, he speaks English. Didn't you hear him say something in English today? And besides he is supposed to speak also French and Italian."

"If I spoke English with such an accent and with so many mistakes, I would never open my mouth. Have you ever heard him say a couple of sentences in Italian or French or Russian?"

"I haven't, but everybody says that he has mastered several languages."

"He spreads such rumors himself. But I think that he doesn't know much about books or about languages."

Tina kind-heartedly said that I was a young bull and that I would see how things were in the course of time. In her opinion, I could certainly not judge the knowledge and culture of an old man who'd devoted his whole life to books and libraries.

"Well, if he devoted so much time to them, why hasn't he written anything himself?"

"He is writing a book."

"Yes, but his writing takes more than ten years," remarked my boss, who entered our office and listened to my angry criticism.

"You won't convince me that such an intelligent and educated man knows nothing. I would have preferred to listen to the description of our boss's travel to Russia, but old gentlemen like to speak. We must show them a bit of respect and understanding."

After my first year in the library, I had to pass several professional examinations in librarianship. It was obligatory for all new librarians, because Slovenia had no university programs that would teach librarianship. Libraries employed people who graduated in philosophy, sociology, comparative literature, art history, Slovenian and other languages. The newcomers first had to train in all the library's departments and then pass about seven courses in librarianship. My main study obligation was still law, so I did not devote much attention to library examinations and did not pass with the highest marks.

One of the examiners confused me. She asked me about the dissemination of materials in special libraries and I started to answer with a verb instead of using a noun. It seemed that this made her very angry. She asked me three times—louder and louder—if I understood Slovenian and then she answered her question herself and shook her head to point out my obvious lack of knowledge and intelligence. After the exam, I asked my boss if I was really so stupid or if the only difference between the examiner's and my definition of dissemination was a different sentence structure.

He laughed: "Your answer was right, but you are obviously not aware of where the examiner comes from."

"Why is that important?"

"My dear girl, how young you still are and how little you know about real librarianship in this country. The lady who examined you is director of the second largest Slovenian library. It can never become the National and University Library, but all fifty employees of that library hate us just like Partisans hated Germans or vice versa. Their director always tries to show that people employed in our library are unprofessional and incapable, while her librarians are technically oriented, rational, intelligent people who will create the future of librarianship."

40
Work and Problems at Home

Tone and I renovated and put in order only the most necessary places in our house: the living room with the kitchen, bathroom, bedroom and room for the baby. However, it was necessary to change the flooring in the house, provide for central heating, tear down the pantry that intruded square meters into the living room and put on the house's façade. My father-in-law suggested that we should also build a balcony, while I very much wished for a sauna.

When we asked for the building permit, my father-in-law rolled his eyes and said that we wasted time and money for unnecessary things. He suggested that Tone and I buy the necessary building materials and then he and Tone would do the majority of work themselves and thus save a lot of money. Tone frowned when he thought about helping his father and firmly opposed handling the façade and central heating themselves. I, too, thought that we should find specialists.

The construction works lasted about six months and were, for those times and considering our lack of experience, quickly finished. We were often desperate to get building materials. We had to wait months for cement, façade sand, bricks and other building materials. We once heard that one of the shops would receive a big truckload of cement and decided to wait for it before the shop opened. However, other people heard about it too and when we arrived at four in the morning, we faced a long line. As soon as the shop opened, the cement was sold out and we didn't get any. Then I remembered the salesmen from my first company, who'd said that it was always possible to buy things. I knew that there was a factory for cement in western Slovenia and asked a truck driver if he could take us there. Perhaps we could buy at least a few bags. Everybody thought that we were throwing our money away, but I didn't see any other possibility. When we came to the factory there were about ten long vehicles in front of us. The truck driver desperately said that he had to be home in the evening. I went around and started to speak with the truck drivers, who were waiting and smoking. I sighed that we would need just a couple of bags and that I did not know how to get them. One of the men said that the company also had a retail trade department and that I should go there and ask for some bags. I quickly ran to a small wooden cottage and the shop assistant said that our driver could bring his vehicle to the front of the shop. In half an hour, we got so much cement that we had enough for all the construction projects.

When looking for façade sand, I had to be even more innovative. We bought as much sand as the masons ordered, but they soon used it all and required that we deliver some more and very quickly. I had to call many Slovenian firms to find out where we could buy the sand. Then I called a farm that was rather close to the place where the sand was produced. I asked the housewife if my husband and I could come and try to get some bags of the sand. The housewife was young, talkative and knew the troubles with building. So, I dared to ask if she knew somebody in the sand factory and if she could come with me so that we would convince the foreman to sell it to us. She sat in our car and spoke with the foreman so long that he finally agreed. A couple of workers produced sand in the evening under the moonlight. Each of them accepted a bottle of beer, while the housewife didn't want anything. I do not remember her name, but I will never forget how she helped us.

During the months when our home was under construction, we lived in the home of my mother-in-law, who took care of Lili and prepared us supper each evening. She asked why I didn't do it, but both Tone and my father-in-law explained to her that we had no electricity and no water in our house. Besides, I had to help them, too.

Tone hated construction works and tried to convince me that we should be pleased with what we had. He was annoyed by simply filling in the numerous papers to get a loan. He frowned even more when it was obvious that he would have to help his father with the masonry work. His father could do everything easily but he was very authoritative when working and very impatient. If Tone, who did not know much about building, did not bring him the right tools or bricks, his father started to scold him.

Tone did not listen to his shouting, but I got angry and stood up to my mother-in-law: "Why should Tone know how to build a house? He did not study construction. His father has no right to shout at him."

My mother-in-law did not need to be told twice, she immediately settled the matter. She gave her husband a good nagging and then asked him, every day, if he'd behaved like a bull again. My father-in-law never admitted that he shouted, saying that he just spoke more energetically.

Although Tone did not like building, he did everything that was necessary and was very happy when the work was finished. Perhaps I did not appreciate his work enough. I enjoyed working because I was prepared to do everything to create a pleasant home. If somebody works with pleasure, they simply don't understand that other people might hate it.

When our house was renovated, we started to invite guests, our relatives and friends. Our house was always full of people: for Christmas, Easter, other holidays, birthdays of all family members and so on. I made a big feast each time. It usually started on Saturday with cleaning and putting things in order, continued on Sunday morning when I cooked, and finished in the afternoon, when our guests ate everything I prepared. We met our friends almost every Sunday, sometimes in our house and sometimes in theirs. Tone had five or ten very good friends from his company who had small children, too. We also invited my college friend, Mara, her husband and my colleagues from the library. Although such parties were always a lot of work, I enjoyed organizing them. I was also happy because they praised our house and the food that I cooked.

I missed compliments because Tone no longer managed to find any good words for me. He only noticed what was wrong. He nagged and nagged that the house was not in order and he found me lacking in many ways. Once he explained for two hours how negligent I was, so I dragged him out of bed at midnight and made him show me what was not in order. When he checked everything and could not show me either unwashed dishes or anything else, he said that he did not speak about the house. He wanted to say that I was a rather careless person. I still don't understand why I started to cry instead of breaking some glasses over his head. I was probably too tired to make a show. The next day, I quickly forgot my anger and said to myself that married people should forgive each other. I think that quite a lot of women in Yugoslavia in the 80s solved problems like I did. Women tended to be submissive and accepting of irrational abuse, even if we were financially independent and could get a divorce rather quickly (except for the slow-moving issue of divison of property). However, many of us loved our husbands, had children and wanted them to have fathers. The women who were Catholic were not supposed to divorce because the Church taught us that married people should live together until the end of their lives.

Tone also criticized my way of dressing. Of course, I wore somewhat different clothes than other women, but people generally liked them. All my friends said that I wore unique things and only old conservatives thought that I was too extravagant. If I heard criticism from people who had no idea about fashion, I laughed. But it hurt when Tone reproached me because I wanted to look good for him.

When we met our friends who also had children, I noticed that other fathers expressed much more feelings for their kids than Tone did. He always claimed that married people should first think about their own relationship and then about children. I considered such thoughts to be nonsense and sometimes said that loving one's husband was one thing and loving children another. But he did not seem to listen. He went off on long monologues about educational principles that he brought from his family, but they were quite out-of-date. My mother-in-law spoke just like Tone and had some even more old-fashioned ideas about education and family life.

What I hated most was Tone's driving. He drove as quickly as possible and always tried to pass other cars. We had a small and slow car, and it was dangerous if he drove too quickly. I grumbled that he should drive more slowly and think at least about his child who sat in the back seat.

"Oh, stop teaching me how to drive. You can't discuss the topic because you don't drive anymore. An experienced driver does not need to obey each stupid rule."

"Didn't you feel that the car slipped because you drove too quickly? Can't you see the speed limit?"

"Come on, I am not going to mind each limit. You remind me of jokes about women who teach their husbands how to drive."

"Every time I sit beside you in the car, I am afraid. How can I explain to you that you should drive in a different manner?"

"With that grumbling of yours, you will certainly not convince me."

Once he arrived home in an unknown car, although he had left with his own. When he came to the kitchen, he grinned and said that he flipped twice and that his car hung on a bush like a pear. I grew quite pale and at first could not believe that it was his fault, but the passengers in the other car explained that he'd driven too quickly. My mother-in-law rarely uttered a critical word against her precious son, but this time she seriously warned him to be more careful. He had a child and a wife, for God's sake! I tried to convince him in a softer way and he reluctantly nodded that we were right. The car was insured, but not in the case of the driver's fault. We took out a loan and bought a new car, but he only drove normally for about a month. In those years, fear entered my bones at the thought of driving with him and I still do not want to be driven by somebody else.

41

Birth and Death

When Lili was two years old, I got pregnant again. I was very sick during the first three months, but then things calmed down and I felt so well that I could dance, run and go for a walk.

During her last years, my grandmother had to be taken to the hospital very often and I worried about her. Her heart didn't function as it should. Every two months, Tone and I had to pick her up and take her to the ER. Neither my mum nor my aunt felt when my grandmother had to be taken to the hospital, and my grandmother postponed it to the last moment.

Each time we took her, I ate my heart out with anxiety: would she return home or die? When we brought her to the hospital the last time, her condition did not improve. I visited her every day, although my friends and relatives said that my anxiety and sadness would influence the baby. Tone thought so, as well, but he understood that I could not just leave her, so he helped me. I was grateful that he was always ready to take my grandmother to the hospital and that he comforted me. During my last visit, I brought her some chicken soup made by my mum. She could not eat it herself, so I had to spoon-feed her.

On the next day, she died.

Up until that time, I thought that I could still keep her alive by regularly driving her to the hospital and convincing doctors to help her. It was not logical to think that visiting her in the hospital and bringing her soup would somehow keep her alive, but I still hoped and prayed. When she died, I was completely broken. I believed in God, but it did not occur to me that death was a new beginning. Slovenian newspapers and books of those times never wrote about dying. They represented the official policy of the Communist Party that denied God and life after death.

I was eight months pregnant when Lili fell ill. She was with my mother-in-law, who always emphasized how healthy her food was, and how many different medicinal herbs she could prepare and use. She certainly cooked well, but I never thought of her food as healthy, because I knew that she was very economical and considered it a sin to throw away even an old piece of bread. I also did not like her herbal products, because they were several years old, and I was once sick when she made me drink one. I immediately took Lili to the doctor who ordered that she should be taken to the hospital. She was afraid that Lili might have meningitis. Lili, who was then almost three years old, was in the hospital for four days. I still do not like to think about that time. She lay in her little bed, quite exhausted, and revived just at the moment when I had to leave. Then she would jump up and beg that I wouldn't leave her. A parent is now required to stay with the child, but in those times, it was strictly prohibited. Doctors also didn't want to give me any information. I remembered that one of my schoolmates was a doctor and asked her if she could help me to at least get an idea about my daughter's illness. She called me after half an hour and said that it was just diarrhea. I could come and take her home. Lili was still quite exhausted, but she soon became her old cheerful, always busy little self.

As soon as Lili came home, my mother-in-law began to offer her herbal products again, but now I'd had enough and refused all her syrups and teas. I was convinced that Lili got sick because of her elderflower syrup. Tone was sure that his mother's herbs could cure many illnesses, so he was perplexed when I clearly demanded that his mother and everybody else stop pretending that she knew more than doctors.

She nursed a grudge, my father-in-law and Tone were silent, but my brother-in-law said: "Mum, I don't understand why you offer the child all sorts of syrups—the girl is quite healthy. Why did you give her that old liquid that you've kept in your cabinet for ages? And I also think that you should be more careful and look after her when she plays outside. A week ago, the little girl was playing in the street when I came home. I told you that somebody could hit her with their car, but you only laughed that people here drove slowly and that there was no danger. If you take care of a child, you should watch her all the time and have her in the garden."

My mother-in-law was quite beside herself and so was I. Tone always said that his mother could look after children much better than I, and I'd believed him. Now it was clear that this was not so.

My second baby was late by almost a week. Tone and my mum thought that a pregnant woman should not be home alone, so they convinced me to stay with my mother-in-law. They thought that the baby might come very quickly and that somebody had to observe me and help if necessary. My mother-in-law was ready to accept me, but I saw that she could not sleep because she was so worried. She constantly asked me how I felt. There was nothing special, except occasional cramps. When they started at regular intervals, I happily informed her that we might have another baby in the evening. She started to tremble and called Tone, but I said that we would have to wait at least ten hours and that there was no hurry. She was even more nervous when I mentioned that I wanted to go for a short walk. I heard that walking could accelerate the delivery and I wanted it to come sooner.

Lili and I dressed and went to the nearby church, in which I had not been for a long time. I entered, prayed that the birth would pass without troubles and then went home.

At five in the afternoon the cramps came every thirty minutes and it was time to go to the hospital. In that moment, Tone and my brother-in-law arrived and asked how I felt. My mother-in-law wildly shouted that they should stop asking stupid questions. They should instead think about what pains I had and stop smiling. Where had they been up to now?! They should get into the car and take me to the hospital immediately, so that I would not deliver at home or in the car. Damned men, she shouted, because of whom women had to suffer so much!

When we left, I felt strong pains and the baby came quite soon. It was a girl again. The delivery was much easier than the first one and no doctor was needed to help me. I named the baby Vali, because that was the name of my schoolmate who'd helped me when Lili was in the hospital.

When our second baby was born, Tone thought that he was an experienced father. He claimed that he was a mature, clever young man who could provide for his wife, who'd just borne their second child. He took the baby firmly in his hands. The house was warm when we arrived home and he said that he intended to make chicken soup for me. He showed Vali to Lili and then put the baby in her bed. I stayed outside and exchanged a couple of words with my mum, when he opened the window and asked me to change the baby's nappies, because she had probably pooped. I did not hurry, because I knew that small babies rarely cared about what was in their nappies.

When I cautiously climbed the staircase, he said that I should move more quickly, and my mum looked at him with a frown: "You should know that she bore a child four days ago and lost a lot of blood. It would be good if you did some work yourself and not forced her to run."

When I entered the sitting room, Vali slept and there was no need to wake her up. Tone just wanted to ask how to prepare the chicken soup. I gave him instructions, then he thoroughly studied my cookbooks, but he thought that his mother prepared chicken soup in a different way. When I went to bed, he placed the pot with the chicken and vegetables in his car and took everything to his mother to help him with cooking. The chicken soup had to boil for hours, so he stayed at their home for the whole afternoon. I was not only alone and had to take care of two children, but we would also be without lunch if my mum hadn't helped me. She brought something to eat, took Lili with her for an hour or two and then returned and admired the baby. Tone arrived in the evening with a pot of chicken soup, put it in the bowls and was convinced that he was an ideal husband. I didn't think so, but I didn't want to reduce his happiness.

In the evening, I was prepared to have to get up and feed the baby during the night, but I woke up at seven in the morning and everything was quiet. I leapt to my feet, frightened to death: did my baby die? No, she was sleeping in her bed. She woke up an hour later, ate and fell asleep again. This birth and early days were really easy: I had no stiches and there were no sleepless nights. The only thing that worried me, were the cramps that tortured Vali each afternoon. I tried everything to stop them. I massaged her belly, stroked her back after breastfeeding, cooked her special tea, but she cried each afternoon, sometimes for two hours, sometimes three. Then she suddenly stopped, ate and fell asleep. I took her to the pediatrician and asked for something for the cramps, but the doctor said that the baby was strong and healthy and that cramps were normal.

Soon after delivery, I started to study again because I did not have any hard work. Lili was an independent girl who did not like to sit on anybody's lap, but always made things and was creative. She often drew, pretended to read books, sometimes played with her sister or with her dolls. Vali usually slept or watched Lili and smiled. All the other family members worked: Tone, my mum, my aunt and brother.

My mum usually came home at two in the afternoon, ate her lunch and then came to me and asked about the children. My aunt and my brother were not especially interested in children. Tone came home at about six in the afternoon, sometimes even at eight or later. His mother called him almost every day and offered him some salad on Monday, new potatoes on Tuesday, eggs on Wednesday or carrots on Thursday. She had a small garden and provided vegetables for our family, but I never accepted her gifts with gratitude. I knew that this was a way to see her precious son as often as possible.

When Vali was about one month old, we organized a family party. My father-in-law suggested that Tone come to his old home, because he was obviously tired. I maliciously said that Tone was married to me and that he should come to our home and help me with the children. I deliberately looked at my mother-in-law because I was sure that it was her who initiated such a stupid suggestion. My mother-in-law innocently said that I was probably tired and could not cook for Tone. I answered that Tone had a very good lunch in his public administration office which Tone always praised.

"Oh, there is a difference between lunch that is prepared at home and lunch in a canteen."

"I would gladly prepare dinner, if he came home at five, like other husbands."

"Come on, you should understand that your husband is an engineer and has a responsible job. He can't come home every day at four or five like other men."

I knew that Tone could come home at five. The problem was that he tried to perform each task so perfectly that he completely forgot all about the time. And besides, his mummy called him every day and asked him to come and take vegetables that we did not need at all.

When Vali was some months old, we started to take trips and were more often together again. Once or twice we even spent our holidays with Tone's friends who also had small children and it was much more pleasant than with my mother-in-law.

After my second baby, I decided to improve my domestic skills and learn how to sew. All my colleagues in the library could make tablecloths, curtains and even dresses themselves and I wanted to show that I was as good a housewife as my friends. I bought a sewing machine and instructions for sewing, my mum showed me some basic skills and I started creating dresses for myself and for the children. My products did not look good and they hung loose on me. Once I put on my own creation when we wanted to visit some friends, but Tone firmly demanded that I should dress in something normal. When my colleagues from the library came to see the baby, I made aprons for all of them. I first colored and then sewed them. They were rather pale and to be frank, one could hardly see the color. Some of my friends found the aprons too big or too small. My colleagues were merciful enough to admire my skills, but I think that they used the aprons just to clean the floor. Anyway, after some months I found out that I was not born for sewing and that it caused pains in my back.

42
Changes in the Library

When I came back to the library, I sadly found out that my boss was leaving us. I asked him why, but he only shrugged his shoulders: "Relationships in the department are no more what they used to be. Since we introduced new job descriptions and new salaries, I cannot enter a room without hearing what's wrong and I'm fed up with it. My new job is much better. I will work as a book reviewer for the National TV, I will be independent, the salary will be better, and nobody will measure the minutes spent in the office."

While I was on maternity leave, the National and University Library had introduced a timekeeper and it almost caused a revolution.

Tina was still madly in love with the father of her son and, from time to time, still jumped through her window to have coffee with him. She still organized Friday meetings in that small forgotten room.

Soon after our boss left, Tina came with the alarming news that we would get a new boss, Mrs. Kos, a rather unpleasant woman: older, who worked in the same library as Tina's lover. Stupid as I was, I immediately spread the news to some good friends in the vicinity, including the anticipated negative aspects.

Mrs. Kos came into a rather unfavorable environment. She surely found her new job difficult because her previous library was quite small and because she had never been a manager.

I was aware that my slandering was wrong, so I started to speak well of her: that she was well-dressed, that she could laugh like a young girl, that it was possible to speak with her about everything, that she was well-acquainted with what was going on in Ljubljana and that she took our negative opinions in a rather sporting manner. The new boss had nothing against the noon coffee and sat with us as an equal, spoke about books, films, TV, culture and so on. She did not have her own children, but was well-informed about the troubles of young mothers, because her niece had children and she was obviously interested in them. She spoke about her library and its visitors and we often laughed at her stories. She had her own critical opinion about the library management. She always allowed us to go out if we needed to.

Mrs. Kos liked to emphasize that she had her system of values and she often mentioned that she wanted to be creative and well-informed. I never found book acquisition to be very creative work, but she was certainly knowledgeable. It seemed that she knew everybody in Ljubljana and especially about their love affairs, towards which she showed a lot of tolerance. I had no idea that there was a relationship between a lady in the manuscript department and an old, shabby-looking man in the acquisitions department. He was so ugly that I didn't understand how a woman could fall in love with him. But Mrs. Kos said that the rumors were true. I still wouldn't have believed it, had Tina not confirmed it.

Both the photographer Miro and I made stupid faces and he said: "Oh, come on, the beautiful, young, dynamic Vera cannot be in love with that fat old man."

But Tina and our boss laughed: "Be quiet, young man, you will eventually see that love is not logical."

The photographer was a quiet boy who often blushed because we were a group of rather loud women, but he did not stop visiting us, even if we sometimes embarassed him. In the morning he came and greeted us, at ten he went out with one or another woman to buy a snack and he also joined us for noon coffee.

Soon after, we got a new library director, Marton. The former director, Berce, had accepted a place at the School of Arts. He would organize a department for the university education of librarians. This was certainly the top achievement that a library employee could strive for. However, I often heard him say that it was the most difficult job that he'd faced in his life. Years had to pass before I believed him. I understood what he meant when I established my own college.

People said that the new library director, Marton, first worked in a Slovenian embassy somewhere abroad and later lectured in one of the Slovenian schools that was established to educate future politicians. He was tall, spoke good English and Serbo-Croatian, and wicked tongues added that he could quickly win women's hearts.

The new director caused a lot of dissatisfaction because it was clear that he had no understanding of librarianship. It was also known that his academic qualifications were rather low and that he became library director just because he was a member of the Communist Party.

Marton managed the library in an autocratic way: all the post first came to him and no letter could be sent without his approval; he could not bear for people to think in a different way than he and nobody dared to even think about resisting. If somebody corrected or completed his words, and only a couple of the bravest top librarians dared to do it, they were soon punished: not allowed to go for holidays when they wanted to, frequently asked why they were late in the morning, or they were required to speak English even though they could not. Everybody had to dance to the director's tune.

I, too, found it rather strange that the director had no understanding of librarianship and that his character was not like that of the former director. But I still regretted that I spoke ill of my new boss and I did not want to repeat the same mistake. I did not like that the new director often corrected my translations, but I had to admit that he knew much more about polite phrases than I did, and he could change my short sentences into larger and more skillful ones.

43

Burnout

*O*ur department got a new employee, Sonja. She was one of the most beautiful women I'd ever met: tall, slender, red haired, educated and she spoke with the pleasant intonation of Slovenians who lived along the border with Italy. She too had a small child and we immediately accepted her at noon coffee and on Friday afternoons.

Sonja was a nice woman, very communicative and liked to socialize. My colleagues started to celebrate birthday parties, created evenings featuring plum or apricot dumplings, had suppers with the first spring salads, and took trips to the mountains. All these social obligations were too much for me, so I started to skip some.

However, Tina, who always felt, that she should encourage my social skills, quickly started to criticize me: "Well, Madame, you've become rather reserved, haven't you? Are you afraid of the new boss? Or do you want to make a good impression with the director?"

Mrs. Kos noticed that I no longer came to all celebrations and she whispered that she, too, did not like so much socializing, but she had to force herself so that others would not say that she was arrogant.

I began to feel that I was imperfect: the director always corrected my letters, I was asocial, and could not include myself in the work place.

When I said as much to Tone, he answered that I should not worry because of such opinions and that I should work in my own way. However, he had even more remarks about my negative points than my colleagues. He often said that he was disappointed because he thought that we would have many more common interests. Now I lived just for my children and studies, I worked and tidied up all Saturday and Sunday and he felt quite neglected. He still thought that I could not dress well and that I was rather dull. Up to that point, I had not taken his critical remarks seriously. Now such thoughts did not want to go in at one ear and out at the other but remained in my head. As soon as somebody said a critical word about me or my work, I thought for hours about whether it was true. I usually came to the conclusion that everything I did was wrong.

After some months, I grew too nervous to go out among people. I thought that I was the ugliest and the worst woman who'd ever lived. I tried to be as unnoticable as possible. If somebody watched me for too long or asked me too personal a question, I started to tremble and sometimes simply quit the room. I lost ten kilos and would start to cry for no reason. I did not know why this happened or what I could do to fight it. Once, when my colleagues criticized me again because I did not participate in a birthday party, I burst into tears and ran away. I was ashamed but could not do anything else. I just asked my boss if I could go home. She showed compassion, lent me money for the bus and said that I should stay home until I recovered. I went directly to my doctor and told her how unbelievably touchy I'd become. She gave me fourteen days of sick leave and some pills that should help me to be in a better mood. I did not want the sick leave, because I did not feel ill and because I had a lot of work.

"OK, how much time do you need to finish the most urgent work?"

"At least two days, so we can order the new literature."

"Go to the office for those two days and then take sick leave. Also go to a psychiatrist and start taking these pills immediately."

"Do you think that I am mad? I don't think it's necessary to go to a psychiatrist."

"Just go, perhaps one visit will be enough. I was in a similar position two years ago and believe me that I know what I am talking about. You look utterly depressed because you are over-tired. Some pills and sick leave will help you to overcome your troubles very quickly."

I did not think that I was too tired and depressed, and I did not believe that pills and doctors might help me. But I did not see any other possibility, so I started taking the pills and went to the psychiatrist.

Everything happened exactly the way my doctor had said: one interview with the psychiatrist was enough. She told me to describe my working day and I started to explain: "I wake up at five, prepare breakfast, dress my children, take them to daycare, go to my office, work eight hours, pick up the children, prepare an afternoon snack and the dinner, play with them, wash them, draw, read to them, put them to bed and try to finish the day with studying. I am worn out in the evening but cannot sleep."

"What do you do on Saturdays and Sundays?"

"I usually stay home and try to tidy up, iron, wash, give a bath to my children and study a bit more."

"Don't you ever go for a trip?"

"Oh, we do, and my husband would like to go every Saturday and Sunday. But quite frankly I get more rest at home than on excursions. These are only additional work: prepare the children, food, behave as a happy, sporting, young woman, go to the mountains, swim... Oh, Lord, I cannot do it anymore! Especially because I am so clumsy, unorganized, asocial, ugly..."

"Have you heard what you just said? You work from five in the morning until midnight and you never have a holiday or free Saturday or Sunday. Don't you think that you have too much work?"

"Well, it is possible. I haven't thought about it."

"OK, now that you see the reason for your fatigue, let's take a look at the criticism that you face. Who says that you are ugly, clumsy, asocial? Your husband?"

"No," I lied. "But I often hear it in my office."

"Think about your friends. Name me one who looks better, is more clever and hard-working than you."

I immediately wanted to say Sonja, but I stopped because both Tina and the photographer said only a couple of days ago that I looked much better and that they preferred my style of dressing. So, I remained silent.

"Why do you think that you are asocial?"

"All my friends in our department say so. Librarians like to socialize and discuss things during the coffee break. And they take trips together almost every weekend."

"Don't you think that this is too much?"

"Yes, I do. But my friends say that this is normal and that I should join them."

"I don't think so. In our health service, there are no such parties and we certainly don't socialize after office hours. I think that your colleagues exaggerate with parties and trips. What do you intend to do with your husband? He doesn't help you at all, does he?"

"He works from the morning until the evening. But it is even more tiring if he is at home. In such cases, I must be even more careful that everything is in order, that I cook something according to his taste and that I appear as a happy young woman. He has an unpleasant habit of watching me all the time and commenting on what I do wrong. Sometimes it seems that I can't hold a spoon the way he thinks I should."

"When you come home today, repeat to him our conversation and tell him my opinion: that such a tempo will ruin you in some months. If he loves you, he will see that this cannot go on and he will do something to help you."

When I came home, I really told Tone about my conversation with the doctor. Before I finished, I started to cry again. He was silent and just nodded that I was obviously really too tired. He assured me that he would not complain anymore and made a plan that we would start going for short holidays each weekend. On the next day, he even brought me flowers which had never happened before. He probably also needed a lot of energy to stop himself from criticizing me.

That month, I passed my last exam at the School of Law and finished my studies. I had been aware for quite some time that I did not like law and that I had no wish to make a career in that area. I long regretted the years that I wasted with studying law. But later I realized that I'd still learned a lot. One cannot simply take a couple of sentences from a legal rule and explain them without considering other laws and one needs to read a law at least three times to understand it. I also learned that laws never offer a solution. Now I am aware that my law studies helped me understand legal cases and developed my skill in writing.

My illness ceased in about a week. I remained at home, took pills, and my spirits rose. I became calmer and slept well. After a week I felt strong enough to go to the office. Tina was, of course, very interested in my illness and I shortly mentioned that it was depression. But she had no intention of sympathizing with depressed patients. She said that such people were too egocentric and too focused on themselves. I should go to a birthday party with her, behave normally and everything would be all right. I apologized that I had a lot to do. I did not yet feel strong enough to answer questions about my illness.

The photographer, whose birthday it was, just smiled and said that I didn't need to go to the party if I didn't feel like it. He would bring some cake to my office so that I would gain some kilos and not look like a skeleton. Tina grumbled that such sulking did not deserve cake, but he wouldn't listen. The next day, Tina remorsefully apologized that she did not mean any harm. Her apology came at the right time because I felt that she'd embarked on a hostile campaign against me.

However, I could forget her merciless opinion because I remembered that we always openly and clearly told each other everything, even the most unpleasant things. Our friends sometimes thought that we quarreled and that we would never be on speaking terms again. But we just turned around and were friends once more.

44
Surprise

Our boss often claimed that ordering new books and journals was one of the most important, difficult and responsible tasks. The titles were chosen by Sonja and by our boss. Ana checked if we already had any of the books that we intended to order, so the library would not buy duplicates. The selection usually lasted until the last moment and then Mrs. Kos asked me to quickly type all the orders on small slips. This work was not creative, and it was actually not my task, because I was supposed to acquire books by exchange with foreign libraries. My boss asked me to do it because I was the fastest typist and never got nervous because of time pressure. Then Mrs. Kos took the orders to the director Marton and his assistant, Mrs. Vidmar, and the three of them made the final decisions. When participating in this process, I always felt that each of us contributed to the best possible purchase of foreign literature. But my boss did not share my feelings. She was insulted if the director and his assistant suggested that one or another book should not be bought. After such events, Mrs. Kos came to the office with a cigarette in her hand and hissed that Sonja did not make the right selection and that Ana and I did not notice that some books were not worth buying. Sonja answered that she found her selection reasonable, while I had absolutely no chance to evaluate whether the selection was good or not. I had to type so quickly that there was no time to think about the titles of books.

The library director, Marton, and our boss hated each other. The director was often annoyed that her employees drank coffee and celebrated birthdays all the time, that she was always late in the morning, and that she wouldn't fire two employees who did not work on anything at all. In response to the director's complaints, she tried to put things in order, but she was not very successful. People continued with their parties, some of them were still late in the morning and she could certainly not fire the employees who didn't have enough work. In those times, it was impossible to fire people whose contracts categorized them as "permanently employed." I did not belong to any of these groups, so I was not interested in what was going on. I sometimes thought that the boss was right, but not always. And I was sure that conflicts could be solved peacefully. Tina and almost all the others were convinced that a department manager should not behave in such a way.

However, I also had small troubles with Mrs. Kos. She sometimes told me what to do by writing instructions on small pieces of paper and leaving them on my desk. I fulfilled her orders, and after a few days or weeks, she would rush to my office and complain that I did not do what she had requested. I started to save her messages, so when she came with a complaint that I did not perform her order, I just found the paper with her message and showed her what she'd required.

Then she stopped nagging, although she often said: "Why don't you think with your own head? You have a university education and it is your duty to think about problems and not just follow my words."

If there was time, I explained to her why I did what I did, but she usually rushed out of my office before I managed to open my mouth. I was at first perplexed because of this strange behavior but then she started to get on my nerves. I was not often a target of her wrath, she more frequently had fights with Tina, Sonja, Ana and others. Tina and our boss became bitter enemies. Mrs. Kos did not show anymore understanding for Tina's relationship with the famous writer, and she criticized her if she took sick leave because her son was ill.

If Tina was absent, the boss maliciously said: "How can she have an affair with that old fool who has at least three mistresses and a wife? Instead of losing her time with a guy who actually hates all women, she should choose someone else and marry him."

She also had a lot of remarks against Sonja: "She has no idea about literature and her dresses show that she wants to attract as many men as possible. I am ashamed that she works in our department. "

Sonja liked to dress extravagantly, but, in my opinion, her dresses were always interesting and suited her. Our boss was also most dissatisfied with Ana because she was late in the morning and not at all interested in her appearance.

Eventually, all the employees in our department felt that we had a common enemy and that we should resist. We were now even more aware of what a good person our previous boss had been and how evil the remarks of the present one were. We forgot that it was her duty to provide for order and discipline in the department.

One time, our boss had a very unfortunate day and criticized everybody whom she saw. In one of the offices, she said that they should stop drinking coffee and start working. When she entered Ana's room, she sniffed and mentioned that something smelled and looked directly at Ana. Then she shouted at Sonja, because she did not know what to do with a book that she'd put on her table. At last she came to Tina's and my office. She sniffed the air but did not say anything. Tina laughed and asked if we smelled, but Mrs. Kos just frowned and said that she would not have laughed if she had known that her famous lover had a new mistress. Tina was in a rather low mood because he had not called for quite some time. She grew pale and, for the first time, I saw that she remained without words.

Then Mrs. Kos looked at the photographer: "Don't you have any work to do? Don't you think that Iris will have an even worse reputation because you stay in this office all the time?"

He blushed but did not move and even laughed: "If her husband hears that she has a serious admirer, he might pay more attention to her."

"Iris, you should be wise and tell him to keep away from you."

On the next day, the boss had a day off, so we had coffee without her. We were all of the same opinion that she should be taught how to behave. Tina and Sonja suggested that we should send a complaint to Director Marton, who should teach her how to manage the department. I don't know if the complaint was written or oral, but it reached the director and he organized a meeting of the whole acquisitions department. I suspected that he would have liked to make Sonja our new boss. However, Mrs. Kos was a friend of the director's assistant, Mrs. Vidmar, who thought that it was we who should change, not our boss. The meeting did not bring any results and our boss openly mocked the fact that our revolution had not been successful.

Tina and Sonja did not yield and requested a new meeting with the director. This time he invited just his assistant, our boss, Sonja, Ana, and me. Our boss and the director's assistant claimed that it was us three who organized the rebellion, while the others just followed us. Mrs. Kos tried to do everything so that the department would function well, while we ruined all her efforts. I expected such arguments, so I brought copies of some papers written by my boss which contained her orders as to what I should do and often also her opinions about one or another employee, even the director. When our boss claimed that she was a good manager who tried to produce a good atmosphere in the department, I simply put some of those papers on the desk. The first one contained a rather evil remark that the director made a fool of himself during his last visit abroad and that he'd ruined the reputation of our library.

Up to then, the director had not supported anybody and had just listened. As soon as he read the papers, he asked our boss what she meant. She tried to convince him that he misunderstood her message, but the paper clearly showed that she spread nasty things about him, too. The director stopped the meeting and ordered our boss to stay with him.

When Mrs. Kos returned, she did not mock us anymore, but went to the doctor's and stayed on sick leave. I was not happy that I'd showed the papers and often regretted that we made such a row, but we had to give evidence about her methods of work. All librarians spoke about it and guessed what would happen. The director finally made a wise decision. Mrs. Kos remained the manager of the acquisitions department, because his assistant convinced him that she knew a lot about acquisitions (and she really did). As it was obvious that the department would not function if there were further fights, he decided that Sonja would become manager of the information department, and I would become a researcher in the research department. I still have no idea how the director found out that we were dying to get those jobs, but both Sonja and I got exactly what we wished. Mrs. Kos was happy that she got rid of us. All the others were pleased because they wanted to stay in the acquisitions department and our boss made fewer wicked remarks.

45
New Workplace

The research department consisted of only four researchers and would need at least four more people. The most important person in the department was not my new boss Mimi, but an old lady, Mrs. Koler, who had the salary of a researcher, even though she had no university education. During the Second World War, she was in the Partisan army and then she'd entered the Communist Party. She worked in the library for thirty or more years, knew everything about it, was very clever and could motivate people to work in a team. Margareta and Marko joined the department just a year ago. Margareta was about ten years older than I was and she'd previously worked with the library director, Marton. Marko was one of Marton's favorite students.

My new boss, Mimi, accepted me in a friendly way, and I felt just like I had on my first day in the library. She suggested that I should start with job descriptions for all employees in the department and do my best to raise our salaries.

"This is quite frankly my job," she said, "but I am offering you the opportunity to show your knowledge of law and win our hearts."

I enthusiastically started with my first task. It was not pleasant work. I first had to gather accurate job descriptions of all employees in the department. Then it was necessary to mathematically evaluate all the tasks of each job. The boss's work should be evaluated with the highest number of points and thus enable the highest salary; Mrs. Koler should not get much less. Margareta, Marko and I should get approximately the same number of points, but lower than those of Mimi and Mrs. Koler. However, all the calculations would be of no benefit if the Workers' Council did not confirm the job descriptions and the calculations. The Workers' Council consisted mainly of representatives from each department who were usually not department managers. They confirmed the most important decisions for the library. Workers' Councils could oppose the director, but that did not happen very often.

The easiest part of my first task was the calculations. I immediately noticed that the points defining the level of salary could be construed exactly as one wanted to. I had to do it just because many people thought that mathematics meant an objectively determined level of salaries.

All department employees were pleased with the points with which I evaluated their positions. But the problem was actually raising their salaries. The politically faultless Mrs. Koler said that she would discuss the matter at the first meeting of the library's Communist Party. Each public institution in Yugoslavia had its Communist Party that contributed its opinion to important decisions.

I asked Margareta, who was a close acquaintance of the director, to present the new job descriptions to him and try to get his support. But things still depended upon the Workers' Council and its twelve members. I saw no other possibility than addressing each of them personally and trying to convince them that they should vote to increase our salaries.

Marko laughed: "You are going to start a campaign like American presidents."

"Well, if American presidents are not ashamed to fight for their position, why should I be? Besides, I will fight for the salaries of the whole department, not just for mine."

Everybody said that I was right, so I really spoke with all members of the Workers' Council, asked them to vote for us and promised that we would support them, too, when they would be in a similar position. Mimi presented the matter to the Workers' Council and she was just the right person to do it: she kindly smiled to everybody and she did not get angry if somebody argued that her department could not show proper results.

"Of course," she said, "we could not do much, because there were only three of us up to now. But now I have Marko and Iris and you will see that we will soon be able to show important results."

Our matter was confirmed by all members and we got higher salaries.

Mimi started to give me all the tasks connected with the law and organization of libraries. She let me work on important matters and always took me with her when she visited one or another of the sixty public libraries in Slovenia. She praised me for working quickly and successfully, and it seemed that Mrs. Koler was of the same opinion.

I got on quite well with Margareta, although I had the feeling that she sought my alliance mainly because Mimi and Mrs. Koler did not appreciate her. Margareta actually never said that I was a good worker— she much more appreciated Marko. She was convinced that he was a genius, intelligent and hardworking and would one day achieve the top place in the library. She sometimes exaggerated so much that women smiled, while Marko's face became red and he left the room.

In about a year, I was acquainted with all the Slovenian public libraries and started to learn how to speak with the municipality men who determined the budget for libraries. My boss and Mrs. Koler were much better than I at negotiating, but they did not criticize my weak negotiation skills.

I enjoyed my work and would happily work on larger research projects, which Marko encouraged. He often mentioned that he dreamt about graduating in a librarianship program in England. I would've liked to go and study in England as well, and sometimes I wondered if it were possible to take Tone and my two daughters with me. Unfortunately, we didn't have the money to pay for the flight, tuition fees and accomodations.

Our boss encouraged us and often suggested that the library should pay for our MA studies, either at a university in England or in Slovenia. When I looked into which Slovenian university program I could continue my MA studies in, I found only one possibility: management. Other university programs demanded that students finish university studies exclusively in their scientific field. Management was offered as a rather new program by a recently established school with the nickname "the Slovenian Sorbonne." The name did not mean that this school was the Slovenian version of the oldest and greatest university, but just the opposite, it was meant ironically. The expression was probably invented by professors of the already existing schools that did not like the competition.

Marko knew the nickname, the Slovenian Sorbonne and laughed, but our boss quickly stopped him: "Well, Marko, people speak evil things about each school. They say that your school produces future politicians and that it is not important if you know anything, but just that you are in the Communist Party."

Marton became president of the Association of Yugoslav National Libraries and needed an executive secretary. He noticed that I did not find it difficult to travel and speak with unknown people, so he suggested that I take over the task. He expected that I would resist because it meant a lot of additional work and no higher salary. So, he invited me to his office and presented to me just how important the work was. I accepted with great pleasure because I wanted to make a career and knew that this was the right way to achieve it. He was quite amazed when I thanked him and promised to do my best. It must have been the first time in his life that somebody thanked him for additional work. All my colleagues mocked at me: "They use you for every dog's funeral."

I did not let my coworkers' jeering spoil my spirits. Instead, I enthusiastically spoke about my work and thus got the bad reputation of a career woman. Nowadays this is fine, but in the 80s and especially among librarians, ambitious women were not appreciated. Working for the Association of Yugoslav National Libraries was actually very simple. We had a meeting every two months, I prepared all the necessary documents, organized a meeting in Ljubljana, and participated in meetings in other Yugoslav republics. All they discussed was so strategic and general that the final conclusions could be signed by anyone. I often wrote the minutes in advance because it was so predicatable.

The library director, Marton, became rather friendly with me, but his assistant, Mrs. Vidmar, clearly showed that she could not forget my impudent behavior towards my previous boss (and her friend), Mrs. Kos. Whenever she could, Mrs. Vidmar found a mistake in my work and I usually had to quietly swallow her remarks if I wanted to advance. Once we had to travel to Belgrade alone because the director fell ill at the last moment. I saw that she was nervous because she was to lead an international meeting, so I explained the agenda to her, the possible discussions, the characters of other national library directors and directly said that everybody spoke only about principles. They never touched real problems. She successfully led the meeting and got applause at the end. When we drove towards the airport, she relaxed, thanked me and invited me to lunch. I thought that we would finally develop better relations, but I was mistaken. Some people never forget and never forgive.

When I had to go to a meeting alone, I did not worry and came in on time and in a good mood to the library in Zagreb. I was the only woman and all the gentlemen were older than me. The representative of Serbia came half an hour late, but nobody cared about his delay. When he arrived, they just kindly asked if he'd gone for a drink before the meeting. He did not answer, but looked around: "Be ashamed, you smoke like gypsies. One can hardly see that there is a beautiful young lady present."

He raised a chair above his head and brought it close to mine. Then he pushed away the chair of his Croatian colleague, looked into my eyes and introduced himself. We all knew his cosmopolitan nature and Serbian charm, so I just smiled. He belonged to a culture that always tried to pay attention to women. After the meeting, he tried to convince me that I should go to dinner with them and sit beside him. But I kindly refused, saying that I had to go home and take care of my children. He was not insulted—after all, he did what a Serbian man was supposed to do.

46
School and Religious Lessons

My two girls grew, and Lili was about to start elementary school. They were both born in the spring, so I did not know whether I should send them to school when they were six or seven years old.

I knew that children in England, the United States and elsewhere started elementary school when they were five or six, but the majority of Slovenians were against it: "What, you intend to steal from them one year of carefree childhood?"

I thought for almost a year about what to do. Lili was very clever and independent, she could draw, write some letters and even tried to cook. I did not believe in the cliché about a carefree childhood and thought that she would have been bored if she had to spend another year in daycare.

So, I enrolled her in school. Although Tone often continued with his insulting behavior, there were moments when we were of the same opinion. He agreed that Lili should be enrolled in the elementary school.

I didn't want to set Lili very strong limits or explain to her that this was a turning point in her life, nor did I want to say that she should be serious and learn all day long. On the first day, she came home enthusiastic, told me that they ate sweets and drew. On the second day, I received a phone call from her teacher. She said that Lili had left in the middle of the school lessons. I called Tone, who quickly picked me up and we both tried to find out what had happened. She was not at home, so we drove through the whole village, but could not find her.

"What if she was kidnapped?" Tone smiled that she was probably bored of her lessons and went to some other, more interesting place. I sat pale with horror and vomited.

"My God, why did I send her to school a year early? Why didn't I let her stay in daycare for one more year?"

Tone went back to his company while I continued walking through the village. I soon found her speaking with a dog in front of a village house and she was in good mood. It took a load off my mind and I decided not to show anger or fear but to try to convince the child that she could not come home whenever she wanted to.

"Hello, Lili, why are you here, why did you leave school?"

"I thought that it was enough for today. It is such a beautiful day, so I went a bit around the village. In the afternoon, I will go to the woods and take our puppy with me."

It was actually a Labrador that my brother had received as a present from his girlfriend. He did not have much time to walk him, so he was happy if Lili took him to the forest.

"Yes, the day is beautiful, but you are now in school and your teacher expects that you will be there every morning. You should not leave before she tells you that you can go. No sooner."

"Why not?"

"Because you must learn how to write, draw and read. Besides, the teacher and I are worried if we do not know where you are."

"I already know everything she speaks about. Today she did not tell me anything new, so I didn't miss anything. And you know that I can come home alone, so you don't have to worry."

The explanation was clear and logical, but children were not allowed to do whatever they wanted to. I used another half an hour to explain to her the basics of school discipline and order. She nodded that she understood, but it did not seem that she would do as we expected.

"Do you have any homework?"

"What's homework?"

"Didn't your teacher say that you should write or draw something at home?"

"No. But I can draw something for her. Perhaps she will like it."

On the next day, she came home in the afternoon, but she took quite a lot of time to get there. After a week, she did not arrive at her usual time, so I had to search for her again. This time I wasn't afraid, and I soon found her.

"Where were you? Why did it take you so long to come back?"

"In the school. Then I went to my schoolmate's. She showed me small kittens and we played with them. It was great. And her parents even gave me lunch."

"Next time you should just go and take a look, stay five minutes and then come home."

I saw that she had no idea what five minutes meant nor why she should come home after school. Luckily, she did not have much homework and she did not have to study. Education in elementary school was obviously a bit less demanding than it had been for me, twenty years ago.

Some weeks later, Lili showed me a small notebook in which the teacher wrote something for me. I opened it and it said: "Dear Mrs. Novak, because you missed the parents' meeting, I would like you to come to an individual hour with me."

"When was the parents' meeting?"

"What's that?"

"I should have gone to the meeting of all the parents, but I didn't know that it took place. Didn't you get any notice?"

"Do you mean that small piece of paper on which I drew a flower? I can give it to you, if you like. I put it in my cabinet."

"Well, if I missed one parent's meeting it should not be a catastrophe," I thought. "Children of the first class cannot have learned much in two months."

Lili's teacher had a rather serious face when I met her and immediately made a rhetorical and accusing question about why I enrolled my child in school when she was only six years old. It was obvious that the little girl took school and life as a game and that she did not understand what school was. She once left school earlier than allowed, she sometimes brought her homework and sometimes not.

"Yesterday she decorated her homework with two pages of flowers and animals, although I told her not to. She also chatters during the lessons and does not want to eat meat."

This was my first hour with the teacher and it started in quite a different way than I'd expected. I thought that the teacher would tell me what a wonderful and gifted child I had and now she complained that I did not bring her up in the right way. She made me angry, but I was aware that it could be harmful for Lili if I gave rude answers.

"Dear Mrs. Novak, I take teaching seriously. We have a curriculum and I must stick to it if I want to achieve results. If you made the mistake of enrolling such a young child, you must now work with her at home. Will you be able to help her? What education do you have?"

I breathed quickly and said to myself that I should answer her politely, but also explain to her that she is a teacher of young children and not a judge:

"I have a university education. I am proficient in English and German, so I will be able to help my daughter. I know that she left school early, but I am sure that she will quickly learn that she should stay in school until noon. In my opinion, it is necessary to have some patience with young children."

When she learned that my education was higher than hers, she became a bit less arrogant but mentioned that the Ministry of Education required results from teachers.

"During the introductory meeting, you said that children only played in the first year and that there was no assessment."

"Well—the assessment at the end of the first schoolyear is really only descriptive, but how shall I produce it if I did not assess them through the year?"

"I see. You tell parents one story and, in reality, work in another way. Okay, I will take care that my daughter does her homework in the future. But it is not just my daughter who chatters. Don't all the children?"

"Yes, but this disturbs my teaching. Children have to respect order."

"Don't you think that this is difficult after only two months of school? They will slowly get used to order, but if you continue like this, they will start hating both you and the school."

"I still think that you made a mistake by enrolling your daughter when she is only six. If you left her home for one more year, she would be an exceptional pupil and you would not have any work with her."

"Perhaps. However, the law allows the enrollment of six-year-old children and the school faculty found that my daughter was mature enough to start going to school. I decided on enrollment after long and serious consideration. As I told you, I will help her to reach your expectations, but please relax the military regime with which you bring up children."

"How dare you speak with me like that?"

"Dear lady, this is my child and we have just said that I have an appropriate education with which to discuss this matter. I do dare to speak and if you don't relax your discipline and order, I will go and discuss things with the headmaster. I will not allow you to destroy her will to learn, so I am asking you once again to be more patient and tolerant. I also do not allow you to force her to eat meat if she does not want it."

"Don't you understand that other children will start refusing meat, just like your daughter?"

"I think that you have no right to force children to eat what they do not want. Besides, this has no connection with teaching."

"I just want to make your daughter a successful pupil. I hope you do not resent if I am frank."

"I, too, hope that you will not feel offended. You must understand that my child is the most important person to me and I will not let anybody suppress her."

"Please come again next month and we shall see how she develops."

"I certainly will. And if things do not become different, I will come even sooner, take her out and enroll her in another school that has a better reputation than this one."

When I said goodbye, the teacher seemed amazed and a bit scared. She was probably used to more remorseful parents who felt guilty. Although I firmly said that I would enroll my child in another school if necessary, I was aware that this would be difficult. Lili was happy among her new schoolmates and already found many friends.

My mum was not quite sure that my behavior was appropriate, but she had no better ideas. My mother-in-law said that it would be best to take Lili out of school and include her in the first grade the next year.

"What do you mean? Shall I tell Lili that she is not capable of first grade and completely destroy her self-confidence?"

I decided that I would check Lili's homework and often tell her how to consider order and discipline. She did not like that she had to show me her homework every day and that I sometimes tore a page from her notebook and demanded that she write it again. When Lili's schoolmate, Meta, came to us, I openly admired her writing and drawings. I hoped that Lili would develop some sense of competition and thus achieve what her teacher wanted.

I talked about my experience with the teacher with my friends in the library. I expected compassion and understanding but all the women, especially Tina, attacked me: "What else did you expect? Everybody knows that it is much better for children if they go to school when they are seven. You are a career woman and you transfer your ambitions to your children."

When I heard that sentence for the fifth time, I burst into tears. One of my colleagues, who was also supposed to be a "career woman" said: "Stop it. You have never been in her skin, your children never showed such knowledge as hers, and you did not need to make a decision.

I am still grateful to her for these words. Besides Tone, she was the only one who understood that such decisions were difficult.

After two months, the situation was very different. Lili became a conscientious, good pupil and at the end of the year the teacher regretfully said that she did not mean to hurt me. My colleagues and my mother-in-law never admitted that I was right. They didn't want to listen, but persistently repeated that children should have a carefree childhood. I still think that a carefree childhood and school are compatible and that this depends on teachers and parents.

When Lili was in the first grade, she also started going to religious lessons and prepared for First Communion. My family members never discussed if children would have a religious education because they found it natural. But I asked myself if it was necessary that such young children learn about religion and accepted sacraments. The answer was clear: of course, it was reasonable. If children started learning math, art, science and so on when they were seven, it also made sense that they started learning about religion. I did not believe that a religious education might mean a reduction of their freedom to choose a religion.

Besides, if I had not sent my children to religious lessons, I would have had to teach them religion myself. If that were the case, I would have deprived them of numerous pleasant events that the Church offered as a part of education: celebrations when children accepted sacraments, Christmas, Easter, and so on. I thought on it, but it was clear to me that children needed the religious education provided by the right institution and not by the lay instructions of a mum. I remembered only too well how I tried to teach Lili German and English: I taught her for a couple of weeks, but then I ran out of time and our lessons finished. It would be similar with religion.

The priest, who obviously counted and remembered all those who participated in the Mass, said to me: "Dear lady, if you intend to give your child religious education, please bear in mind that you have to be a model. It is not just your daughter who should come to Mass every Sunday, but also you and your family."

I did my best to attend Mass and I took both girls with me. I did not like those Masses. Outside the church, the priest spoke with a normal, matter-of-fact voice but when he started the Mass, he became most dramatic and emotional. If he expressed special enthusiasm over Jesus or his mother, his voice grew quite unnatural. His sermons were not systematically constructed, his statements lacked evidence, and his judgements were, in my opinion, from the previous century. However, the worst was his singing because he was absolutely tone deaf.

He was better when he taught children because he liked to explain the bible stories and was not too strict when they chattered. I usually sat outside the classroom and waited for Lili, so I heard everything he said.

When my neighbors saw that I drove Lili to her religious lessons and to school, they often teased me, asking if I thought that gypsies might steal her. I stubbornly answered that the street was dangerous for children because cars drove 80 or 100 kilometers per hour and there was no crosswalk for the school or for the church. I soon got a bad reputation that I spoiled my children.

It would have been much more comfortable to sit at home, but I would worry all the time. And if something happened, I would be horribly unhappy while my neighbors would shrug their shoulders and say that it was destiny. I wrote to the municipal authorities several times, explained the problem and asked for crosswalks, but the clerk responsible for traffic just irritably answered that children should get used to the traffic.

Sometimes I had no time to drive Lili, so she had to stay at home, and I wrote an apology about why she was absent.

Lili once said that the priest raised his eyebrows and smiled: "Can't you walk? It is not so far."

Lili beseeched me to let her walk around alone, but I remained as solid as a rock.

Teasing continued until a car hit my neighbor's daughter when she went to her religious class. The poor little soul lived just an hour after the accident and then died. I did not know whom to pity more, the poor girl or her parents. From then on, people stopped reproaching me that I spoiled my children. Other parents started to drive their kids to school and to religious classes. It seemed that even the priest finally recognized that I could estimate what was dangerous and that neither my closest relatives nor representatives of the Holy Church could change my opinion.

When First Communion approached, the priest reminded parents that we should be a model and go to Confession and Communion ourselves, too. It seemed that he looked straight at me. He was right, I thought reluctantly. Who knew if Tone would be prepared to go to

Confession with other parents and their children? Tone took the whole event in a sporting and cooperative way and did not protest at all. He just asked that I teach him the confessional forms and prayers again. Confession was in the afternoon and I was so tired that I fell asleep after lunch. My neighbor rang at the door: "Aren't you going to Confession? The priest told me to remind you that all the family should come."

"Didn't he say that the Confession would be after four? Has he finished with everybody?"

"No, but hurry up, otherwise he will continue panicking."

I put on my coat and off we went. The priest asked why we were so late, and I admitted that I fell asleep. He was perplexed about how somebody could sleep in the middle of the day as he said he could hardly sleep three hours per night, but then he must have guessed the secret of my tiredness, and his face changed. He smiled and suggested that I not kneel but sit during the Confession. I expected that he would scold because of my absence from the church, but he was surprisingly tolerant and kind. He did not let me think long about my sins but just asked if I hated anybody. If I really thought about hatred, I could have told him that I was often angry at my mother-in-law, my previous boss and many other people. But I didn't even remember it and the priest did not go into details. He quickly gave me absolution and sent me out.

47

The Third Child or My Career

I got pregnant again when I was in the middle of my time in the Association of Yugoslav National Libraries. I was aware that it might be difficult to appoint somebody who could replace me and introduce him or her to the work. I was acquainted with everything and everyone, while my replacement would have to start from the beginning. I also remembered how angry my director in the business firm had been when I was pregnant and thought that this would happen again at the library. My first boss in the library and the previous library director had not been bothered when I'd expected my second child, but they were exceptional people. Even if Marton and his assistant, Mrs. Vidmar, would not find my pregnancy annoying, there was still a possibility that my career, that I'd hardly begun, would stop. I was supposed to pass the exam to become a library adviser and had to prepare and defend a rather long and demanding research topic that would include economic, legal and organizational aspects of the libraries. If I went for maternity leave, it would be almost a year before I could start visiting libraries again. And the new baby might eliminate the dreams that Marko and I had discussed during the coffee break: to enroll in a master's program. I already dismissed the possibility of studying in England, but I still hoped to enroll in a Slovenian university.

Although I was aware of all the possible consequences of the pregnancy for my career, I was happy to expect another baby. I looked forward to going through the early stages of motherhood once again because for me, there is no bigger miracle than carrying and giving birth to a new human being. I looked forward to breastfeeding once again, to watching the baby smile for the first time and to accompanying the child to school. No, all the careers of the world were quite incomparable to having a baby.

When I told Tone, he seemed happy, although he did not expect the third child. He did not say that he would help me, and I quite frankly did not expect it. I reconciled myself to the fact that he was a good worker, that he cared about technical things in the house and that I could discuss a lot of things with him. One might ask if this was love. It was, although it changed.

All the family members were happy that we would get another child. My two girls looked forward to the baby and they wanted a sister. Lili was seven and Vali was four years old at the time. Even my mother-in-law praised me, although it was implied that I still did not quite deserve to be the wife of her golden son.

This pregnancy was different from the previous two. I was not so sick, so I did not need to take sick leave. I also decided that I would hide it as long as possible, although I knew that hiding my pregnancy could not last long. I was in a predominantly female organization and women would soon notice that I'd stopped drinking coffee and gained weight. I opted for another style of dressing to hide my waist.

Neither Tina nor the photographer was pleased with it: "Well, this dress is nice, but the previous ones were better. Where do you have that blue one that is tight and has a belt?"

"I am fed up with that old style and I need some changes."

When all my dresses were really too tight, and I had quite a belly, I decided to announce the truth.

When the director and I made a work plan for the Association of Yugoslav Libraries for the next year, I looked down and sighed that I would not be able to participate next year.

"Why not? You work so well. Everybody knows you and relies upon you and you want to stop? Look, I am aware that you are not paid for this work, but just think that you will be able to make a career in Yugoslavia and not just in the Slovenian arena. Perhaps you will be able to continue studies in England? Don't you find it rewarding?"

"Of course, and I like the work. But I am pregnant. I will be on maternity leave next year. Excuse me, I know that you relied on me, but it just happened."

He got up, gasped and said: "Oh, that's good news. Congratulations, that will be your third child, won't it? Nice, nice."

When his assistant entered the room, he told her with a pleasant smile that the library would get a new baby. She, too, smiled and congratulated me.

"Well, what shall we do now? Shall I immediately appoint somebody who will replace you or would you continue to work in the

Association, eventhough it means traveling?"

"I can still work for at least four more months. I never have trouble in the last months of pregnancy."

"In the coming months we will have to fly to Belgrade several times."

"Flights are easier and more comfortable than trains. No problem."

They began to feel at ease, and I was pleased, as well. Who would have thought that two people, with whom I had not always been on good terms, would accept my pregnancy with such understanding?

Now it was time to tell the news to my colleagues. I did not expect any negative thoughts, but rather joy. In those days, many parents had just one child, so a woman who had three was thought to be a rather hardworking person. I came back to my office when my boss was celebrating her birthday.

When I took a piece of cake, one of the women whispered: "Haven't you gained some weight, Iris?"

"Yes, and I will gain even more."

"What?"

They realized that I expected a baby and they clearly showed their pleasure and enthusiasm. Everybody congratulated me, asked when the baby would come and said that I was brave because I dared to have three children in such bad times. Librarians always had a habit of complaining about alleged "bad times".

Neither my boss nor Mrs. Koler showed any anger or grumpiness because they had children, too. Margareta remarked that the library director might not be pleased, but everybody said that the library would not collapse because of one child.

I accompanied the director to Belgrade until the ninth month. Sometimes I was very tired because the meetings lasted until four or six in the afternoon. Once I could hardly keep upright and there was no free seat at the airport. Marton surprised me by somehow finding a free seat for me. As I sat down, one of the stewardesses gestured that the director should come to her.

He spoke with her for some time and when he came back, he said: "I haven't had such an interrogation in my life. The woman wanted to know the date of delivery and I had to assure her that you were not going to deliver in the plane. Now you must stay at home."

In the last month, I started to prepare things for the new baby. I already had a lot of clothes and linens, so I mostly just had to wash, iron or mend these items. I often sat with Lili, Vali and with children from my neighborhood and we sewed.

My mum liked to observe us and once she asked, gesturing to some articles for a baby girl: "Why are you putting these things aside?"

"Because they are for girls."

"What makes you think that you won't need them?"

"I think it is going to be a boy."

"You have a good imagination. You and Tone probably want a boy, now that you have two girls."

I wished that it would be a boy, especially because I knew that also Tone wanted a boy, although he did not say anything. But I actually expected a boy because this pregnancy was different. I was not as sick, and the child was much stronger than the first two. It kicked so often and so strongly that everybody could notice it.

In the end, I really did get a boy. He was so heavy and big that we could hardly believe it. He had a very strong voice and was always hungry. When Tone visited me, he smiled as I had never seen him smile before, and I asked if he was so happy because it was a boy.

"No, of course not. If a man gets a child, he is happy."

"But this is your third child and you did not show any special happiness when Vali was born."

"Perhaps I didn't know how to show it," he answered.

I came home four days after delivery and Tone immediately suggested that we should prepare a celebration for our relatives on the next Sunday. Was he really not aware that a woman could not prepare a party in the first week after she'd borne a child? But he was so happy that he simply had to show him to all the members of his family. He said that it was not necessary to prepare anything special, but we could make coffee and he would bring some biscuits.

Of course, I did not consent to such a disgrace. I organized a big party where we presented each of our babies to the family: with hors d'oeuvres, soup, several main dishes, salads and desserts. I'd prepared plans for a festive lunch before I'd gone to the hospital, so I only had to buy the ingredients and cook them. I started to cook on the Friday before and barely managed to prepare everything by Sunday afternoon. Luckily the baby slept all the time, except when he ate. Lili and Vali tried to help where they could.

Tone was of no help when I made festive dinners. He worked until the last moment, took a shower, and then came to the sitting room and asked what the guests would like to drink. We usually only had water, some juice and wine.

But sometimes a guest answered that they would like beer or schnapps and Tone would ask me: "Beer, Iris, where do we have beer?"

And I had to say that we didn't have any.

I also got mad when he started to take a look at the glasses to see if they were clean. For God's sake, before the guests arrived, I'd washed and wiped all the dishes and yet he would check to see if they were spotless! And he did it in front of all the guests. His behavior during the parties was strange. Instead of sitting and chatting, he ran around to find the glasses, offered coffee at the beginning of lunch instead of after, brought the wrong glasses and God knows what else.

Tone's father did not behave any better. He usually first went to my mum and my aunt, evaluated whether the pigs were fat enough and advised them how they should farm. My mum found it annoying because she was from a farm, while my father-in-law cultivated only some vegetables in his small garden.

However, this time he came to us, and I noticed that he had tears in his eyes. Then he stammered: "Congratulations, Tone, you have a son!" He was also most pleased with the name that we had chosen for the baby, Martin. He congratulated me, opened his wallet and gave me quite a lot of money.

Tone's cousin, his wife and their two daughters admired my boy who slept in his basket. The man said to his wife: "Just look what a good wife and mother Iris is. She has a responsible job but was still ready to have one more child and now they have a boy!" She was not pleased with this sentence and snarled that he could go and deliver one himself.

Now that we had the third baby, Tone often came home earlier in the afternoon and liked to play with him. The little boy got used to his father taking him into his arms immediately upon coming home, so he always raised his hands towards him. It was a beautiful year in which I felt that we were a family and that we loved each other. We did not go for trips to the mountains or to the coast as often as before. But I preferred that we stayed at home. Our house became almost too small, but we didn't mind.

After six months, I had to start working again. Lili was in school and Vali and Martin went to daycare. Martin did not cry when I brought him to the nursery, although he was so small. He was curious, and his surroundings interested him. In the first year, he often caught a cold or some other virus, but nothing serious.

48
Master's Degree

My colleagues could hardly wait for me to come back and start working. The library director, Marton, had a lot of plans and Marko was happy that he could discuss the possibilities of master's studies again. I did not intend to make definite plans immediately, but Marko firmly decided that we should raise our education and encouraged me to join him. I knew that he was right: among Slovenian librarians, there were only few doctors and masters and there were no university programs that would educate librarians. I was aware that further studies would help me to raise my knowledge, develop my personality and perhaps even achieve a leading position. My friends often asked if my work and family life were insufficiently interesting and if that forced me to continue studying. I don't think so. My work and my family were interesting enough and I loved them. But I always craved new knowledge and I hope that I will feel like that until the end of my life. I have always been aware that my never-ending desire to learn something new was a blessing and that it was my duty to try to reach for new challenges.

I enrolled in management studies as a part-time student at the University of Maribor. This was not as impressive as an MA in England and I had no previous knowledge about management and organization, but there were no other options.

Our lectures were short, and the teachers only gave us an outline of what we should learn. But I was still grateful because I remembered that the School of Law did not provide any lectures for part-time students.

On the first day of my management studies, I came to a classroom with about 60 adult students, among whom there were only three women. One of the teachers said that perhaps 10 of us would finish the studies and that we were too old to study. I was only thirty-five, but many others were forty or fifty years old and I found the teacher's statement to be very insulting. They knew that we were adult part-time students and they earned quite a lot of additional money for teaching us, but they still dared to mock us.

At the School of Management, women were always at the center of events because there were so few of us, and both schoolmates and professors tried to include us in discussions and invite us for drinks. I was rather shy and silent because I felt that I did not know anything about the themes we dealt with. I read the textbooks, listened to my schoolmates and slowly got acquainted with some basic ideas. When we discussed projects and finances, I could not hide that I didn't know anything about them. Although I'd worked for many years, I had no experience in these two fields.

The first exam assessed our knowledge gleaned from five courses referring to research methods. We had to pass exams in at least three of the courses. I decided for statistics and two other courses, although I knew that the majority of students failed statistics. It was common knowledge that the teacher of statistics always prepared a new exam and that students always got at least some questions which they hadn't studied. I studied for a long time and did all the exercises except one, which I could not solve. If I could not answer just one of the questions among several hundred, there was a rather small statistical probability that the exam would contain exactly that tricky question, right? But it did: the exam included the only question that I'd never managed to solve. I first answered all the other questions and then started to work on the last one. And then, a miracle: during the exam it suddenly struck me how to solve it.

We had to wait for the results for a long time, although just one-third of the class sat for the exam. The secretary was kind enough to tell us the marks by phone. Eight of us passed and we continued with our studies. The next courses were not so difficult, and I studied them with interest and ease.

Among my schoolmates were a couple of tradesmen who sometimes spoke about their work. They knew much more about business than others who were directors in public enterprises.

I remember how they laughed when we spoke about investing and the director of a big state firm said: "I am going to take out a loan to start a new operation."

"What if you can't return it in time?"

"We'll go to another bank, get another loan and pay for the first one."

"And when you have to pay the second loan? Will you take a loan in the third and fifth and tenth bank? If private firms did such foolish things, the government would put us in jail. You, gentlemen in the public enterprises, can afford it without punishment."

"Oh, really? Isn't it common knowledge that tradesmen cheat the state wherever possible, professor?"

The teacher was an old man, but he was energetic and clever and quickly answered that tradesmen were under such state control that they could hardly do something wrong. Some of my schoolmates did not like this statement, while the tradesmen looked around with conscious superiority. Our arguing was never meant as an insult but always finished with laughter and with the feeling that we'd had a good discussion. Our open debates made my studies interesting and I sometimes thought that I might establish my own business.

I first started to speak about it with my brother-in-law, who married into a tradesman's family. My brother-in-law often agreed with me, but when I mentioned that I was thinking about my own business, he grinned: "You have absolutely no sense for business. You're better off staying in your nice quiet library."

I did not find it necessary to defend myself because I felt like that was true. But I thought to myself that he should wait, and I would show him one day. Perhaps I would establish two businesses!

After some time, I expressed my thoughts to my closest colleagues in the library: Marko and Margareta. It was actually Marko who suggested that all three of us imagine our goals after five or ten years. He didn't want to start, and Margareta just smiled.

So, I took initiative and said: "I am going to become a businesswoman and will have a big house, a BMW and a fur coat."

They both knew that I did not like big cars and fur coats but they understood that I was thinking about my own business. Marko immediately asked what I intended to do, but I had no idea.

As I was so open, he dared to proclaim his wishes too: "I would like to become director of a library and travel all over the world."

"Oh, yes, I am going to travel, too. Where shall we meet? Seychelles?"

"OK, Seychelles."

Margareta laughed at our boasting and modestly said: "I can see myself right where I am now."

None of us believed that our wishes for the future would really come true. Aside from Margareta, of course.

The Workers' Council considered Marko's and my request to pay our tuition fees and give us some free days for studying a couple of months after I'd already passed my most difficult exams. They made the decision that the library would pay all the costs for Marko's accommodation, flight to England and the tuition fee. But the assistant director, Mrs. Vidmar, strongly opposed covering my tuition fee and study time. She said that the library had no interest in supporting studies in management. When I heard about it, I jumped up and ran directly to her office.

Her secretary said that she had a meeting, but I opened the door and shouted: "How can you say that knowledge of management is not important for the library? You said yourself that every person in a leading position needed it."

I didn't wait for her answer. Even though she had some important people sitting in front of her, I didn't think about how she must have been embarrassed. I also didn't think about how my future master's degree was the perfect education for her position, and she had no management education. All I knew was that it felt unjust, and everybody else in the library agreed with me.

Marko could not believe it and said that he would tell the director to support the full tuition fee and free days for me. Perhaps he did so, but I took further steps myself. I wrote a complaint to the Workers' Council, went to all the members, and told them what a crying injustice I faced.

Members of the Workers' Council tried to convince Mrs. Vidmar that the library needed somebody with knowledge of management and that it was unjust that Marko got the money to study in England while they didn't approve the cheaper Slovenian tuition fee. But, Mrs. Vidmar insisted. Finally, she made me come and present my arguments to the Workers' Council. I had to explain why the library needed somebody with knowledge of management and work organization. Although I did not expect such an appeal, I did as she asked.

She coldly stared at me and started with a long explanation that the library needed, above all, librarians and not managers.

But I interrupted her: "Look, Comrade Vidmar, I am not going to listen to your long stories with which you are trying to supress me. I told you that we needed better work organization and how much organizational work I already perform. I think that everybody understands and supports my opinion. Vote on it. I am leaving because

I have so much work that I don't intend to waste my time with boring stories."

The majority of the Workers' Council secretly smiled and stared at their feet, save for the director's assistant and my previous boss. Then they voted and confirmed that the library would pay my tuition fee and study leave.

When we had coffee in our office, Marko and my boss, Mimi, laughed and congratulated me: "Nobody has ever dared to say something like that to Mrs. Vidmar. You were right, but you were as sharp as a knife."

I was sorry that I had to be so aggressive, but I simply didn't know what else I could do. If I'd left Mrs. Vidmar to spread her explanations, she would have spoken for two hours until everybody was fed up with her and they would have yielded just to be able to go out for lunch. Luckily, the president of the Workers' Council was on my side and quickly suggested voting. I was happy that I won the battle, but I knew that I'd won an enemy who was much stronger and much more dangerous than my previous boss, Mrs. Kos.

49
New Tasks and New Atmosphere

Mimi told me to prepare a register of all the Slovenian libraries, because Slovenia did not have any. The register of Slovenian libraries required a lot of data collection, but I started to work on it with great enthusiasm and I managed to convince almost all the libraries to send me the necessary information. Then I had to process the data. In those days, people had just started to work with computers and all the men in the library were very enthusiastic about them. I think that the library had only one computer, and Marton suggested that I should make the register on it.

"What computer? We have only one and my colleagues won't lend it to me."

"We could buy one."

"How? The library probably has no money for it."

"We have money, but there is a stupid administrative barrier that does not allow importing equipment from abroad. If an individual bought a computer and gave it to the library, we could get it. I am sure that you could find a way."

Of course, I could. I bought a computer abroad, donated it to the library and they covered my travel expenses in the amount of the purchase.

I thought that the data would be entered by a secretary or by a student, but Mimi told me that I should not require the secretary to start working on a computer. She had enough work because she typed for our department and for the administration. Marton also refused my idea to hire a student. He thought that I should learn how to work with computers. He already worked on a computer at home and he was much older than I. So why shouldn't I start, as well?

This made me angry and I hissed that he wanted to make me into a simple typist. It came to my mind that I could leave the work undone. But I worked too hard and could not leave it unfinished in a drawer. So,

I started to work on the computer. I soon learned the main rules and worked quickly, but I still complained that I was just a typist. I didn't want to hear the director's opinion on how we would, in the future, all write our work on computers. I worked and worked and entered the data until I got an inflammation of the eyes. At last, I managed to finish a database of about 800 Slovenian libraries and prepared a rather simple but extensive publication with just the basic data and without photos.

Marton, Mimi and Marko liked to boast that the National and University Library started to introduce computers and that we had just made a database of all Slovenian libraries which contained the addresses and types of libraries, the number of their books and their specialities.

Margareta made a most unhappy face when they spoke about it and said that certain things should be considered before publishing the database as a book. When I asked what was wrong, she said that I should not have entered the library of the School of Theology among university libraries.

"Why not? You know that this is one of the oldest and richest libraries in Slovenia."

"You entered it as a university library, but the School of Theology is not acknowledged as a part of the University. You should know that the Faculty of Theology is not accredited by the State and that its graduates are not recognized as people with a university education."

"You know that this is just politics. I don't intend to omit such a good library from the register just because of politics."

"The fact is that the School of Theology is not a part of the University and its library cannot be registered as a university library."

She could have said that before I sent the materials to the printer, but I would not have listened to her anyway.

However, Margareta continued her whispering and asked Mimi and the director if they found my work all right. After all, Marton was in the Library Communist Party and should represent the official opinion of the State and be against it. Mimi laughed that Margareta was more orthodox than Stalin, and Marton said that it was important to make a register of all libraries. If that had happened in the 50s, the book would have never been published. But at the end of the 80s, nobody was interested in such political sophistications. This ended my friendship with Margareta, although we still tried to remain polite towards each other.

The second year of my graduate studies approached, and I was working on my master's thesis. The theme was the organization of the library system and my mentor was a small, quick-tempered professor who often loudly shouted at my male colleagues but was always very kind towards women. I wrote and wrote and showed him my work, but he always found more I could introduce into the thesis. I corrected the work four times and he was still not pleased.

My boss told me that Mrs. Vidmar had started with evil suggestions that I would not graduate in two years, as was required by a contract, and would have to return the tuition fee and the costs of my study leave. My colleagues and I knew that these were repercussions for my having publicly embarrassed her.

When I told it to my mentor, he finally said that I could defend the thesis. On the day before the oral presentation, I was so nervous that I called him several times and asked about the details of the presentation. When he was fed up with me, he said that I should drink a glass of milk and go to bed.

The oral presentation was official enough, but the committee consisted of three lecturers whom I knew, and they asked just two or three questions. I finished in half an hour, phoned home and to Mimi and informed them that I passed. With the greatest pleasure, I brought the certificate to the director's secretary.

My boss, Mrs. Koler and Margareta congratulated me. Marko sent a written card from England, while my former colleagues from the acquisitions department did not care about an MA. They were not ambitious and were much prouder of me when I got my third baby.

The old lady in our department, Mrs. Koler, suggested that I should now start working on library architecture: "Nobody has dealt with this question yet, so this is a big challenge."

"It sounds pleasant, but I have no education in the field of architecture and building. And besides, I expect that I will now start to work on library organization. Don't you think that we need to make a lot of changes?"

Quite frankly, my studies did not give enough knowledge for me to simply sit down and write a good plan of reorganization. But the old Mrs. Koler clearly explained that the new organization would be made by Mrs. Vidmar, Mrs. Kos, and one of their friends who also did not like me. I thought that Mrs. Kos had absolutely no idea about organization and that I should work in the team. But I was, of course, not welcome.

Instead of starting to study library architecture, I was stupid enough to insist that I should work on reorganization. I still regret it. What interesting work I skipped, just because I was so stubborn!

The atmosphere in the research department grew worse. My boss became very careful about what she said because she knew that the library director Marton and Mrs. Vidmar quickly learned about imprudent statements and then had called her to account for them.

I once complained about it to a colleague, and he said: "Do you think that my department is in a better position? I work until seven or eight because I can do more in the evening, but nobody pays me for it. They require that I arrive early in the morning and that I produce results. They don't want to see that, at this point of computer development, it is still impossible to guarantee results. I'm seriously thinking about leaving the library and establishing my own business."

"What kind of business? For computers?"

"Of course."

I admitted that I, too, dreamt about my own business. I sometimes thought about opening a secretarial service or a firm dealing with book design or a personnel search agency. I most liked the idea about a personnel search agency, or as it is sometimes called, "headhunting." I ordered all the books about entrepreneurship that I could and read them. One of them contained a description of an employment agency. Then I found a list of addresses of such agencies abroad and I wrote to them to get information about their work. Some of them answered and I learned a lot of new and useful facts. An agency from the United States suggested I launch a franchise. But when I saw what I could get for the amount of money they required I refused their offer. They wanted $50,000 for advising me on how to equip the offices, how to arrange the files and how to perform marketing. The marketing step might have been interesting, although marketing in Slovenia was different from in the States. But I knew that I could organize the offices and the files much better and cheaper than the Americans.

Marton and Mrs. Vidmar now both drove me mad and I saw that I could not expect any advancement while they were on the board. So, I looked at job advertisements and found three or four institutions looking for someone with my education. I wrote applications and they all invited me to their interviews. Two positions were in public administration and one was in the private sector: the largest school for foreign languages searched for a new director. My friend, Mara, had worked there for a long time, so I asked her if she could get some information for me.

"I spoke with the deputy director yesterday and he said that they had almost no applications. You are ideal for this place! You have the right education, a good approach to people and I am sure that you will be successful. You should, of course, be aware that this language school is a snakes' nest, but I don't think that there will be a better candidate than you. He even invited me to send an application, but I certainly won't. I am leaving the place."

"What happened with the last director of the school?"

"She had a fight with her employees and gave a written statement that she no longer wanted to be director. She thought that the teachers would beg her to stay, but they gladly accepted her leaving."

"Don't you think that I should have some more knowledge about pedagogical work?"

"You speak as if you have none. You give lectures for your fellow librarians, don't you?"

I'd had just a few lectures and I found my lecturing poor, but perhaps teaching might not be so difficult. After all, I'd studied to be an English and German teacher.

I went to an interview. The employees greeted me very kindly and I liked them. We spoke for about an hour and then they said that they would inform me of their decision. They invited me for another interview and suggested that I present my ideas and plans for the development of the School to the Workers' Council. They asked all kinds of questions. I showed understanding and compassion for the teachers who worked mainly in the afternoon and were nervous before lessons. When the accountant asked me about some financial questions, I directly answered that I did not know much about finances and accounting and he seemed very pleased to hear it. This meant that I wouldn't be able to control him. In a week, I was informed that they'd accepted me as director.

50
Everything Changed

Our youngest child brought a lot of happiness to our family. Both girls were old enough that they could sometimes take care of him, feed him or change his nappies. Lili was nine, Vali was six and Martin was two. The whole family observed how he started to raise his head, fix his eyes and stare at something for a long time, how he started to crawl and then walk.

During his first months, he enjoyed it when Tone held him in his arms, and it made my heart thrill when I watched them. As soon as Martin could sit at the table, we placed him in a special chair as an equal member of the family.

Each time I served a meal, my little boy showered me with compliments: "You cook so well, how beautiful, how wonderful you are!"

The child gave me more praise in one week than my husband in our whole life. I mentioned that Tone could try to imitate Martin, and Tone started with his old excuses, saying that he was not like other men who flattered women. He always spoke the truth and I should appreciate it, instead of expecting stupid courting behavior that was beneath him.

"I'm not speaking about courting. What I want to say is that you could sometimes praise me if I am well-dressed or if I cook something good. I do not expect you to bring me flowers."

"Why should I speak such nonsense? You are certainly well-dressed, because your closet is full of clothes. I just don't know why you always look as if you were going to a business meeting or to a concert. Other women dress in a sportier way. And I also don't know why I should praise the food that you prepare. I eat everything, isn't that enough?"

Martin interrupted him: "Mum cooks well, the best in the world."

Tone stared at him: "Well, I wouldn't believe that some people can flatter women even when they still wear nappies."

"That's not flattering—it's a sign of love. The little creature loves me and tells me that, while you don't care about me anymore."

"Oh, come on, don't speak like that. OK, if you want to, I will from now on start saying that I love you and that you cook well. Tomorrow, in the evening, I will be the first to praise you."

On the next day, he came to dinner, sat down, placed his spoon beside his plate and tried to invent an appropriate compliment.

But Martin already stroked my hand and chirped: "What a good cook you are. I love you so much."

Tone laughed and yielded. He said that he was obviously not born to give compliments. I often asked myself how he could change so much in just ten years. Before we married, Tone often praised my appearance, clothes, character and work, but after marriage, he saw and commented on only my mistakes. I long consoled myself that this happened because he was brought up in a family that complained and criticized all the time. My mother-in-law always blamed women from the neighborhood, saying that they did not work hard and that they just spent money for clothes and for hairdressers. My father-in-law suspected that his neighbors tried to poison his hens and ruin his trees. The sentence: "You are to blame" was pronounced at least ten times per day. Before we married, I often said to Tone that it was funny and abnormal to accuse one another and that they could also tell each other something nice. Tone quite agreed and suggested that we should not follow their example.

But Tone did bring this behavior into our family. He claimed that he wanted to clear up all misunderstandings and thus provide for a good marriage. He thought that we would solve all our problems, if he told me, at least twice a month, what mistakes I'd committed in the past. He expected that I would regret my faults, promise him to improve and we would love each other again. If I opposed him and listed his own mistakes, from always being late to not helping me at home, he denied everything and said that I saw problems where there were none. I listened to his sermons for several years and I often cried when he finished. Perhaps he thought that I cried because I regretted my faults but, in reality, I was so tired after his long brainwashing that I could only cry.

It took years before I came to the conclusion that I could not stand it any longer. Only slowly did I understand that such confessions and blackmailing was abnormal and unjust, and I knew that I would, sooner or later, break down if I continued taking him seriously. I can't remember what Tone scolded me for when I last listened to him. I just remember that he analyzed my mistakes for several hours and then I had to nurse a child who fell ill, while my "ideal husband" finally fell asleep and slept soundly until the morning.

The next day, I said: "I do not want to listen to anymore of your accusations that you call sincere discussion. If you start with it again, I will take my things and sleep in the children's room. And I don't care what you think about me. I work as much as I can. Perhaps not always correctly, but three times more than you."

He answered that I'd made a fatal mistake because I refused his attempt to solve disputes by communication and that it would be my fault if he divorced me. Since I continued to be firm and did not want to hear his friendly advice, he sulked and remained silent for weeks. I knew this behavior of his from the time before our marriage. It was weeks before he stopped sulking and said what insulted him. He had developed sulking into an art form. But I was strong. I decided not to apologize anymore. If he was silent, I could be silent as well, and even longer than him. I had so much work with my children, my job and studies that I often didn't even notice if and why he sulked. I think that the children even preferred his being silent and coming home late. Neither Tone nor I discussed our behavior, either with our children or with my mum and other family members.

If I'd had no children and if I were not religious, I would probably have started asking myself about a divorce. Divorces were rather common in those times and easy to do. The children were almost always given to their mother, and their father had to pay a small allowance for their expenses. The family property was usually divided equally among both partners.

I didn't think about divorce because I still liked him. He wasn't always so awful and could give help and support. I also found my promise in front of God and the Church important and everybody said that children needed both a mother and a father.

Tone often mentioned that he thought about divorce.

"Go and start the legal procedure. I am not holding you back," I usually answered him.

There was no need to be afraid that he would really start the legal case. Divorces required too much work, and he would probably regret remaining without children. It was too complicated. So, he somehow reconciled himself with the situation as it was.

Before I began to work in the school for foreign languages, we invited Tone's family to a picnic and my mum joined us in the garden. It started well but finished in disaster. Tone said that he was proud that his wife would become a director. He also liked the idea that we would have more money.

My mother-in-law grumbled that I would now certainly not have enough time for children, but I quickly returned the attack: "You'd better tell your son to take a little more care of his children and suggest that he should come home before eight in the evening."

"Don't make a cock-and-bull story. I know that Tone likes his family and takes care of his children."

That was a bit too much for my mum: "If your precious son took care of the family, his children would have starved by now. He has never come home before eight this week and he came twice around midnight. I already thought that he had another woman."

Tone laughed sarcastically and explained: "On Monday, I had to check the work of our department in northern Slovenia, on Tuesday I went home to pick up the lettuce that my mother prepared for us and I stayed at home until the evening. On Wednesday, we had a meeting in my office, on Thursday, we located a station on a mountain and yesterday I went home because my mother offered us eggs. I have a lot of work to do and, besides, I provide my family with food. And what do I get for my efforts? A wife who looks as if she has eaten a lemon, instead of showing some happiness when I come home. And if you are asking about other women: I have a colleague who likes to speak to me and shows much more happiness when she meets me than my wife does."

And his mother nodded: "Yes, women always liked Tone because he has a good figure."

He continued: "Perhaps it is time that I start speaking with other women, because Iris doesn't want to change."

It is hard to believe that such a quarrel developed during a family picnic. My mum rose and said that she should leave to feed the hens, my brother-in-law said goodbye because he had a business trip early the next morning and I took the children to the bathroom. I was not quite aware of what I was doing, because I felt as if I'd been slapped in the face. I mechanically washed and wiped them and trimmed their nails. When they fell asleep and Tone wanted to discuss further, I told him to shut up and to go to that wonderful colleague of his.

"All right," he answered offended.

He sat in his car and drove away. My mother-in-law called me next morning and told me that he'd slept at home. This was really too much. I was convinced that this was the end of my marriage.

51

In the New Area

Although I really liked both librarianship and my friends in the library, I decided to become the director of a language school. In librarianship, Director Marton and his assistant, Mrs. Vidmar, would never allow me to advance to a leading position. I also couldn't immediately establish my own company because I wanted to develop a new business and it required a lot of time. As director of a school for foreign languages, I had the opportunity to get plenty of practical experience with management, personnel, and finances. I would be independent, have a good job and a much higher salary than I'd ever had before.

When I said that I was leaving, the personnel officer and the director's assistant required that I return the money that the library had invested in my studies. I curtly answered that they could offer me the position of second director's assistant, as it was known that Marko would get it when he returned from England.

The library director said: "You can leave if you want but you will have to return the tuition fee and the costs of the study leave."

I shrugged my shoulders and gave notice. I knew I would have to return the money because it was defined in the contract between the library and myself.

I suspected that the personnel officer would try to keep my worker's booklet, a document necessary to start work in a new organization. I also assumed they'd force me to sign a paper saying that I would return the money immediately. It was not legal, but many institutions practiced it. On my last day in the library, I came rather early, went to the secretary and asked if she had already filled in my worker's booklet and stamped it. She quickly performed her work and said that the personnel officer would give it to me later.

"Why?"

"I am not sure, but I think that she wants to speak with you."

"She can speak with me, but I want my booklet." And I pulled it out of her hands. It was very easy because she did not expect it.

"But Iris, give it back, she told me twice not to give it to you."

"You did not give it to me. Tell her that I took my worker's booklet because I have to show it in my new institution."

"Oh, please give it back or else she will scold me again."

"She won't be able to do anything if you tell her that I pulled it out of your hands and left."

I took leave of my colleagues and went home. Later, I was told that the personnel officer and Mrs. Vidmar went mad and calmed down only when the library director promised that he would do all he could to get my tuition fee back. The majority of librarians laughed, because it was really silly that I had to steal my own workers' booklet.

Before I started working, I read dozens of books about management, finances, organization, and private enterprises, but the theory did not prepare me for real world.

On my first work day, there was a long queue in front of the school and people angrily hissed when they saw that I went to the door. They were our students, who wanted to get a good place and came hours before the school opened. When I stammered that I worked for the school, one of the clients shouted that I should make employees work and not just drink coffee.

Peter, the deputy director, with whom I would have to closely work in the future, was already waiting behind the door: "Didn't I tell you how stressful our work is?"

"Well, I don't find it horrible at all. Isn't it great that we have so many clients who are fighting for our courses? Why don't you start enrolling them?"

"We have been waiting for you so that you could see the situation and organize work in a better way."

"Come on, let's start immediately."

"OK."

Then I took a look at all the classrooms and offices. My room was the smallest in the building, which was about 500 square meters. In the National and University Library, I'd had an office about ten times larger, and I was not a director. My office in the school had no direct phone line and the school had no business car. Since I did not choose my new job for money or prestige, I didn't care. But my face became sullen when I saw the small and humid rooms in the cellar that were obviously classrooms. The classrooms on the first floor were big and bright, but I was told that they were awfully hot in the summer.

"For God's sake, do we also teach in the rooms in the cellar?"

"Of course, where else would we put all the people who want to study in our school? We rent classrooms in another school in the center of town—but do you know how expensive those are? We will go bankrupt because of them one day."

I immediately decided to go and check those premises, ask about the price and find out if it was worth organizing courses in rented classrooms. I found out that the classrooms in the secondary school were big, bright and not expensive at all.

The long queue of students continued for several days. Then we had to arrange placements and solve problems with students who wanted to enroll but could not because there were no free places. It seemed that the secretary of the school, Stane, enjoyed verbal fights. He argued and quarreled and finally found places only for those whom he liked. He was an older, bald man with glasses, very simply dressed and had only a secondary education and both Peter and one of the administrative clerks told me that Stane had been in the school since its beginning. He knew all about the business, whom to contact if we wanted to achieve something at the municipal office and he could successfully calm down teachers and students. But he was extremely disorganized and absent-minded. He mixed up all the papers, enrolled people in the wrong groups, and did not register new employees in time. I found it strange that I liked him more than the deputy director, Peter, who was an English teacher, wore a suit, a white shirt and a tie, spoke eloquently and could be very kind.

On my first working day, I was in the school from seven in the morning until eight in the evening, because Peter suggested that we should discuss enrollment at the end of each day. I quite frankly didn't know why we should have the evening meeting, so I finished it in five minutes: I simply said that the enrollment would be good and that we should be happy.

"Is that all?" asked Peter. "I thought that you would suggest a different organizational system and some improvements."

"After the first day, it is impossible to suggest changes. However, you have been here for ten years and you organized the enrollment. If you have any suggestions, go ahead."

When he saw other teachers nodding, he said: "Do as you wish.

I wanted only the best for the school, and I expected that the new director would have new solutions. Don't blame me if the number of enrolled students is smaller than a year ago."

"Oh, my God, I will have difficult life with you," I thought. But I didn't want to be sarcastic or aggressive and said: "Come on, don't be so negative. I am sure that we will have even more students than in the last years."

"All right, we shall see at the end of the week. You can go if you are in a hurry, but I will examine enrollment in my classes."

On the next day, I decided to make my first suggestion: "I think that such evening meetings are quite unnecessary and a waste of time. This week, we shall invest all our energy into enrollment and then we will discuss it at the final meeting."

The teachers seemed pleased. Peter raised his eyebrows and remarked: "I don't know what you mean. Are you aware that both previous directors stayed at school from the morning until the evening? Do you intend to leave at four, just like office employees?"

"I intend to leave at three, because I normally arrive at seven. And I am sure that the school will not break down because of my working time."

"All right, you're the director."

How nice. I thought that my life in the library was intolerable because the assistant director and one of my bosses sometimes made teasing remarks. But in the new workplace, where I expected more respect, Peter flung more critical and sarcastic remarks at me in one day than I'd heard in the library in a year and he did it with the sweetest possible face. And I was well aware that it would not be possible to fire him. The Trade Union and laws in Yugoslavia protected employees to such a degree that one could hardly believe it nowadays. I very much regretted that I left librarianship, because I knew it so well and I loved it. I regretted that I'd left so many good friends, such a beautiful building in the center of town, and many other things. But there was no way back. I would at least learn a lot in my new environment, and it would help me to open my own business.

52
Problems of Management

O ver the next days, Peter tried to encourage me to perform some urgent tasks necessary for normal functioning of the school. He said that I should develop more business contacts. He mentioned that some teachers drank or took drugs and that I should fire them. I should also tell both previous directors that they should no longer come to the school. And, in front of all, I should prove my sovereignity by firing the secretary, Stane, who really compromised the school's reputation.

I could have put Peter in his place and required that he stop bossing me around. I could have said that I was the boss. The library director, Marton, had taught me how to do it. But I was a different character and did not want to lead in an autocratic way. Firstly, I wanted to introduce equal relations, teamwork and good atmosphere. The second reason why I had to be patient was that I knew very little about school management, while Peter had been employed there for years and knew everything. I simply depended upon his help, so I had to let him act like this.

I had to force myself to show much more determination, self-confidence and knowledge than I really had. I visited the mayor of the city and some other more important officials with a bottle of wine and they seemed quite happy and interested in our language services. I also went to the directors of some competitive schools, bearing flowers, and tried to find out if they might be interested in cooperation. It never came to anything, but when I visited them, I noticed that they did not represent any special competition. They were in other parts of the city, had fewer students than we did, no better premises and they did not invest in their teachers' education.

The former two directors continued to come to the school every day. The first one, who was its director from the beginning and retired two years earlier, hired some rooms for the Third University, which was a school for old, mainly retired people. She was the mother of one of our teachers. She did not cause any trouble, and warned me that I should be careful about Peter, because he was an unparalleled hypocrite.

The other director, who had resigned, was still a teacher at the school. When I started to work, she was on sick leave. When she returned, she immediately came to my office to introduce herself. She behaved according to the rules of business etiquette, but I did not like her. I was aware that she was deeply hurt, rather unsure about her further career and that she tried to hide it through energetic, strict behavior, so I tried to be as kind as possible. She offered me help and introduced me to the Chamber of Commerce, which had founded our school, and to some more officials in the municipal office. During those visits, she described the characters of all the employees. I don't think that she said a good word about one of them. She explicitly pointed out that I should spend a lot of time watching the secretary, who was absolutely incapable of performing the work for which he was paid.

"Why didn't you or the first director fire him?"

"Oh, come on. This is Yugoslavia, not America. I would like to see if you could fire anybody. You can choose either to lead the school or to lead legal procedures against fired employees. You won't have the time and nerves for both. You know very well that a fired employee can make endless complaints and that he would be protected by the Trade Union, by the Communist Party, by the social court, by journalists and who knows who else."

"I don't want to make a fuss, but why didn't you move him to another position, if he is so disorderly?"

"No, it is not possible to move him. He doesn't want to go anywhere. He has too much information and you simply cannot work without him. If you move him, he won't give you any information and will do everything to show your colleagues how incapable you are. Stane needs permanent checking and repeated reminding. That's the only way you can make him do what he should."

I walked with her and listened to her for about a month, but it became more and more obvious that I should either think just like her, and that meant having a most negative opinion about all the employees, or resist her and she would start hating me, just like she hated everybody else. How could I work in an organization and hate all the employees? And why should I hate them? The majority were very nice people.

When she scolded me that I was too soft, I told her that I intended to work in my own way and that I did not want to share her disappointment, although I understood her.

Her look was full of scorn when she said: "You will be sorry for this."

After that, she rarely skipped the chance to criticize me when she was with other teachers. She had a lot of remarks: that I wasted money because I ordered a special phone line for my office, that my daily meetings with Peter were useless, and that I shouldn't have stopped inviting the representatives of the Chamber of Commerce to each meeting. Even my dresses disturbed her. I was afraid that the employees might join in her opinion, but they didn't.

I soon experienced Stane being a difficult problem. Everything that I was told about his lack of organization was true. In the first days of my employment, he should have registered me with the Office for Social and Health Insurance. The registration should have been made within eight days of someone starting work, and I asked him every day if he'd done it. But he always had much "more important" things to do.

"All right, if you don't have time, give me my workers' booklet and other documents and I will register myself."

"I don't know exactly where your booklet is now. Wait a day or two. They never make problems, even if the registration is delayed."

As he did not register me on the next day, I started to fish through his drawers. Then he immediately found my booklet and other papers, quickly ran to Office for Health Insurance and settled the matter. When he returned, he stated that he'd had to run so quickly that he was almost run over by a car.

I had no idea what to do, so I called the son of my friend, who worked as a lawyer for a big enterprise, and asked him for advice. He thought that it would be the best if I started to look for a new secretary and move Stane to another place. I asked the administrative clerk Beta, a thin, small girl of twenty-five, if she might be able to replace Stane, if necessary.

"Yes, of course, I always replace him when he goes for holidays. I put in order all the papers, but then he mixes them up again. I am rather annoyed that I cannot have order in the office. And he is not at all grateful for what I do. He complains about me all the time."

After some weeks, Stane asked if he could have longer unpaid holidays, because he wanted to go to the United States with his wife. I told him to give the young clerk all the information and signed that he could have holidays, although all the employees, especially the previous directors, grumbled: "Instead of punishing him, she gave him holidays."

When he was abroad, I suggested new job descriptions and a small raise of salaries in administration. Stane became a personnel officer and the young clerk, Beta, was placed in his position. All the department leaders, the Workers' Council and the Trade Union approved it.

Stane had caused problems for almost everybody, so there was only one teacher who said: "Do you think it is okay that you fire an employee who has been here for 30 years?"

"He won't be fired. He will be placed in another position and he will have higher salary than before."

"There aren't any free offices. If you leave him here, nothing will change."

"In the morning, there are many free rooms. But I think it will be best if he works in the library."

"That room is in the cellar and humid."

"All rooms in the basement are a bit humid. If they are good enough for our clients, one of them should also be good for Stane. Or perhaps you can give him yours?"

Beta got a slightly higher salary and jumped with joy. In the first week, she fulfilled all expectations. She came to her office at six in the morning and left at eight at night, if necessary. In a week, she organized all the materials, was very kind with the students and gave me much more free time to think about future business plans.

When Stane returned to the office, I immediately called him to my room and told him that he should, from now on, perform the tasks of a personnel officer.

"Who suggested it? Beta, I know. She's hated me from the first day, that lizard."

"Sorry but this is quite your fault because you are so disorganized. Just remember my workers' booklet."

"Aren't you going to ever forget that booklet?"

"I will forget it, but you made a lot of mistakes. Evaluate yourself, Stane. You are clever and you know that you don't like papers and that you always quarrel with our clients. Be happy that you are still employed and that you will get a higher salary."

"You could not fire me."

"You're right, that would be difficult. But I can move you to a job with a higher or lower salary. If you prove that we don't need a personnel officer, we have just one more job free: a janitor. Be careful how you perform your work and how you behave."

Quite frankly, he had no order even in this new role. But he was at least removed from the central office and he could no longer make trouble among clients. He first tried to resist my decision and sent a complaint to the company Trade Union. But the Trade Union consisted just of women who were happy that he was no longer in the central office and their final statement was that my decision was right. When he proved that he would no longer make any trouble for me, I moved him to another, better room and we more or less continued with normal communication.

The two previous directors expressed different opinions about my action. The old lady admired me because I'd done something that she had not succeeded in doing. The second director, who had resigned, said that I was lazy. Instead of monitoring Stane's work and making him perform his tasks, I shut him in the cellar. But I had neither the time nor the desire to control him. He was an adult and his duty was to work in the best possible way.

On the outside, it seemed that I was very successful: the school had even more students than it had before, we employed several new teachers, I made the necessary personnel changes and started to think about the enlargement of our program. But although I showed self-confidence, I was actually rather unsure. I had no one who could advise me when I didn't know what to do. The library director, Marton, wrote to me and offered me help, but I refused him. He had first helped his assistant encourage me to leave the library, then he required that I return the tuition fee (which I returned easily because my salary was much higher than it had been in the library) and now he offered to be my advisor. I thought that he was shameless and that he wanted to earn money on my account.

The second person who could be of help was Peter, my new assistant. I am still sorry that we could not be friends. He was a handsome, tall, energetic, clever, smart man whom people often stared at. I, too, liked him when I first saw him. But I immediately noticed that he tried to do everything possible to cause troubles.

Even if I had not picked up on it myself, other teachers would have taught me the truth: "He is the most horrible, quarrelsome person in the world. Be careful and don't trust him for a moment."

Stane and Beta said that Peter wanted to become director himself, but the Workers' Council was against him. Peter, of course, denied this and told me that he had to devote time to his family and that he was not a career person. The accountant once said that Peter had a lot to say about me when he was with other teachers.

I tried everything to get into his good books. I suggested that we call each other by our first names as employees in Yugoslavia usually addressed each other as "Comrade" or "Mrs." or "Mr." I gave him a small present because he introduced me to my work, I asked him to come to my office frequently because I appreciated his opinions, I admired his business ideas, his knowledge of English, his sense for the commercial part of the business, and I often praised his clothes. I tried to be kind and honest, told him what happened in the school, always confirmed that he could have holidays when he wanted, and I did not monitor his lectures, just to prove my trust and friendliness.

I sometimes felt that he liked me and that we could be great colleagues. There were moments when he showed real happiness when he saw me, told me that I was a beautiful and clever young woman and it seemed that we both enjoyed working together. But it would only last a couple of minutes. In the next moment, he would sullenly whisper what the teachers said about me in the teachers' staff room, explained that he really did not know what the accountant did with all the money we earned and suspected that the teachers drank and took drugs. He quarreled with the head of the German department or stated that he would organize a strike if I did not convince the accountant to immediately raise our salaries.

Peter's unexpected and frequent requests to raise our salaries were tiresome, especially because the accountant always resisted. However, I immediately recognized that Peter was well-informed about when the government would freeze the level of salaries and I knew that we should listen to Peter and not to the accountant. Peter's wife worked in the government and was near the source of information.

Peter had unbelievable talent for selling the courses. As soon as a new client popped his or her head round the door, Peter found out which language the client did not speak and convinced him or her to start studying.

We sometimes observed him and laughed: "Just look at him, he has stopped a good-looking young woman again. I bet he will convince her to enroll in his courses."

She usually did and usually visited his classes for a very long time. I am sure that he acquired the majority of our clients.

I don't know if I have ever been so patient with anybody else, aside from Tone. I tried to show him that I was his friend and not his enemy and that it would be wonderful if we could work together, but it was hopeless. He used every opportunity to slander me, especially in the teachers' staff room. He tried to convince the teachers that the school desperately needed a savior, a strong, commercially competent manager like himself. I was never in such a strange situation: I appreciated him, and in some moments admired him, but I felt like he was a bomb about to explode.

I was also rather shy when I found myself among the teachers. They were my employees, but it was difficult to make contact with them. Their working time was in the afternoon, when mine finished. Of course, I could wait for them or come to school in the afternoon, but it wouldn't help. They had their lessons and were nervous, as teachers usually are before they start teaching. Besides, they did not like it when I tried to speak to them during breaks, because the majority made a quick survey of what they were going to do during the next lesson or tried to take five minutes' rest.

Between the teachers and me were department heads who did not like to see that the teachers would come directly to me and interrogated them each time to learn what we were talking about. I never felt so miserably pushed away from people who performed the most interesting work, from whom I wanted to learn something and whom I appreciated. Of course, I went to the teachers' staff room every morning, checked the information and messages, and looked at their books and materials, but I wanted to learn more about their work and the small things that made our school special. I was very interested in the mentorship of new, young teachers, but nobody wrote about it— that knowledge was transferred only as oral tradition. I only ended up learning a couple of things from their reports before their department heads took them.

My communication with the majority of teachers was stiff and unrelaxed until the last moment I spent in the school. The majority probably still think that I was haughty and avoided them.

53
Different Views of the Family Life

After our last quarrel, Tone took his mother to a spa and remained there himself to have some rest. When he came home, he tried to reestablish good relations. However, only after five minutes, he started with his accusations again. I first answered with short sentences and when he began criticizing, I went to another room and shut the door with a bang. I no longer asked him to pick up the children from school, to help me with domestic work, to take me to the cinema and I stopped telling him what happened in my school. I did not want to visit his relatives and friends anymore and we did not take trips with the children.

At first, he could not believe it. Then he sulked for months—or maybe years. I don't remember, anymore. Then he cautiously tried small talk and sometimes I answered, while on other occasions I curtly said that I had no time to speak about the weather. I saw that he wondered what he could do to improve the atmosphere, but I did not want to help him. If he felt at least a smidgen of respect towards me, he should try and mind his tongue. If not, he could sulk for the rest of his life. I spent fifteen years with my father, whose behavior was nearly identical. And now I was strong enough to bear it and fight for myself and for my children.

In the summer, he tried to organize holidays with his mother and with the children again, but I coldly answered that the girls could go with them if they wanted to. Martin had to stay with me because he was still small.

"What about you, don't you intend to go for holidays? Look how hard you work and how tired you are. I think that you need and deserve some rest."

"I have been telling you for ten years that I hate camping, where I have even more work than at home. I hate going for holidays with your mother, who thinks that I am her slave. And if I am so poorly dressed that you are ashamed of me, you can be happy that I will not be with you. Or perhaps take the admirer from your office with you and have her wash, clean and cook for you."

"I don't know what you are speaking about. You know that I appreciate your work and see how hard you work."

"Of course, I do. One must, if others are always on holidays."

At first, he did not believe that I did not want to go with him and the children. When I did not move and did not help prepare anything for the journey, he frowned, picked up his mother and both girls and off they went. I missed my daughters, but I had my little son with me. To forget the pain, I started to decorate the house and air the rooms and the cabinets.

When Tone, my mother-in-law and the girls came home, they did not look happy. Tone and his mother had quarreled. The girls said that they did not want to go to the seaside with them anymore because their grandmother was an old, boring pest and Tone was reading newspapers all day long. Tone and his mother actually brought me a present— some wooden thing from the market. I pushed it onto a shelf and threw it into the wastebasket at the first opportunity.

Over the next years, Tone and I spoke about what was necessary, but he remained in his office until the evening. He had a lot of business trips that lasted several days. He came home just to sleep. He only talked when he had problems in his department. During those moments, I tried to listen to him and give him advice.

I often asked myself if my behavior was right, and sometimes I even discussed it. The Church always presented the family as a sacred thing. I never heard any priest repeating the words of the apostle, Paul, who said that it was better if a man were not married. In my whole life, I met just one priest who dared to say that it would be useful if women taught men a bit of respect. Once, I spoke about family problems with one of the younger priests in my parish, who was convinced that married people were happy because they were not as lonely as he was.

"Why do you think that you would be happier if you were married?"

"I would have somebody on whom I could rely, who would support me and to whom I could go, even if everybody else disappointed me."

"And if you quarreled with her and you no longer loved each other?"

"I would be a good husband. I would take care that we would love each other."

"How?"

"We would discuss things, clear up misunderstandings and certainly find a good solution."

"What kind of solution would you find in a case where the husband is sure that his wife should think just like him otherwise he sulks and beats her?" Tone never beat me, but I was being dramatic.

"In each community, there must be a leader. But he should be capable of accepting the opinions of others. Discussions can solve everything."

"Good. Now explain to me how to solve my marriage. My husband is also convinced that discussions can solve everything. When we start speaking, it is only he who speaks and does not listen to me at all. If I am not of the same opinion, he claims that I am wrong. He repeats it for such a long time that I am too tired to continue listening to him. And I also do not want to."

"There must be a solution. Perhaps you could more easily yield because you are a woman. I know women who at first let their men think that they are right, but later they slowly make them accept their ideas."

"Oh, you think that I should be a silly, little blonde who has patience with her husband and lets him brainwash her every week. Why? Am I dependent upon him? Does he give me money to survive? Does he take care of his children? Of our house?"

"Yes, but look, your children urgently need their father…"

"What for? My husband and many others leave in the morning and come home in the evening. On Saturday and Sunday, he visits his parents, during holidays he reads newspapers. So, what does he do for his children?"

"Well…this does not sound good. But I would take care of my children and would not suppress my wife."

"When would you take care of children? You said that you work all day long. You have meetings in the evening. You work on Saturdays and Sundays. You must visit sick people and so on."

"If I were married, I would organize my time in another way…"

"Oh, stop it, I know the bluff. You would not spend a lot of time with them. You would also lay all the work onto your wife."

"You don't understand how it is to be alone. And you don't know what it means to really love somebody."

"Oh, I am not capable of loving somebody, while you are?"

He was much younger than I and made me angry, so I dared to speak rather passionately.

"Excuse me, I did not want to say that. But it is very hard to know that you've met the woman of your dreams, and you have to sacrifice her because of a rule that was made by the Church and not by God."

"Well, let us imagine that you stop being a priest, marry that woman, have children and a family. It would be a paradise, wouldn't it?"

"Yes."

"What about the next time, when you fall in love with another woman?"

"What do you mean?"

"I mean what I said: with another woman. Do you know any man who is still in love with the first woman he met? Are you going to say that being in love with somebody is something permanent? You know that being in love lasts some months or in the best case some years. Then it expires, doesn't it? Religious newspapers write about it, don't they?"

"Why, yes, but serious and responsible love cannot just die."

"The number of divorces proves that love dies. People frequently fall in love and each time think that they found the love of their life."

"You don't understand."

Later it proved that he did not understand. He really left the Church, married, had two children and later found out that his wife was impossible, so he divorced her. Then he met a new woman with whom he fell in love but was a bit more cautious and did not marry again.

54
Children and Religion

When Lili went to elementary school and to religious lessons, we started with family prayers. I think that Lili brought the idea from her priest. Martin was usually the first who went to bed and then started to call: "Girls, come here, let's say our prayers."

If we did not come immediately, he continued calling us for so long that we hurried to his room and prayed. Tone came from time to time, but he was rarely at home when the children went to bed and he was not always prepared to pray. After praying, Martin gave each of us a big hug and suggested that we continue discussing things. Sometimes we spoke for ten minutes and on other occasions for a whole hour. The children spoke about school, their teachers, their friends, their dog, funny stories that my mum told them and so on.

When I went to bed, I took a book and read until I fell asleep. I started to read books on religion, especially about the lives of Saints. I read four large books several times. It was obvious that many Saints built up their piety on stubbornness, but the books were written with love and tolerance. When I knew them almost by heart, I borrowed the books of Theresa of Avila. I remembered that my secondary school teacher mentioned her as an important Spanish author. When I started reading about her life, I did not believe that I would finish it, because I didn't like the baroque style of her writing. But I found her autobiography fascinating. It was such a good picture of the 16th century, of life in nunneries, of relations among different social classes and also of her visions of God.

I once spoke about it with our priest and said: "I can see now why peoply decide to go to the cloister."

He did not exactly agree with me: "Oh, come on, Theresa of Avila perhaps had her visions. But don't think that this happens to all the monks and nuns in the cloisters. They must be quite realistic and, as far as I know, they much more frequently ask themselves if they should leave the cloister and marry than have visions. Their life is not easy."

I did not let him destroy my interest and continued reading everything about Theresa. I felt that the woman spoke the truth and believed her, although I'd never had any spiritual experiences. I even tried to learn the interior prayer, as she called a deep conversation with God, but I was not successful. I did not try to achieve it by all means, because I knew that my way was different from hers. And anyway, even Theresa of Avila wrote that she continued to learn how to pray for twenty years and that it was difficult.

When Lili was old enough to start with her confirmation lessons, the priest asked me to teach one group of children.

"Yes, but…I don't have much pedagogical knowledge."

"Of course you do, you work in a school."

"But I don't teach. My knowledge of teaching is poor, and I don't know how to teach children."

"Why don't you read one or another book, if you think that you need special knowledge. I don't manage to do everything myself. We have some young girls who try to teach, but they really don't have either the knowledge or the experience."

"All right, if you don't require special teaching knowledge, I can take a group."

I borrowed a lot of books and started to prepare. Before each lesson, I made an effort to find something new that would be interesting for children. It would be easiest to repeat what was written in the textbooks, but the children had already read that, and they would be bored listening to it again. So I made a plan for each hour. I would include a part of the information from the textbook and then make a discussion or a quiz about certain notions: what is Heaven, what is Hell, what can we do to be less bored during the sermon, why do we go to church and so on.

Some of my colleagues who taught children prayed with them during the lessons and made the children learn all the prayers by heart. I sometimes forgot to pray, or we just crossed ourselves. I told them that they could say something to God if they wanted to and that they should not forget to pray at least when they were in distress. The priest must have heard about my teaching, but he never said anything. He didn't even require that we pray at the beginning and at the end of each lesson.

The priest was in our parish for almost twenty years and then decided to go to a monastery. Before he left, he came to our house and asked me if I could edit the sermon for his last Mass. I remembered how I first had not liked him, because he'd seemed so out-of-date. I still laugh when I think of his Che Guevara cap and his trenchcoat from the 50s. I'd always thought he had such poor sermons, and he had no ear for music. But now his leaving brought a tear to my eye. I felt as if I was going to lose somebody whom I liked and respected, although he had his flaws.

When he humbly stood in front of me and asked me to correct his sermon so that it would not be too sentimental, I had to collect all my courage and strength to produce a laugh: "How did you know that I always wanted to correct your sermons?"

If I had not made a joke, I would have burst into tears and a mother of three children and director should not cry, should she?

I crossed out all the lines that I found too sentimental and which might make people cry. I also corrected a paragraph that praised the new priest as an unbelievably good spiritual guide.

I soon met the new priest because I had to go to the church at least three times per week: to the Mass on Sunday and to religious lessons with Lili and Vali. He seemed nothing special, although the majority of women admired him very much.

We first spoke when I came to pick up Lili and he accepted me with a wide smile: "Oh, hello. So, this is your sister, Lili?"

I stated, full of dignity, that I was Lili's mother. But, being honest, sister did not sound bad at all, especially because he'd obviously meant what he said. But his best point was his sermons. He did not preach with the help of a slip of paper, but improvized. His sermons were long, they lasted twenty or thirty minutes, but we listened to him with open mouths. My mum did not want to go to any other Mass than his. She said that he could really say what a priest ought to say. Besides, he was also a good singer and was social.

Up to that time, the Slovenian Church had no Scouts. The State organized an alternative movement of young people who spent a part of their holidays in nature, and learned how to survive in the forests without their parents, similar to American Boy Scouts, but this movement did not include religion. Our new priest started to introduce a similar movement which involved religion and accepted both boys and girls. My two girls enthusiastically decided to join it. That meant that they would go to the Scouts' meetings every week, camp out in the open and prepare to survive in nature. I found everything rather dangerous and without any appropriate supervision, but the girls insisted that they wanted to become Scouts. My mum and Tone thought that this would be good for them, as well.

The first experience was difficult for me: children in groups of three or four made a three-day trip to the moors and had to spend the night in a barn. What if it rained, what if there was thunder and lightning? What if they met a psychopath? What if they got hurt? My God, I thought, those priests really have no sense for children and no responsibility!

I gave Lili a lot of advice, told her that she should call home if necessary, equipped her with a first aid kit, and explained what she should do in the case of a storm. After three days, she came home muddy, bitten by mosquitoes and scratched by straw because they slept in a hay barn. She was enthusiastic and said that her group experienced extraordinary things. The barn was beside the chicken coop, and the cock started to crow at four in the morning and crowed for hours. They'd fall asleep for two minutes and then he'd crow again.

After that, they camped on the moors for fourteen days and were even dirtier. After one week, the parents could come and visit them. It was expected that mothers would bring as much food as possible, so that the hungry children could eat. They cooked while they were out there, but mainly pasta with tomato sauce. I started to prepare fried chicken, Russian salad, tomato salad, cake and fruits. I prepared food for ten people, because I knew that everybody would be hungry. At first, we had a Mass and then the children ran to us and asked if we'd brought anything to eat. They ate and ate, as if they had not eaten for a week. Then they started to explain about all the wonderful things they'd experienced. The priest walked up and down, from one family to another, got acquainted with parents and ate if he was offered food.

When he came to our table, he sat down and said: "I know that you want to interrogate me about how we organize life in the camp and I am ready to answer all your questions."

Tone laughed, although I did not see anything funny. I thoroughly examined how it had been during the storm, asked if anybody was hurt, how they provided for the wounds, if he had the phone number of the ER (he quickly told it by heart), if there were any quarrels among children, and if there were any snakes. When he'd answered all my questions, I relaxed. While we spoke, he lay on a bench and continued answering my questions. Many people gathered around our table and I didn't even notice that they laughed and nudged one another.

At the end of the interrogation, the priest sat up and said: "OK, the Confession is finished. Will you give me absolution?"

55
High Anxiety

had been director for more than one year, but I still did not feel at home. I was unsure and stiff when I spoke to the teachers and I still enviously listened to their conversations when they came from their foreign language classes. I found it a bit snobbish, but very elegant and attractive. I now know that they were really absorbed in the foreign language and that they needed some time to switch back to Slovenian.

I had an unpleasant fight with the accountant, who was much more loyal and honest than Peter, but he wished to have full control over the financial and accounting arena. I did not like accounting and was happy at first that I could leave him to figure it out. But with time, I was forced to press him to raise salaries, I had to tell him that he should stop giving loans to enterprises that were in danger of bankruptcy and I had to say that he should explain financial reports in a way that the teachers and I could understand.

He hated raising the salaries because it gave him a lot of work, and he had to change everything very frequently, at least every two months. Our teachers had the highest salaries in Slovenia and the Service of the State Finances, an inspecting body for all firms that could poke their nose into everything, often asked him to give reasons for his changes.

At first sight, it seems strange that a school lent money to other enterprises. However, our school was actually also a company that earned a lot of money. Financial methods, like mutual funds, were limited, so our accountant looked to other methods to earn money from the capital. But it was risky to give loans to enterprises that could go bankrupt. If that happened, we would have lost considerable sums.

He never gave me any definite answers regarding loans. If I asked how much money the school lent and to whom, he said that he did not know it by heart. He emphasized that I should not worry because he personally knew the accountants of the firms to which we had lent money.

All the employees, including myself, were annoyed when he explained the financial reports. Today, I know that the majority of accountants report using professional terminology and that they find it difficult to use lay expressions.

But in those times, the teachers and I often exchanged glances and asked ourselves: "What is he trying to say?"

If anyone demanded an explanation, he answered in such a way that the one who asked felt like a complete idiot. The employees stopped asking him, and they started to come to me to demand information in words normal people would understand. So I asked him to speak in more everyday language. He did not like it—he thought that I wanted to monitor him.

Nowadays it seems unusual that employees were involved in discussions about finances, but in socialist Yugoslavia it was common that all employees, and especially their representatives in the Workers' Council, required detailed financial reports from the accountant and from the director. The annual reports were a nightmare for each director and accountant because the employees required a lot of data and the majority did not understand that money should be used also for investments and not just for salaries.

I once read in the Official Gazette, which published the most important legal, public and business data that an enterprise to which we had lent some money just a week ago went bankrupt. I went to the accounting department and asked the accountant if he was sure that we would get the money back. He snarled that he would inform me when he had time. I shouted that I wanted the report immediately and that the money that he had lent to the other firms should be in our account in two hours. I slammed the door so that the building shook.

He knew that he was wrong because lending money was not even registered as one of our activities, so he got all the money back in our account on the very same day.

He later came to me to say: "Director, you should understand that we must invest money in something. If it is simply put on the account, we earn miserably small interest from the bank. If I try to earn money from the capital, this is good for both our company and for the company that cannot get a loan from the bank. I repeat that this is not at all risky because I know the businesses, their directors and their accountants and I can require the money back immediately. It is not quite legal, but it is a good way to benefit from our business's capital."

"From now on, I want regular information about everything that is going on in finances. We will first raise salaries, because they are not frozen at the moment. If necessary, work until midnight. In the future, we will raise salaries as often as possible."

In those times, it was urgent to raise salaries. Inflation in Yugoslavia was so high that it's difficult to believe today. The government froze salaries every other day and those who did not raise them at the moment it was allowed remained on a much lower level, not just in that moment but also in the future.

"Well, if we continue like this…"

"Stop with your explanations. I will decide how to continue in the future. I have just found a financial adviser who will check all our financial data and will tell me what to do. You'd better be careful how you perform your accounting and not make any mistakes, otherwise you will be fired. From today on, you will ask me for written permission every time you want to go out."

Going out was his weak point. He always came in on time, worked for eight or more hours, but he had to take some air. So, he usually went out to the Service of the State Finances, paid the invoices and then had a meal. If he remained out longer, Peter often noticed his delay and told me. I never made a problem of it and never asked where exactly he was and for how long. If I had to work with something as boring as finances and accounting, I would also need some fresh air. But now I had to take serious measures, and when he sent his clerk to have me sign the permit, I refused.

His coworker said with a trembling voice: "But, director, the accountant simply must go to the Service to pay bills. It is not possible to work without it."

"Bring the permit for yourself, not for him. By the way, which school did you finish?"

"The secondary school of economics."

"That's the same as your boss."

"Yes, but don't think that I am capable of leading the department. I don't have enough experience."

"You have been in our school for several years."

"Yes, but you know that managers always hide their knowledge and data."

Although the accountant showed that he had no intention to make further trouble and that he would remain loyal (and he did, although I declined to sign his permits to go out for several months), I still hired a financial adviser. She explained the basics of finances to me, taught me about balance sheets and, told me that we had a lot of money and paid high taxes and high rent for our building. If we invested the money in a new building, we would not need to pay such high taxes and would slowly get rid of the rent expenses.

Peter laughed when he heard about my fight with the accountant, shook my hand and whispered: "I love it when you are so energetic." We started to make plans for the new building. Peter knew a location in the vicinity where magnificent new houses were being built and suggested that we should buy one.

I searched the whole city before we opted for Peter's suggestion. I liked to go to construction sites and ask what was being built, and I also enjoyed examining real estate ads.

But Peter was only interested in the place he'd first suggested: "Listen, stop visiting those old buildings because old houses smell."

That was true, but it was possible to renovate old buildings so that they did not smell anymore. It seemed to me that old buildings had souls, while new ones were without them.

The investment analysis for construction was made by a well-known construction firm and we made a plan to get the necessary additional sum of money by loan or by shares. Shares were, in those times, something quite new in Yugoslavia. I had no idea about them, but the accountant claimed that he would do everything necessary.

When I wanted to hear how exactly, he said: "Why should shares be something special? They existed in old Yugoslavia and they are normal in capitalist countries. When we need to pay, we will arrange both shares and the loan."

The representatives of the firm that made the investment analysis warned me that shares in Yugoslavia were not at all an everyday practice, but they were sure that we would get a loan. Today, I know that we would have gotten it very easily.

However, the advisers had some doubts regarding the premises that we wanted to buy: "Dear Mrs. Novak, we must tell you that these premises still don't have the building certificate. It is possible that you might wait for them much longer than you planned."

I could not believe it because the building was almost finished, and we only needed to add furniture. I didn't know much about construction, but I knew that it was necessary to have a building license before one started building. Especially here, in the middle of Ljubljana.

Because the advisers insisted that we make a precise plan, I organized a meeting with the representative of the firm that was selling the building and with our advisers from the competitive construction firm.

After we exchanged the common polite phrases and ordered coffee, I directly asked the director of the selling firm when we could move to the new premises.

"You were there, dear lady, and you saw that the premises are actually finished. The façade, windows, and doors are ready, and the part that you want to buy is still for sale. Everything else is already sold. We still have to do landscaping, but this can be done in a week.

"Do the premises have all the necessary certificates?"

"Of course, do you think that it is possible to build without a license in the middle of Ljubljana?"

I looked at the adviser who represented our interests and he said: "Sorry, Janez, but I have to tell the truth. You must understand that the lady is my client. The people from the municipality say that you don't have either the location or the building license. And you will still have to ask for the service license... It will be necessary to wait for the premises for at least one year or even longer."

"How dare you say something like that? Take it right back or you will be fired tomorrow. You know very well that we have close contacts with both the mayor and with the president of the city council!"

"I know that you have good connections. I am also sure that you will, sooner or later, get all the licenses. But at present you don't have any, and the lady must know this. Oh, come on, there is no need to get excited. You know that our roles will be changed when we work with the next client: I will then stand humbly before you and answer your questions. Let's discuss how long the lady will still have to wait—she doesn't need to move immediately."

The director of the selling firm was bright red and sweated as if we were in the middle of the summer. Then he mumbled: "All right, the municipality is making some trouble because of the taxes, but we will settle that very soon. Perhaps it will really take a few months before you can move in."

I couldn't believe it. They'd built a big complex in the middle of Ljubljana, with hundreds of flats and business premises, and they even did not have the location certificate.

We politely said farewell to each other, and the seller said: "Dear lady, don't worry. If you give us an advance on the account, we will pay the taxes and immediately get the location and building certificates."

It did not occur to me to pay an advance onto their account. In that case, we would be dependent on them and I certainly did not want to depend on somebody so unfair.

But our adviser did not find the matter dishonest: "It is not so bad. They simply did not pay the taxes and now the municipality does not want to issue the location certificate. He will, sooner or later, get it. That happens in all construction firms. But we represent your interests and want you to know everything. Do you wish to wait, or would you like us to find you another place for construction?"

Of course, I wanted another place. The advisers exchanged glances, and, in my opinion, they shook their hands when they were outside. They were paid for their investment analysis and managed to get a new client to whom they would be able to sell premises and thus earn much more money than for the analysis alone.

In later years, Peter got many benefits. He was my assistant, he had holidays when he wanted, he could go abroad to refresh his knowledge of English and now he required that the school pay his phone costs, because he often called to find substitute teachers. There were a lot of replacements needed because the teachers sometimes got ill themselves, or they had to care for their children or parents. In such cases, the department managers had to work hard to find another teacher or had to replace teachers themselves.

I thought it made sense that the school would pay the phone costs, so I supported Peter's suggestion and the Workers' Council confirmed it, as well. Peter immediately required an amount that exceeded all reasonable costs. When I showed his invoice at the meeting of the department leaders, the accountant got crimson with rage and the new lawyer laughed that it was impossible to incur such costs, even if one phoned to America every day. Others were of the same opinion so we refused the payment.

Peter got mad and said that I was incapable because I could not defend his rights.

I'd had enough of him. I did not shout but said in a very quiet voice: "Please leave my office. And I am sorry that we have to end this in this way."

Of course, I was so angry that I could have bitten him. I so often forgave his unloyalty, his straightforward and his hidden attacks, his lies, and now he thought he could shout at me? But besides being angry, I was also very sorry. He did not always make trouble, but could be very helpful. And now, instead of putting all my energy into the business, I would have to waste it on quarrels with an employee.

The next day, he made a loud speech in the teachers' staff room about the injustice that had happened to him, but his colleagues did not want to listen. He sent a complaint to the Workers' Council and his requirement was refused again. He should have known when to stop, but he did not. He started to shout again, and I quietly invited him to my office. Perhaps he thought that I would find another way to enable the payment.

A couple of days earlier, Stane had brought me Peter's new business cards that were produced in the nearby printing house. Under his name was the title: MA in English.

Peter often said that he'd finished his master's studies in the United States, but many of his enemies stated that it was just a course in English. Now I asked Stane to bring me Peter's personal file. The certificate about Peter's American education was at the top and it clearly showed that he'd completed just a course that had lasted for a few months, which no institution would acknowledge as a master's degree.

I took his business cards from my drawer and pushed them under his nose: "What's this?"

"I can't believe that you would poke your nose into my business cards."

"You claim that you have master's degree, but you don't."

"I told you that I finished my MA in America, but I did not have it nostrified. And I finished it without any support from my institution. Unlike you, who had all your studies paid for by your firm."

"A master's degree lasts for two years, while your course lasted a couple of months. You know very well that nobody would recognize these courses as an MA."

"Oh, yes, of course, this damned country does not recognize any foreign qualifications."

"Are you aware that you committed fraud? A criminal offense?"

"What criminal offense? Don't be silly. The school would benefit if it had more MAs than just you."

"Let's call the lawyer and he will tell you about punishment for fraud on official documents."

"All right, all right, if it bothers you so much, I will take the business cards and throw them away. I can even pay for them, if you want."

"Of course, you will. I already refused the bill. And in the future, I will refuse quite a lot of other bills."

"There is no proof that I required that the printing house put an MA under my name."

"The printing house sent your order with your signature. And you don't have to look for it, because the order is not here."

He finally remained silent.

I suggested: "Look, Peter, maybe I could forget that you committed a criminal offense. But be careful not to make me angry again. I do not want to hear any more lies or any more baiting. I also do not want you to continue coming to my office and pretending that we cooperate. I will soon establish my own firm and quit. Then you can become director, if your colleagues want you."

When I left, he fought hard to become the director, but the Workers' Council refused him.

56
My Own Business

U p to that time, the government had treated private entrepreneurs almost as though they were swindlers who were supposed to earn lots of money and steal the property of Yugoslav citizens. It was widely known that private business owners tried to pay as low taxes as possible. But, in the 90s, everybody started to speak about small businesses as a way to save the limping Yugoslav economy. Some lecturers started to teach how to establish one's own business, but they spoke mainly about the possible legal forms of business and how to register them. There was nobody who could describe possible new products and marketing. So, I ordered some foreign books and read the most interesting chapters at least ten times.

I wanted to start a business that would be a first in Slovenia. The books I read mentioned agencies that helped to search for personnel—headhunters. Personnel search and selection in Slovenia was performed by personnel departments in big enterprises, or through advertisments for smaller firms. There was also the Employment Service of Slovenia, but that mainly dealt with the unemployed.

I wrote to numerous foreign employment agencies and some answered and gave me advice. I then made a business plan. Some parts were easy to do because I'd studied management and led a private company. It was difficult to make the financial plan because I did not know how to define costs and income. Nobody knew anything about it and I also had no idea when Slovenian firms would start to order my services, how many would be interested in becoming my clients and how much they would be ready to pay. I made a lot of calculations and decided to offer my services at the lowest possible price.

After the business plan was ready and I mapped out the workplan for individual weeks, I started to look for a location. I wanted to find one or two offices in the center of Ljubljana, in the vicinity of banks and ministries, with parking and low rent. I examined all possible buildings in the center of Ljubljana and finally found exactly what I wanted: three furnished offices. They belonged to the municipality of Ljubljana. I only had to decorate the rooms, change the curtains and rugs and add an additional cabinet.

I put in the application to register my business and it took about three months before I got the official decision that the company could start functioning. While I was waiting for the decision of the court, I had the necessary forms printed, I wrote a booklet on how to look for employment and Tone helped me buy a new computer. I only knew basic things about computers, while Tone was an expert. Although we only interacted for the most necessary things, he was willing to help if he was interested. By the end of the year, everything was ready, and I published a small advertisement that the personnel agency accepted applications from people who wanted to change jobs.

I also called a young journalist and asked him to write an article about my business. I was afraid of journalists, because people said that all they did was criticize or change what you'd told them. It was my first interview, so I was a bit nervous. But I had to do it.

In the end, the article written by the journalist was so nice that all my fears disappeared. In the coming years, I had many contacts with journalists because they always liked to publish articles on employment practices. I never had problems with them.

However, there were some difficulties with the Employment Service of Slovenia, who did not appreciate a private company in their area. As soon as the journalists published my opinion that the unemployed should be taught how to search for jobs, an old gentleman from the Employment Service angrily warned me that I knew nothing about employment, and that they might make an appeal to the minister to close my business. The Employment Service of Slovenia was a part of the public administration and they often behaved as if they knew everything, while other common people should not think about or discuss their field. It was them, the almighty government, that was to make decisions and give information.

Unfortunately, the Ministry really could decide that employment issues were a matter of State interest and that private businesses should not deal with them. I was well aware that they could immediately close my business. I don't know why I had no troubles because I'm sure that the Employment Service suggested that the Ministry stop my business. The only reason I can think of for why they left my company alone was that the number of unemployed citizens started to increase to alarming numbers.

During the first two months of my private business, I was still working as the director of the school for foreign languages. When the company started, I used my holidays to hire and introduce six students who would work with the applicants. They accepted, and their duties included registering people interested in changing jobs and answering the phone. After I used all my spare holiday time, I only went to my company for an hour or two every day.

The phone rang for hours. Everybody was interested in how they could apply, how much they would pay for it, and talk about the possibility of employment. We never charged anybody who wanted to change jobs or get a job—the firms paid us to find them people.

Several firms called to say that they needed employees, but most of them wanted salesmen that were rare in our database. I immediately had too much work, but there was no income. The invoices to firms were sent three months after they accepted our candidate—when they were sure that our candidates were what they wanted. I'd saved some money for paying the rent, the employees, and electricity, but if I left the director's place in the school for foreign languages, I would not receive any income at all.

When my company launched, it caused a storm in the school for foreign languages. Peter made a fuss, even though I had threatened that I would start a legal case against him. One might have thought that he would be happy because he could run to be the new director. However, he knew that the employees did not like him and that they would accept him only in the case of an emergency.

He was whispering to everybody that I only worked for my own company and that I was partaking in unloyal competition. It seemed that some teachers believed his words and did not trust me anymore. So, I decided to organize a meeting of all the teachers and explain my business.

The accountant was a bit embarrassed, but bravely said: "Do you think that it is wise to speak about your business? Why would you have to explain about your personal things? There is no need for everybody to poke their nose into your affairs."

His words touched me. After all our quarrels, he was still honest and loyal.

But I knew that my employees were interested in it. Almost

everybody came to that meeting, although there was nothing else special on the agenda. My information that I established my own business came right at the end of the meeting. I described its activities and said that it was not in any way competitive with the school of foreign languages. I also said that I would give notice in a couple of months. Nobody rose to show that they would like to leave the meeting and head home, as usually happened.

When I wanted to go, a very young teacher from Peter's department, who started to work just a month ago, asked: "Do you consider it appropriate that you will use your business contacts from our school for your own firm?"

"Of course. If there is opportunity, I will gladly call everybody whom I know. This will not do any harm to the school."

"Well, I don't know, but newspapers say that this is unloyal…"

"It is unloyal to establish the same business. I told you that I was not going to offer courses in foreign languages."

"Will you be able to work for our school and for your firm? Maybe you'll only do work just for your business?"

"I intend to work as I have to date. I have employees in my own company who can manage without me for now."

"Some directors work from the morning until the evening, but you don't."

"Yes, indeed. I work eight hours per day and have since the moment I came to the school. If you check the financial results and the number of students at our school for all 35 years, you will see that the school has never had as much money and students as under my leadership."

"That's true, but it might be still better."

"Perhaps. But as long as we have the highest salaries among Slovenian teachers and the school functions so well, nobody can be upset with me. I perform my duties and I perform them well, don't I?"

My employees had no more remarks. When I was leaving, the accountant whispered: "Congratulations, you pulled it off."

The last two months in the school were not pleasant. People started to search for a new director. Three groups were formed, and each tried to promote their own candidate. I felt as if all my employees waited for me to finally quit so that they could appoint a new director. This made me give notice two months before I intended to. I was not sure that my own business would bring any money, but I could not endure in the school any more. No income for such a long period of time was a surprise but I had to face it.

Several colleagues came to me and said goodbye. People in the administration, whom I was with every day, said that they would miss me. During the last week in the school, the weather was rainy, but I still remember the moment I closed the door behind me for the last time: the sun suddenly appeared, and I considered it a good omen.

57
Even More Work in One's Own Company

Tone and my family were very helpful when I established my own company. It meant a lot to me that Tone did not oppose my business, and was ready to buy a new computer, prepare the necessary programs and teach me how to work with them. I'd worked with computers for a long time, but I'd just learned to press the keys. I never wanted to really understand all the secrets of computers, whereas Tone was deeply engaged in all their functions. All the employees in his department had computers and he immediately said that we should buy the best possible one for me. We bought it in a time when the Yugoslav government allowed the import of things of small value, so we went abroad with the children and declared that each of us had bought one-fourth of the computer.

Then we put it in a small room next to the garage, where I had the cabinets with paper files. The computer sometimes got stuck and I often didn't know how to continue, but Tone patiently helped me. He tried to explain how things really functioned, but I didn't want to listen to him. I found it a pity that I would use my energy for such uninteresting and mechanical things. Of course, I could have left the work to one of the employees in the agency, but I entered the data much faster than anybody else and this work also helped me remember a lot of information by heart.

This new period of friendliness between Tone and me was unexpected. He might have hoped that we would get back on friendly, supportive terms and was also happy that I'd opened my own business.

In any case, it was a sign that love does not die in a moment, but that people must ruin the ties between them for a long time to have it truly end.

When I left the school for foreign languages and remained in my own company, I often felt anxiety. In the first months, I had no income, and many costs. The other, unexpected source of negative energy was my clients. Most unemployed people didn't believe that it was possible to find a new job. The majority were convinced that getting a job required personal connections. I knew that this wasn't true, but it was hard to listen to negative opinions day after day.

The only income that I received in the next months wasn't even from the business. I was given a small amount of money for English courses I taught in a big Slovenian industrial firm in Trbovlje, about forty kilometers from Ljubljana.

The industrial towns around Ljubljana often asked for the courses of our school, but we almost never answered their inquiries because we did not have enough teachers who wanted to teach outside Ljubljana. The worst problems were always with Trbovlje. Nobody wanted to teach there because the journey took a lot of time.

Before I'd left the school, the managers from the coal mine in Trbovlje asked me for two beginners' courses in English, I mentioned it to the school and Peter answered that I should refuse them because we didn't have enough teachers.

Then I said that I might take them on myself, and my colleagues laughed: "Do it if you want to. You will probably stop after a month or two because you will be fed up with the travel and with the place."

In those days, our family car was mainly used by Tone, so I knew that I would have to travel by train. But I needed the money, so I made a contract with the coal mine, took a textbook of English and started preparing. I was horribly afraid of teaching adults. When I thought that I would stand in front of ten or twenty people who would expect an experienced teacher, I felt sick. When I first sat on the train to Trbovlje, I wanted to get out and then force one or another teacher to teach instead of me, or even cancel the course. But my fear that I would be penniless in the coming months was even stronger, so I remained on the train and prayed that I would somehow manage it.

When I prepared for the course, I saw that the teacher who wrote the textbook had tried to make students speak as much as possible. I used her method more than she had because I was afraid that my students would hear how my voice trembled. During the first ten minutes, my heart pounded, but then I started to feel a pleasant atmosphere spread through the classroom. Students mustered all their effort to speak English, they repeated the words, kindly looked at me, smiled and let me feel how they appreciated me. They knew that I was the director of the language school and considered it an honor that I was ready to teach them. I was touched when I saw them working so hard and being so grateful.

I felt bad because I didn't think my teaching skills were up to par. However, I tried hard and successfully brought several courses to their completion. I stopped teaching after two years, when my own company started to bring in some more money and because the travel really took up a lot of time. The courses gave me a lot of practice and I became aware that I was not only capable of teaching but had a much better feeling for it than many of my former colleagues.

I had set myself a murderous tempo: I got up before five, prepared breakfast, drove the children to school and to preschool, went to my office and worked there until twelve. Then I bought what we needed at home, picked up my children, cooked lunch, helped them with their homework and continued to work for my company from home. Sometimes I worked until two or three in the morning.

Tone often tried to persuade me to stop working so much or find a normal job with normal hours. I was convinced that he did not understand anything about entrepreneurship and that he was only nagging. But I remember that he looked concerned and repeated that I would work myself to death.

I did not want to hear it at the time. He had a safe job in public administration and could not understand that private businesspeople had to work as much as the clients wanted. During the first year, I received an order on New Year's Eve. Instead of going to a party, I searched for appropriate candidates for the job so that I could send an offer. I never found it difficult when I had to work hard during holidays.

When I began to work at my company full-time, I started to interview the candidates, process the job seekers' data and enter them in the database. I read a lot about job interviews and sat in on the committees that selected personnel, so I mastered interviews very quickly.

But it did take a few months before I created a useful database of job seekers that allowed me to quickly search for appropriate candidates.

One of the main problems of my work was that employers wanted ideal people who, frankly, did not exist. Several times, an employer, who had obviously only finished the eight years of elementary school and didn't have the slightest idea about behavior or business, required an economist with a university education who would sell his products door-to-door. Some employers expected that women would not go on maternity leave, and one employer even demanded the appropriate astrological sign of her future employee.

I tried to be as kind as possible, but such requirements made me angry and I told them that they could not demand such things.

There were even more problems with job seekers. While Slovenia was a part of Yugoslavia, Slovenians did not know anything about job-seeking. Some candidates thought that I had very good connections with numerous directors who would immediately accept the recommended person. Several unemployed candidates called me after a week or two and shouted that I did not know how to perform my work, because I had not yet offered them any job. I very much wished to answer that I never would find them a job, because their education or behavior was impossible, but I didn't.

Such people often made me moody, but they also taught me to restrain my outbursts of anger that had sometimes caused me trouble. Before I'd started to work in the school for foreign languages, I'd thought that anger was quite a useful emotion. If I loudly scolded a person who made me angry or banged the door, I expunged my negative feelings and, at the same time, informed people that they should change. I did not understand why I always had stomachaches after such outbursts. I was old enough to know better and I was an educated person, so I should have known that I was doing something wrong, but it took a long time before I was fully aware that I should control my anger attacks.

Now that I had my own business, I found that my anger was useless. Not just useless, it was harmful. If I got angry and gave rude answers, I could be sure that the person would spread negative opinions about my company and about me. I learned that I should speak as quietly and sweetly as possible. In many cases, I felt that a person wanted to complain or fight as soon as he or she called.

I would take a deep breath, decide not to get angry, and recite the sentences that I'd learned by heart: "I am sorry, but we cannot promise that we will find you an appropriate job. For this reason, we do not take any money from you."

Or: "We are looking for something appropriate, but there has not been anything so far. We will inform you immediately when we hear about the right job for you."

In the beginning, I still felt anger, but with some practice, I learned to pronounce such sentences automatically and with a kind voice.

The first year was difficult and the company barely survived. Slovenian firms were not used to such services and they found it cheaper to perform them themselves. Although my company had an extensive database of available candidates, we did not always find appropriate candidates. I also did not invest much in marketing. The company managed to survive because I was used to being careful with money and because I had courses in English for students in Trbovlje to offset the losses. Outwards it seemed that we were very successful as the company was never in the red and it never took a loan, but I was often nervous and thought that we might not succeed. I sometimes even thought that it would be better to close it and find a new job.

In the second year, my company started to bring in a small profit. Personnel search and selection became a daily routine, and employment interviews took less time. I did not become careless, but after 1,000 interviews, I really knew what I was doing.

When basic tasks in the company became routine, I started to think about how I could enrich the activities and bring in more money. I wrote an instruction manual for those seeking jobs, several brochures for companies, and articles for newspapers. The book for job seekers, with advice on what they could do to get a job, was short, just about 100 pages, but it was the first of its type to be published in Slovenia. The brochures for firms on how to organize the search and selection process were written on just a few pages and contained ideas about how to find appropriate candidates, how to organize the selection procedure and what laws to consider. For example, several Slovenian directors thought they could require that women wouldn't get pregnant which was, of course, illegal.

These brochures were regularly sent to Slovenian firms. My company published them itself because we were also registered for publishing. Writing books and brochures was easy, but I found out that books for job seekers did not sell well. People simply did not believe that they could improve their job-seeking skills.

Directors of big companies said that they were ready to pay a lot of money if I could teach their workers, who were at the point of being fired, how to find another job. I once made a deal with a director of a major company that I would prepare lectures for his employees who would soon lose their posts. I told him that I could only lecture about different strategies, but the people would have to find the jobs themselves. It took me quite awhile before I convinced him that people would not immediately find a new job, especially because the unemployed received good financial support after dismissal. About thirty people came and listened to me. We spoke for three hours before they managed to get their hatred of the manager off their chests and only then were they ready to listen to what I had to say about job-seeking.

I also prepared a longer, six-month course about job-seeking for one of the Slovenian municipalities and I told the mayor even more firmly that they should not expect that the unemployed would find another job within a couple of weeks. They understood and agreed with the contract terms. In the end, 60% of the participants found employment. At the time, I thought that I was not very successful, but later, when such courses were organized by the Employment Service of Slovenia, I saw that I did perfectly well with this result.

I was rather unhappy because of one of the participants. He had a university education and worked on statistical analyses. When he lost his job, he started to work on data about unemployment. He sought information that fed his hypothesis that it was impossible to find employment. He really didn't find a job and then he called a well-known editor of a leading Slovenian newspaper and informed him that my course was thoroughly unsuccessful. The main editor called me and asked for details about the contents, participants and results of the course. I kept data about each participant's ways of looking for a job and about the number of letters of application that he sent to different companies, so I invited the editor to come and take a look at the documentation. Although he was first convinced that my course was throwing money away, he finally agreed that the analyst, who was his former schoolmate, was just out to prove his own opinion.

I also embarked on research projects in the area of employment. I decided to start when I met the dean of the School of Social Sciences. She'd been a model when she was younger, and even in her fifties, she was very beautiful with blonde hair, clothes like Marilyn Monroe and full make-up. I sat beside her during a meeting, felt inferior and didn't dare to look at her. I was very surprised when she started to ask me about my opinion regarding unemployment and invited me to present my work to her university students.

After my presentation to about sixty students, she offered me a position as her assistant at the school. I only had a few lectures each week and didn't need to leave my job. I had no idea how much of an honor this was.

The dean suggested that I should teach students about real work cases so that they would know what unemployment meant and how to look for a job. The work was not very difficult, and I got a lot of teaching practice.

Under the influence of the dean, I prepared some research projects in the area of employment and was surprised when they were approved by the Slovenian Ministry of Science.

One would expect that my numerous and contemporary ideas based on practical work would enable me to establish cooperation with the Ministry of Employment and with the Employment Service of Slovenia. The Ministry of Employment was the highest body that decided the politics in the field of employment. The Employment Service of Slovenia registered and monitored the unemployed people and provided for their social allowances. Both governmental institutions should have been aware that Slovenian unemployed people needed more than politics and monitoring. Namely, they needed courses that would encourage and teach the unemployed how to find jobs.

At the beginning of the 90s, they were still fully aware of their importance as a part of the government. However, the number of unemployed people in Slovenia rose very quickly and the unemployed blamed the Employment Service for not trying to find them jobs and only sitting in their beautiful offices all day. They must have been among the first Slovenian governmental institutions to experience the feeling that they were no longer on a pedestal. I tried to make contact with them before I opened my company and one of my former colleagues who worked at the Ministry promised to help me. But the majority of his colleagues in the Ministry looked down on me. They said that I was just a small private businesswoman who had no idea about the complex employment problems. When I sent them a copy of my latest book on looking for employment, they scoffed that it did not mention the Employment Service of Slovenia, but gave advice on how to individually look for employment. Two of the most important employees of the Employment Service said that this was a completely incorrect approach.

I was once invited by one of the most important firms for the education of adults to give lectures to personnel officers, and almost 100 people sent applications to attend. The organizer was very happy that they invited me, as that was quite a large number for Slovenia. The Employment Service of Slovenia sent three of its employees and they ruined all my enthusiasm for further lecturing. All three came almost an hour late and with scornful expressions on their faces. When I offered them some of the most recent foreign books about employment, they said that they came to listen and not to look at books. When I continued, they tried to object to almost everything that I said, and they made remarks every five minutes. They continued this for two hours and I hardly endured it.

After the break, other participants also started to give comments, but these were directed against the people from the Employment Service of Slovenia and supported my statements. Then all three left, again with scornful grimaces. I was so demoralized that I did not want to continue with such courses anymore and even wanted to stop lecturing. I told my former schoolmate, Mara, and she said that this was normal and that such things happened to every lecturer. She was a teacher and had seen it many times before.

Two more years had to pass before one of the more important representatives of the Employment Service asked if they could visit me and if I could tell them how I worked with the unemployed and what troubles I faced. I didn't know why they asked, but I offered them coffee and answered their questions.

The next month, I had a speech about unemployment at a political meeting. The organizers asked if I knew any foreign guests whom they could invite as a guest speaker, so I contacted an employee of the Austrian Ministry of Employment, whom I had met during a career fair in Vienna. She presented so many measures to combat unemployment that we were rather surprised. Slovenia had no encouraging brochures on how to search for jobs, aside from my little, despised booklet published by my company. Austria had a lot of brochures that covered the topic and more, such as where to look for information about vacancies and how to open one's own business. The representative showed them with great enthusiasm.

At that meeting, there were many people from the Employment Service of Slovenia, including their director, and I gave him my book about job searching. After that, the Slovenian Employment Service started to publish different brochures and began to organize workshops.

They invited me to submit an application for my company to work for them as a job club that would encourage the unemployed to search for vacancies. Job clubs were new to Slovenia, but they were actually similar to what I had organized for a municipality some years earlier and what I always wanted to do—to help those who really needed and wanted a job. About 100 companies sent in applications but, when it was necessary to start working, only ten of us remained. We were supposed to accept a group of about 20 unemployed people each month and teach them how to search for job. After six months the Employment Service expected that 60% of the unemployed would find jobs.

The Employment Service gave us fourteen days of training on how to perform the job club program. I hired a new social worker and we started. Each month, we got a new group of about 20 people, among whom some were quite desperate, while others were happy that they received the monthly allowance for the unemployed and finally enjoyed some peace and had some time for themselves. There were a few alcoholics in each of the groups. The majority had only completed elementary school, but some had finished secondary school. The participants of the job club started by complaining about their former employers and only later seriously wrote job applications and went to employment interviews. When somebody got a job, he brought homemade biscuits, we made coffee and had a small party. This activity was completely different from my agency's activities of personnel search and selection. The personnel search and selection meant being on the side of the companies, evaluating the candidates and sending only the best ones to firms. The job club meant working for the unemployed, encouraging them to send letters of application when they didn't meet all the requirements, writing letters of recommendation for them, and offering them computers to search vacancies and write applications.

My general feeling was that people were grateful because we listened to them, advised them on how to behave, taught them how to write job applications, and explained individual companies to them. We achieved good results and continued the program for several years.

58

Independence

n the 90s, Slovenia saw not only new entrepreneurial values but also freedom of the press. Almost all the newspapers expressed a strong opposition to the thought that Slovenia had to be part of Yugoslavia. I never liked politics, but it soon became such an important part of everyday life that it was not possible to avoid it. The TV transmissions and reports, newspapers and reviews openly and frequently criticized the Federal State of Yugoslavia. Some journalists wrote quite unbelievable stories: that Slovenia would declare its independence, separate from Yugoslavia and establish its own state. I sometimes mocked how easy it was to whisper about independence but that it would be impossible to realize it.

Tone was employed at the Ministry of Defense for years and once said very clearly: "I think that we will have our own state as soon as this year and it might be better than it has been thus far. But we will not achieve it without sacrifice. You can be sure that there will be fights."

He was much more interested in politics than I. He was always very well-informed about happenings in the government and at the Ministry of Defense, but I still did not care about his remark.

I scornfully thought: "Men cannot survive without politics and soccer."

In the spring of 1991, he said that he would probably not be back home soon.

"Why, are you going for a business trip?"

"No. The preparations for the independence of Slovenia have started and I will have to be on duty all the time."

"But they will let you go home in the evening."

"They said that I would be able to go home just from time to time. I will try to come at least once a week."

"In my opinion all the politicians, together with your bosses, exaggerate. I am sure that there will be no war."

"From your mouth to God's ears. Let's at least hope that the war will not last long. But I tell you once again that it is serious and that it is necessary to be ready."

"And how shall we get ready? What could we do if the enemy starts bombing us?"

"Buy some food supplies. If it comes to bombing, go with children to the garage or to the forest."

He left and did not return for a month. He sometimes called, but never spoke about where he was and what he was doing. He just asked how we were at home. Over the next months, he sometimes came home for an hour or two, with the military jeep and in a military uniform, and Martin's face shone when he watched him. His daddy was a soldier, he drove a real jeep and once he took him on his lap and let him turn the wheel.

Before the celebration of our independence, his driver brought him by for a few minutes and he told me that the war would start very soon. He had no idea what would happen and how long it would take. We took leave, but I still could not imagine that there might be a war. My God, we were at the end of the twentieth century and it was full of wars. Was it possible that people still had no idea that wars made no sense?

I was anxious and fell asleep rather late. In the morning I woke up late, so I quickly dressed Martin and took him to the preschool, while the girls had no school and could sleep longer. When driving the car, I felt that the road was full of holes and I thought that it should have been repaired. When I arrived at the village center, I saw a large group of men in front of the pub. It amazed me that they wanted to drink before seven in the morning, but I had no time to think about them, because I was late for work. In front of the preschool there were no parents and children. Only the headmistress and the teachers walked about.

I said hello and wanted to leave Martin in the classroom, but the headmistress asked: "Dear Mrs. Novak, do you really intend to leave your child here? You certainly must be aware that you are leaving him here at your own risk."

"What do you mean?"

"If a bomb falls and something happens to the child, we will not be responsible."

"What bomb, what are you talking about?"

"Didn't you listen to the radio or watch TV? And your house is beside the road, you must have heard the tanks!"

"No, I didn't hear anything."

"You must sleep soundly. So, you don't know that tanks passed by during the night and that people in the next village stopped them with their cars and tried to prevent them from attacking the airport?"

Now I understood why the road was so ruined. The tanks.

"My husband said that something like that would happen, but I didn't believe him."

"Listen to him now. And switch on the TV so that you will be a bit better informed. What shall we do with Martin? No mums left their children in the preschool today. They all stayed with their children at home."

"The others can stay at home because they are employed in public administration. I earn only if I work. I will probably have to go to my office."

"I am sure that you will have no clients today. In my opinion, you should stay with your children. And besides, you can probably work at home, as well."

"Yes, of course. But I must at least hang a notice on the door of my agency."

"You'd better call a neighbor to hang it instead of you. Don't even think that you will reach Ljubljana. In the next village there is a roadblock and it is possible that the police will confiscate your car and put it on the road to stop the tanks."

Martin and I went home. I ran to my mum and told her what happened. She already knew it, because she heard the tanks and listened to the radio. She very much agreed with everything that the preschool headmistress said. I was curious what had happened in the next village, so I decided to go there by bike. I really did not wish for my car to be confiscated.

On my way, I met some soldiers who were in a good mood. When I asked them about the roadblock, they said that I should ride one more kilometer. If I wanted to, I could go there, but not too close to the cars.

After five minutes, I arrived at a crossroad with a ruined tank, about twenty ruined cars and cement blocks that would prevent tanks from continuing their journey. It was a horrible sight and I finally was aware of how serious the situation was.

I must have made an appalled face because one of the soldiers said: "Don't look so desperate, young lady, we will soon chase them away from Slovenia. Get bravely on your bike and go home."

When I came home, I collapsed in front of the TV set and left it on all the time. I don't know if the Slovenian TV broadcasted any films in those days. I only remember reports about the measures with which Yugoslav government threatened Slovenia, stories of a chopper that was shot down in the center of Ljubljana, tellings of incidents at the border and how Yugoslav military aircraft left Split to bomb Ljubljana. We felt miserable and caged. I still cannot forget hearing a foreign politician, sharply and arrogantly stating that his country would never declare Slovenia as an independent country.

Before the war started, I sometimes wondered why people in such a situation did not go abroad. Only now did I see how difficult that would be. I could have put my children in the car and crossed the border—but I would have left Tone, my mum, my brother, my aunt and other numerous relatives and friends at home. It would've had to have been much worse for me to be ready to leave them.

The most difficult experience we faced one night when all our neighbors started to say that a convoy of Yugoslav tanks would drive to Ljubljana, and that Slovenian soldiers would attack them from the forest behind our house. We would find ourselves between the tanks and the bombs. One of the neighboring families went to the forest and made a shelter. Our family and some neighbors sat in front of the house which was farthest away from the street. We spoke constantly and, for the first time in our lives, felt that we were friends. I managed to get a phone connection with Tone. He did not know anything about an attack or the movement of the Yugoslav Army and we relaxed. Nothing happened, and at two in the morning, we went to bed in our houses.

Over the next days, the situation was similar. We continued watching TV and listening to the radio. Once, the TV broadcasted a meeting of the Yugoslav government. The journalists reported that Serbian women had broken into the governmental palace and required that their sons should return from Slovenia. They did not intend to lose them in a country that did not mean anything to them.

I thought: "You couldn't have done better! God bless you, sisters."

After a few days, we were informed that an agreement had been made and that the war was over. We could not believe that we'd been saved.

I was afraid that the war would mean the end of my small business. But people soon began to work at full speed, and at the end of the year, there was no financial sign that business had stopped during the summer.

I was proud that Slovenia became an independent country, but I knew that there would be negative changes as well. For example, the Slovenian economy would lose the Yugoslav market, which would result in great damage. As well, the wars in neighbouring republics might not end as quickly as the one in Slovenia. These things made me afraid for the near future.

59

Doctorate

When I registered the research activities of my company, I thought that I was doing something that would bear no fruit. Research organizations employed PhDs, while I had only a Master's degree. Besides, I was aware that I didn't know much about science. I could not make a really deep study in one field because I'd changed my course of study fields from pedagogy to law, to management and to library science. It was true that I really loved librarianship, but many years had passed since I'd left it. However, the employees of the Ministry of Science did not look down upon me—they were very kind and many of them gave me advice. I soon recognized that I would be able to apply to only a couple of research projects, because the majority had to be led by somebody with a PhD. So, I decided to get a PhD at whatever cost.

It was difficult to make a decision on the area of my doctorate because I had many options: I could have chosen from foreign languages, work organization, librarianship, employment, and teaching. It seemed that I had the best chance to earn a PhD in management because I already had a master's degree in it, but it did not interest me very much.

I finally decided to write my theme on the comparison of university programs and the work of Slovenian school departments. Several teachers said that it was a good idea, so I asked the Senate of the School of Management to approve my theme. They never sent an official answer, though I often asked them when the theme would be approved. They always answered that I should start studying and writing because approval of the theme was a long process. They appointed my mentor who advised me on what to read and how to improve my work.

A year passed, but my theme was still not officially approved. When my mentor corrected 200 pages of my doctorate paper, he had no special remarks, but he said, a bit embarassed, that I should once again require that the faculty approve my theme.

I should have heard the alarm in his voice, but I didn't. I sincerely wrote to the Senate that I'd been awaiting the approval of my theme for more than a year, that I had almost finished the thesis and that my mentor had corrected it.

I did not get a written answer, but the dean called me to his office and said: "Dear girl, you cannot work on this theme."

I gasped and almost fainted because I was so shocked: "Why not? Many teachers and my mentor find the theme appropriate. I already wrote it and the mentor corrected it."

"Yes, I know that you have been waiting a long time, but I cannot allow such a theme. It is very nice that you are critical, but if I allow such a theme, I will get enemies in all the departments that you analyzed. I quite understand you, because I was a young rebel, too. I wanted to make my PhD about the influence of membership in the Communist Party on careers. But I was not allowed to write about it. And it was quite fine, because writing on such a theme would have ruined my career and I might have been sent to prison."

Tears started to run from my eyes, and I cried when I remembered how hard I had worked to find the study programs of the departments that I compared and how much work had been necessary to define the parameters that I'd wanted to analyze.

Both the dean and my mentor were embarassed. The dean said: "Don't look at it as if it was the end of the world. Think about the theme once again, send the application and you will be a doctor of science very soon."

My mentor watched me with compassion and said that he would be happy to help me with another theme, but that we had to consider the dean's opinion.

I went to my car and wept during the journey from Kranj to Ljubljana. I felt that I had never faced such injustice. They'd given me a mentor, let me write 200 pages and, in the end, said that the theme was not appropriate! And it happened because the dean did not dare to make an evaluation of what is good and what is bad in the academic world. Today, all the schools have to evaluate their quality and they have to check it in much more detail than I wanted to.

When I passed the School of Arts in Ljubljana, still weeping, with red eyes and nose, I remembered that one of my colleagues from the National and University Library had told me that the school recently accredited a PhD in librarianship and had asked if I wanted to enroll.

A week ago, I'd told him that I'd already written the dissertation at the School of Management.

I parked my car, went to his office and told him what had happened.

He smiled: "Look, we would like somebody who could evaluate the quality of our work and compare it with other foreign schools. Don't cry over that school in Kranj, and start studying at the University of Ljubljana. Come on, sign the application, bring the plan of your doctor's thesis and start working."

This was a great comfort! I could work on my doctorate at the University of Ljubljana, which I liked, and which was older and more renowned than the School of Management in Kranj. I could further develop my knowledge of librarianship and my mentor would be my first director from the National and University Library, whose kindness I could never forget. In a few hours, my despair changed to euphoria.

Of course, I had to start from the beginning. I got two mentors who had a lot of remarks about my work. Librarianship had advanced in the last ten years. My mentor from librarianship told me everything I did not know, helped me with style and grammar, and gave me all the knowledge that he had. I accepted it with all my heart.

My second mentor, from pedagogy, was a young, sharp lady who could look into somebody's eyes and say: "My dear, you don't know anything about it. Take these books, read them and then we will continue speaking."

If I did not read quickly enough and send her new written pages, she wrote to the other mentor that I had not sent anything. When I sent her my draft, she wrote pages of remarks. My knowledge of pedagogy was even worse than that of librarianship, but I worked hard to learn. I read everything that she ordered and more. When she required that I make comparison between some foreign university programs in librarianship, I wrote to about 200 libraries and asked them for their programs as they were not on the Internet and I had to gather everything by post. I received about 40 programs in return and made a comparison.

She was finally impressed and praised me for the first time: "People usually make such comparisons among four or five programs, while you made yours among forty."

My mentor in librarianship required only two rounds of edits, but the pedagogy mentor made me review it six times. In the end, I produced 400 pages.

I am still convinced that it was a stroke of luck that the dean of the School of Management refused my theme. And I know that it was a privilege that the University of Ljubljana accepted me back and that I could be mentored by teachers whom I loved and respected.

I also started to participate in international conferences. They helped me to collect references necessary for project applications and to get acquainted with the most recent findings of academics from throughout the world.

I received the first invitation to a scientific conference via the dean of the School for Social Studies. I considered it for a long time and found it very difficult to apply.

Wasn't I vain—how could I think about presenting a paper at an international conference abroad? I had never been to a large international meeting and never written anything important. Quite frankly, I was even a bit afraid to travel abroad. What if I'd already forgotten all my English and German?

After the conference I could see that this had been a silly concern. I ran a language school and I'd been teaching English in Trbovlje and elsewhere. And yet, I was still unsure and worried about it.

Brushing my concerns aside, I started to write.

Organizers of scientific conferences usually required that we first send them a short abstract of what we were going to discuss, then send the complete paper and make a presentation. I thought that they would refuse my abstract, but they answered that the abstract was confirmed and that I should write the complete paper. I had to write in English, but that was not a problem. I was much more afraid of the oral presentation, even though it was only about fifteen pages.

But it was the time before my presentation that was the most difficult part. Communication with Austrians was tough because they spoke a different German than I'd learned at University, and I had to speak in front of foreigners about a theme that I had not completely mastered.

I thought: why was I so stupid to think that I would be able to make a public presentation about business education? How could I have been so vain to come speak in front of all these doctors from the universities of Vienna, London, Munich, New York, Glasgow, Paris, Madrid and God knows where else?

If I could've crept down under the table unnoticed and hidden, I would have. But the main speaker announced my name and looked in my direction, so I placed myself behind the microphone and started speaking. At the start, I felt that my voice trembled from time to time. But it quickly passed, because I had to focus on the presentation. And so, it went by rather quickly and without mistakes. And not just that, the doctors in the audience even applauded and asked me questions. Before I'd finished my presentation, I'd been nervous and had stayed alone in one or another corner. After it, I felt a weight off my shoulders and I started to speak with other participants of the conference and make trips around the town in which we stayed.

As I had successfully survived my first international scientific conference, I decided to participate in at least one per year and always prepare a paper. I continued for many years and I am not sorry that I did so. It is true that the conferences did not bring in any money—quite the opposite, each year I used a good deal of money for the conference fee, for accommodations and for the flight. But each time, I had to study a lot of books and articles and I learned new things.

And besides, I saw the whole world.

60
The End of Childhood

Long after my mum retired, she and my aunt continued to work in the field, to pick mushrooms and regularly attend Mass on Sundays. When my mum approached her seventieth birthday, she felt pain in her legs and could no longer go to the forest. She sadly observed us going there and was happy if we brought her mushrooms that she cleaned and pickled or cooked.

She also had trouble with her heart. I was worried, but her doctor said that many people had heart disease. She also had diabetes and had to take injections, but this wasn't very dangerous either. Once, she fainted because she did not have enough sugar in her blood, and scared me to death. My aunt came and told me that mum had fainted, so I quickly ran to her and called the ambulance. It was late in the night when they drove her to the hospital. When I woke up the next morning, I was depressed because I was afraid that she might already be dead. But my aunt came again and told me that mum was already home and that I should not worry because she felt good.

Then she started to complain that she had stomachaches. She'd claim that she'd eaten too much or that she ate greasy food. I suggested that she should have her stomach examined but even the idea that she should swallow a tube made her vomit. I could easily understand it, so I did not force her too much.

When Tone was fifty years old, he organized a big party in a nearby pub and invited all our relatives. Our relationship did not improve but I got used to saying that there was no such thing as a perfect marriage. My mum liked the food so much that she ate quite a lot and when she came home, she had horrible pains. I decided to have her examined by ultrasound.

The doctor who examined her cried: "Oh, no wonder it hurts. You have a big tumor on your pancreas. I will send you to the hospital for a further checkup."

I did not want to ask the doctor about the details and was grateful that she was so tactful and did not shock us with all the information at once.

My mum did not show any special reaction and I hid my fears when I drove her home. When we arrived home, I took a medical encyclopedia and it was clear that she probably had pancreatic cancer. The book said quite plainly what the signs were and how much hope there was. None.

The doctor sent her to the hospital, but I knew that it was all in vain. The doctors did not even operate or perform chemotherapy. It was hopeless.

When my mum went to the hospital, she asked my brother to cook for himself and for my aunt every day. She had a lot of dishes in her freezer that had to be just taken out and cooked.

She remained in the hospital for more than a month and never complained about food or personnel. She knew a lot of doctors and nurses because she'd worked in the Oncological Institute before she'd retired. She also immediately found friends among the patients in her room.

The doctors examined her and always came to the same conclusion: that they could not give her any special therapy. I hoped that they could operate on the tumor and I visited all the doctors I knew. My children's doctor even invited me to her home and explained exactly why the operation wasn't possible. Other doctors said the same. I wrote dozens of letters and emails to the best hospitals in the world, sent them the translated opinions of Slovenian doctors, but all the answers said that doctors in Ljubljana did for my mum everything they could. Just one Austrian doctor said that he could stop the cancer with a freezing procedure. I did not know what it meant, so I asked the main specialist in the Oncological Institute in Ljubljana.

He sat down with me, was very kind, but clearly said: "You should stop. Do you think that you can have your mother driven to Vienna?"

My mum was usually so weak that I could hardly drive her to the doctor in Ljubljana.

"Do you think that your mother will recover after freezing the tumor? Perhaps she will die three months later. It is not worth it to torture her, to drive her to Vienna and back, to send her among foreign people whom she will not understand. You must reconcile yourself with the course of life. We are born, we live, and we die. You will die, too."

His words crushed me, although he spoke with a compassionate and kind face and held my hands.

I considered myself utterly stupid and clumsy, but I had to ask: "What is it like to die?"

He did not mock me, as I was feared he would, but quietly answered: "Don't be afraid, death is not as difficult as I you might think. She will fall asleep. That's all."

"I hear so often how people with cancer suffer…"

"There is no need to suffer. She will get morphine. I will give you a prescription immediately. See that she takes it regularly. You should be quiet and accept the matter. This is the best way to help your mother. It is the best that you take her home and take care of her."

It was difficult to go to my mum and tell her that she would not have an operation. She understood that there was no solution, and it was a shock for her. Tears came to her eyes, but she did not cry. She immediately prepared to go home. I didn't know what to say and how to comfort her.

"Well, everybody has to die, and my hour is approaching. You must understand that one is disappointed when they hear such news. And I am afraid of pain."

I repeated the doctor's words and it helped her calm down. When we came home, she was so tired that she immediately went to bed.

I went to the nearby pharmacy to get morphine and I gave her half the pill. It did not seem that the pill helped because my mum screamed with pain. Quite desperate, I called the Hospice.

When the nurse heard about the quantity that I gave to my mum, she asked: "Did the doctor prescribe this quantity?"

"No, he prescribed a stronger dose, but I only gave her one half. My mum is afraid that she might get addicted to morphine and that she will, in the future, have to take more and more pills that will not help her anymore." That was the common opinion about morphine among people who did not know much about medicine.

"That's wrong. She must always take the whole pill and exactly on time. She should not wait until the pain starts. Don't be afraid that she'll become an addict."

The nurse also told me that I could call again and that she would come whenever I needed her. Towards the end, she would give her a bottle with a constant flow of morphine, and she would not suffer at all.

My mum lived for nine more months, which was a bit longer than the doctors expected. She sometimes felt so well that she sat in the sun, took a walk in the garden and even tried to cultivate her flowers. I came to her every day, often many times. She usually lay on a small sofa in the kitchen, because it made her feel that she was still in the middle of life. Whenever I entered, she took a seat, smiled and said that she had no pain.

I was trying hard not to show my sadness. It was often difficult to overcome tears and put on a happy face. Sometimes I brought her a plant or fruit, although she always said that it was a waste of money. Until the last weeks before her death, we would sit in front of the house, look out at the garden, the trees, the woods and the sun. We were often silent.

I knew what we both thought: "My God, we love each other so much and there is so little time left."

I sometimes hear people say that it would be necessary to shorten the suffering of such patients by euthanasia. My mum never mentioned such a thing and I, too, never thought of it. Morphine helped her not to suffer. Those nine months were the most precious for her and for me and for all of us. We spent as much time with her as was possible.

Tone and my children knew that my mum was dying. They did not speak about it, but they paid her a visit every day. In the last two months, she was very weak and told me that they should stop coming because they made her too tired and she did not wish them to see her in such a miserable condition. In the last week, a visiting nurse and another nurse from the Hospice started to come. The first one was clumsy, with words as well as with her work. She urgently required that we rent a hospital bed.

"How will my mum climb onto that bed? It would be difficult even for me."

"Your mum can't lie on this sofa. And I don't understand why she is dressed as if she were going out. You should understand that she will not be able to do this anymore."

My mum frowned and said: "Go to your office, nurse. My daughter will take care of me. And thank you for your stimulating words."

The woman tried to apologize, but she finally left. Then I asked for help from the nurse from the Hospice. She was a real blessing. She gave her a small bottle with morphine, massaged her legs (she even taught me do it), and told her some jokes. My mum even looked forward to her visits.

For the last three days, my mum was more or less unconscious. I called the priest to give her the Last Rites, but I am not sure if she was aware of his presence.

My aunt thought all along that my mum would recover. I didn't want to tell her about the cancer. She was a simple soul and might have bothered my mum with her ideas on how to recover.

But in the end, she recognized that mum was dying and came to me:

"Come on, do something so that she recovers."

"I cannot do anything more."

"Why can't you? You could always do anything you wanted to. Try hard."

I barely managed to turn around before I started crying. I told her to go and take care of her sister.

My aunt was a great help when my mum was ill. She sat at her side all those nine months, phoned me at my office if she needed me, came to my house and asked me for help even during the night.

In the morning, my aunt and my brother came and told me that my mum died. I had told my brother that he would have to provide for the funeral. I simply could not do it. I just looked at a photo of my mum as a young girl and could not believe that my beautiful and good mum had died when she was just seventy years old.

During her last year, we had not gone on holidays, so I bought tickets and convinced Tone's brother and his family to go with us to London. I also took both my aunts with us. My father's sister, Fani, lived in northern Slovenia and visited us just once per year. However, my mother and her sister-in-law were great friends and called each other at least three times per week. I, too, liked Fani very much because she was so similar to my mum. My aunts had never flown by plane and enjoyed the flight. They were not at all afraid, whereas my sister-in-law trembled during any turbulence. I liked that we traveled so that I could forget my sadness. I had a lot of work with translating, and taking care of my children and aunts, so there was no time to think about my mum.

My friends expressed their condolences and then kept silent.

Just one of them, whose parents had died a year earlier, looked me straight in the eyes and said: "Now you have no more parental support. It's time that you assume your mum's place and offer help to your children and all others who will need you."

It sounded rather insulting, but I was well aware that she only wanted to transfer my thoughts from mourning for my mum to other activities and stop my useless sadness.

My mum was really a great support. I can only hope that I filled her place well.

Printed by Amazon Italia Logistica S.r.l.
Torrazza Piemonte (TO), Italy

42490213R00188